10⁰⁰

Best w
to

Pa olleen Lane

Sincerely

Reynold M. Wik.

HENRY FORD AND GRASS-ROOTS AMERICA

Henry Ford
and
Grass-roots America

Reynold M. Wik

Ann Arbor Paperbacks
THE UNIVERSITY OF MICHIGAN PRESS

For
Helen Bryan Wik
Denis Peter Wik

Preface

Since one cannot escape past experiences, it can be said that this book originated in 1920 when my mother bought a Model T Ford to provide transportation for herself and eleven children on a five-hundred-acre farm in Faulk County, South Dakota. After eight years of rugged service, little stamina remained in the vitals of that car, but its mechanical career marked the memories of those who knew it intimately. Later this nostalgia lured me to Dearborn, Michigan, to savor the history of the Model T technology, to learn something about those who created it, and to speculate on the social impact of the most famous automobile ever built in America.

Needless to say, my quest for information has been aided by a host of helpful people. I am grateful to the officials of the Ford Motor Company for giving me permission to use the huge collection in the company archives without restrictions. For assistance in using these materials, I express my appreciation to Henry Edmunds, Richard Ruddell, Stanley Graham, Wynn Sears, and Alice Benns. In the Department of Agriculture in Washington, D.C., Wayne D. Rasmussen provided research material. In Europe, Horst Korner located newspaper files in the Welt Archiv in Hamburg, Germany, while Professor Alfred Weber of the American Institute of the Free University of Berlin gave assistance. In London, John Clarkson directed me to periodical literature in the Ministry of Agriculture, Fisheries, and Food Library in Whitehall Place. The Mills College Library assisted by securing a complete file of *The Dearborn Independent* for my use in writing this volume.

Historians who have aided the project in some specific way include Melvin Kranzberg of the Case Institute of Technology, Lynn T. White, Jr., of the University of California at Los Angeles, and Ernest S. Osgood of Wooster College in Ohio. John B. Rae of Harvey Mudd College and Franklin D. Walker, professor emeritus of Mills College, read the manuscript and made constructive suggestions for revision of the text.

I am grateful for financial assistance provided by research grants awarded by the Guggenheim Foundation, the Social Science Research Council, the American Philosophical Society, the Ford Motor Company Fund of Dearborn, and the Faculty Research Fund of Mills College.

Many individuals contributed useful information, all of whom know the life of rural America in the midwestern states. These include the Elmer See families of Walled Lake, Michigan, the Bryan families of Silver Creek, Nebraska, and the A. O. Stewart families at Sioux Falls. Over the years, my brothers and sisters who grew up at Norbeck, South Dakota, have shared their ideas with me about life on the farm; thus my thanks to Victor, Lillian, Elsie, Milton, Elvera, Viola, Irvin, Harold, and Nicholas. I also appreciate the aid of the following people who have talked about their mechanical experiences in the 1920s: Oliver M. Olson, Ed. Haselhorst, George Steffenson, Henry G. Bossman, Cleo Fiscus, Charles Hulbert, Fred Venhauer, Lawrence M. Bryan, and Charlie Ingalls.

I am especially grateful to Marion and Irvin Wik of Walled Lake, Michigan, who provided a comfortable home over long periods of time when I was doing research in Michigan, and to Dr. Ray M. Johnson of Dallas, Texas, who gave the manuscript an editorial reading. Lilliam Wendt and Virginia Mahoney typed the first draft, while my wife, Helen, assisted with research and has given timely aid over the years to an extent which goes beyond any recognition which can be put down on the printed page. Our son Denis is helping restore a 1922 Model T in our garage and thus is learning something about the Tin Lizzie which provided lively motoring during the roaring twenties.

REYNOLD M. WIK
Mills College
Oakland, California

Contents

I.   Henry Ford: The Emergence of a Folk Hero   1

II.   The Automobile Alters the Rural Scene   14

III.   The Ford Name Spreads Across Rural America   34

IV.   Barnyard Inventors and the Model T   59

V.   Henry Ford's Tractors and Agriculture   82

VI.   Farmers' Faith in Henry Ford   103

VII.   Ford and the Farm Cooperative Movement   126

VIII.   Ford, Science, and Rural Ecology   142

IX.   Ford's Politics and the Common Man   162

X.   The Great Depression and the Ford Response   180

XI.   Ford and the Little Red Schoolhouse   196

XII.   "Dear Mr. Ford . . ."   212

XIII.   Ford in Retrospect   229

Notes   243

Index   259

Illustrations   *following page*   108

I

Henry Ford: The Emergence of a Folk Hero

Anyone in the United States who has reached forty-five years of age was born in the age of the Model T. This remarkable era began in October, 1908, and ended on May 26, 1927, when the last of the 15,007,003 Tin Lizzies rolled off the assembly line of the River Rouge plant in Dearborn, Michigan.

Today, millions of young Americans retain fond recollections of the incredible Model T. For many it was the first automobile seen, driven, or owned. For those who knew the car, their experiences were vivid and, for the most part, gloriously memorable. While it may have been as ugly as sin, the "jalopy" gripped people's imaginations, it got hold of their affections, it captured their esteem and won their hearts. A farmer's wife near Rome, Georgia, writing to Henry Ford in 1918, commented "You know, Henry, your car lifted us out of the mud. It brought joy into our lives. We loved every rattle in its bones. . . ." [1] In writing her memoirs, Mrs. Sinclair Lewis referred to the sentimental value of the Tin Lizzie. She recalled that her husband had been thrilled to see *Main Street* in the bookstores of New York, and receiving the Nobel Prize had been gratifying, but it was a safe guess that neither of these experiences had topped the moment when "He stopped the Ford neatly in front of the stone carriage step and called out to father and mother and me as we sat on the porch after supper, 'How about a little ride?' " [2] After driving the Model T from Minnesota to California in 1916, they sold the car to two girls attending the University of California in Berkeley. As they watched the car move away with its new owners and saw the shiny fenders and tiny red kerosene tail light disappear in the distance, Mrs. Lewis unashamedly cried.

Those of us who drove the intrepid Model T realize that the machine impressed us more than any other car we ever drove. Perhaps the reason for this attachment lies in the fact that the car meant personal mechanical involvement. We worked on the machine, we took it apart, made adjustments, added accessories, pampered it, tinkered with it almost daily, worried and brooded over it, cussed it when it failed, and bragged about it when it performed superbly. Creative imaginations could cope with most of its idiosyncrasies. When it refused to start on a subzero morning, we took a corn cob, stuck it on a wire, dipped the cob into the gas tank, touched a match to provide a torch and heated the manifold. At times, a gallon can with some gasoline was lit and placed under the oil pan until the flames made the oil sizzle. Some took the tea kettle off the kitchen stove and poured the hot water over the carburetor. Frequently we were annoyed with its tendency to foul up the plugs and misfire and to run so hot that it looked as if the radiator heated the motor rather than cooled it. But the car's simplicity gave us a chance to pose as doctors with all the satisfaction of making diagnoses, providing patient care, and following the signs of recovery. Having felt its heartbeat and nursed its electrical impulses, and having babied it along prairie roads through torrid heat and biting cold, we developed an affinity for the Tin Lizzie that could never be duplicated with modern automobiles which require the repair service of an expert.

Although the passage of time tends to cloud memory, historical research can recapture some of the spirit of the past. After driving a Model T on a Dakota farm in the 1920s, it was my privilege, thirty years later, to do research in the Ford Motor Company Archives in Dearborn. This study indicated that the Model T could never be dissociated from its creator Henry Ford and those associated with him, who designed, manufactured, and sold it around the world.

Much of my research was done in Henry Ford's home in Dearborn where most of the Archives were housed during the 1950s. It was interesting to walk through the fifty-six rooms of the multimillion-dollar gray stone house built on the banks of the Rouge River. One could see the bowling alley, indoor swimming pool, the pipe organ, the comfortable library, and the bathrooms equipped with circular shower fixtures which sprayed the bather from all sides simultaneously. Everything in "Fair Lane" reflected luxury and good taste. Here was Ford the billionaire.

Looking out the windows, one could see the dam across the

river which generated electricity for the home. Beyond a large rose garden lay hundreds of acres of corn fields, while sheep grazed in a pasture surrounded by elm trees. This pastoral scene seemed to typify the feudal Middle Ages. Here was Ford the farmer; and all within seven miles of what is now Kennedy Square in downtown Detroit.

Ironically, Ford at times decried the study of formal history, yet he amassed one of the most voluminous historical collections ever accumulated by an American industrialist. Apparently he hated to throw anything away. As a result, it is estimated that the Ford Archives include at least fourteen million documents, two-hundred and fifty thousand photographic prints, and ten thousand books.[3] Obviously, no individual could live long enough to read every word in the entire collection. Sidney Olson, a journalist, claims the archives hold enough paper, that, should each sheet be stacked on top of the other, the column would rise six times higher than the Empire State Building.[4]

This mountain of Americana includes business records, production figures, newspaper clippings, and correspondence from people scattered around the globe. One cannot work in this material and not conclude that Henry Ford had a sense of history; an awareness that the printed page had historical value. Among the more intimate items are Edsel Ford's letter to Santa Claus when he was eight years old, as well as the small notebooks which Henry always carried in his coat pocket. Here he jotted down thoughts which came to him as he went about his work, many of them in epigrammatic form, as if to distill philosophic concepts into a memorable phrase. In one of his wallets he carried a newspaper editorial, now yellow with age, which declared the writer cared not who made the laws of the land as long as Ford made its Flivvers.

A dominant theme in the entire collection is Ford's relation to rural Americans. Most of the personal correspondence pouring into the offices in Dearborn was addressed to Henry Ford and originated among the lowly—the farmers, the working men, and the people in the small towns of the nation. These letters were written in simple, candid prose, because the common man was too busy to concern himself with literary expression. Few farm hands could shock grain all day under a blazing sun and then spend the evenings writing in the style of William Shakespeare or Thomas Jefferson.

The researcher finds it difficult to determine the real Henry Ford, since he seemed to have elicited strong opinions from writers who resorted to hyperbole. Edwin Markham called him another

Abraham Lincoln, while H. V. Kaltenborn, the radio commentator, referred to him as the "Mussolini of Industry."[5] "One of the world's greatest industrialists," wrote Joseph Stalin, "May God preserve him."[6] Chauncey De Pew tabbed him "conqueror of the front page," and Theodore Roosevelt complained that he got more publicity than the President of the United States. Will Rogers saw him making more history than his critics ever read. The *Prairie Farmer*, in 1918, believed Ford received more free advertising than any other person in the country, while a Chicago newspaper editor jibed, "One need not mention Ford—he mentions himself."[7]

In addition, Ford's life evoked such a volume of opinion that the plethora of words obscure insight rather than aid clarification. Something of the scope of these opinions can be seen in the press. The editor of the *Rural New Yorker* in 1923 observed that there were stories about Henry Ford whenever people met and the air smelled of gasoline. Arthur Brisbane, writing for the Hearst papers, claimed no American had been written about more extensively during his lifetime than Henry Ford. Charles Merz, of the New York *World*, in 1926, concluded that Ford was the most quoted American citizen, while many small town weeklies declared him to be the best-known man in the nation.

Similarly, an examination of newspapers in the Welt Archiv library of Hamburg, Germany, reveals an obsession with Henry Ford. The Germans, impressed by the Detroit factories producing over one thousand automobiles daily, called mass production "Fordismus," while Henry Ford's biography *My Life and Work* in 1925 became a best seller in Berlin. The *Frankfurter Zeitung* on January 19, 1923, pointed out that Ford built a low-cost car costing only four million marks, whereas other automobiles cost ten million marks. He was, the *Zeitung* speculated, the only rich man in the United States who could be elected to high office. A Spanish newspaper in 1924 referred to Nietsche's superman, but declared, "Henry Ford is the superman."[8] Parents in Russia were known to name their children "Fordson" while people in Leningrad, Moscow, and Kiev used the word "Fordize" as a synonym for "Americanize." The New York *Times*, on May 22, 1932, claimed Ford's name was known in every remote village in Asia, while only the elite in these countries knew such names as Coolidge, Hoover, Edison, Mayo, or Morgan. The Ford name was even more potent internationally than Hollywood movie stars. Ford had become Uncle Sam.

When the Model T put America on wheels, some wits facetiously predicted people in the future would be born in automobiles, live, marry, and die in them, with their bodies cremated by the heat of the engine, all without having put foot on the ground. Will Rogers, with tongue in cheek, quipped, "Brigham Young originated mass production, but Ford was the guy who improved on it. . . . He changed the habits of more people than Caesar, Mussolini, Charlie Chaplin, Clara Bow, Xerxes, Amos n' Andy, and Bernard Shaw."[9]

The archival materials, naturally, reveal contradictory views of Mr. Ford. The more critical believed him an ignoramus baffled by foreign affairs, naïve in politics, confused by the laws of economics, and innocent of the skills in handling human relations. Knowing machines but not men, stated Marshall W. Fishwick, led Ford to follow such cruel labor policies that his employees cursed him in sixteen different languages.[10] The Wisconsin *News* claimed he made a good car but failed to stick to his work because he wanted to instruct the cosmos. Peter F. Drucker insisted he "invented nothing, no new technique, no new machine, not even a gadget."[11] Kenneth Galbraith discounts Ford's ability as a businessman and credits the major success of the company to James Couzens.[12] One of the company secretaries, Harold M. Cordell, thought Henry "didn't give a continental damn what anybody's opinion of him was."[13] Arthur Vandenberg, in 1922, wrote that Ford had to his credit "more erratic interviews, more dubious quotations, more blandly boasted ignorance of American history, more political nonsense, and more dangerous propaganda than any other dependable citizen that we have known."[14] E. G. Pipp, a newspaper man, believed Ford had good impulses, but these did not interfere with his own vested interests for "he was as selfish a man as God permitted to breathe."[15]

On the contrary, Harry Hopkins, the New Dealer, admired Ford and gave him credit for being the first to realize that mass production depended on mass consumption. The historian Allan Nevins insists that he had the most spectacular career in American industrial history, was an attractive figure, and in many ways a genius. Fred Smith, an official of the Ford Motor Company, believed Ford appealed to a wide cross section of the public. In describing the funeral of Henry Ford in 1947, he stated, "You never saw anything like it in your life. People would cry, others would try to touch the coffin, and reach over and touch him and so forth. People in all walks of life, Negroes, Jews, Gentiles, Chinese, Japanese, Hindus. . . . They came from all over. . . . The traffic was tied up for miles.[16]

Although much has been written about the "Motor Magnate," evaluations of him are inconclusive because he was a complex person. He was endowed with enough contradictions and enigmas to frustrate a score of biographers. Roger Burlingame believed he confused his contemporaries and there was no reason to think he would baffle the historian less. The historian John B. Rae, in 1969, insisted that Henry Ford defied interpretation. He asked, "Was he a simple man erroneously assumed to be complex, or an enormously complex individual with a misleading aura of simplicity?"[17]

As the years pass, historians are confronted by a Henry Ford legend which has thrived among those addicted to hero worship. Frequently, what Ford did at his River Rouge factory was of less importance than what people thought he was doing. When Ford hit the nail on the head, the public never forgot it; when he scored a complete miss, oblivion quickly blotted out the incident. In time public opinion embellished the story of the House that Henry built. But the legend went beyond the bounds of ordinary hero worship, it became an obsession, a canonization creating a Zeus of American mythology.

Henry Ford can be understood only in the context of his times. His dramatic success paralleled the growth of the nation following the Spanish-American War, when increased urbanization, industrialism, and the impact of science and technology produced rapid change. The nation was reaching, in Thomas Jefferson's words, to "destinies beyond the search of mortal eye," and the dynamo had, as Henry Adams prophesied, become the symbol of the age.

In a day when chauvinism thrived, Americans had a tendency to idolize prominent leaders, and Henry Ford became one of them, along with William Jennings Bryan, Woodrow Wilson, and Theodore Roosevelt. Mark Sullivan thought this type of glorification had become a little absurd.

Ford was fortunate because he appeared on the national stage at the right time. Virtually unknown in 1908, he escaped the censure of the muckrakers who heaped abuse upon business leaders at the turn of the century. The belated rise of the automobile industry spared its champions much of the vilification leveled at the vested interests.

Had Mr. Ford bothered to peruse some of the literature appearing prior to the birth of the Model T, he could have seen something of the wrath of zealots who hated men of great wealth. Ida M. Tarbell, in 1902, claimed John D. Rockefeller controlled 90 percent of the oil refining in the country and made $45 million annually. She accused him of unfair competition and of using old friends for personal gain. His religion was hypocrisy and he played golf only that he might live longer and make more money. Even his face, to her, reflected craftiness, cruelty, and repulsiveness.[18] The *Christian Advocate* in 1906 claimed the steel companies made a profit of $140 million, half of which resulted from the protective tariff. Who pays the $70 million? William Jennings Bryan often quoted J. P. Morgan as saying, "America is good enough for me," and then he would add, "whenever he doesn't like it, he can give it back to us." [19]

Paradoxically, Henry Ford as the nation's wealthiest man in 1922 was spared this vituperation. Perhaps he never realized his good fortune. Judson C. Welliver, writing in the *American Review of Reviews* in 1925, pointed out that Ford and Rockefeller had much in common. Both were builders and leaders who devised methods suited to the times. Each dramatized his achievements in business, each received great publicity, and both appealed to the popular imagination. But the Standard Oil Company was founded in 1870, thirty-three years before the Ford Motor Company. During these three decades the American public saw business antagonists fight each other for survival. The game became so vicious that legislation was passed to protect the public. This transition occurred around the time Ford became a national figure. Since the steam had vanished from the muckraker crusade, the common man did not view Ford as a malefactor of wealth or a robber baron. He escaped the sinister image associated with the older crop of tycoons. Farmers and the folks in small towns tended to look kindly on Ford and all his works, but they still regarded John D. Rockefeller, who refined the gasoline burned in the Model T, as a tool of Wall Street.

In addition, Ford had the good fortune to reach his zenith in the 1920s, the golden age of American business leadership. The industrial executives now had unprecedented prestige and almost universal respect. The *Outlook* in 1929 described modern industrialists as refined, cultured, and well-rounded. Instead of being preoccupied with money, they were reading poetry, going to operas, art galleries, joining book review clubs, and singing in the church choir. James Harvey Robinson claimed the new business leader refused to spend all his time on the golf course because he was too busy anticipating change and thinking scientifically.

This high degree of respectability could be seen in the establishment of a school of business at Harvard University, while many universities conferred Doctor of Commerce degrees on successful entrepreneurs. Andrew Mellon received eight of these degrees in six years and Herbert Hoover picked up twenty in ten years ranging from Penn College in Oskaloosa, Iowa, to Oxford University. Even after the Teapot Dome scandals, Will Rogers commented, "Well, the old boys were not so bad, they were just unfortunate in getting caught."[20] Meanwhile Glenn Frank, the President of the University of Wisconsin, wrote articles in 1928 proving that business uplifted morals and pointed to Jesus Christ as a super salesman who had merchandised salvation to the human race. Bruce Barton in *The Man Nobody Knows*, the best seller in nonfiction for 1926, insisted the Master was not a febrile figure on an Italian canvas, but a virile he-man, go-getter in business. He was the first advertiser, the premier group organizer, the master executive, the champion publicity grabber of all time. Indeed, business had become almost a holy thing.

Cast in this company of the elite, Henry Ford became an oracle. His material success gave his opinions weight in matters far beyond his ken.

Yet the creation of a hero required more than wealth, a favorable press, and a public conditioned to the virtues of business leadership. In the making of human gods, as one historian observed, the figure "as the public receives it, is molded from a mixture of honest, but always fallible interpretations, colorful but dependable folklore, enthusiastic efforts at mass hypotism, and sometimes plumb dishonest hornswoggling."[21] Eventually idols are accepted on faith, and the myth and reality merge into a syndrome in which opinions rather than facts become the grist. But as Emerson explained, who cares what the facts are as long as a constellation is hung in the heavens as an immortal sign.

One ostensible reason the Ford legend flourished was because the man epitomized values dear to the hearts of the average American. Rural Americans tended to believe in him because he mirrored the thought of the grass-roots elements in society, and so extended a blanket blessing on all his works. Here rests the origin of the Ford halo.

Traditionally, the average American expected his heroes to be men of action, men who worked and stayed in the harness until they dropped. This virtue had credence in a frontier society where a man's worth depended on what he could do, not where he came from. A rugged pioneer insisted he could put on his own coat better than someone could put it on for him. Here class status meant little, utilitarianism much.

Ford exemplified this Puritan ethic of hard work. Instead of re-tiring at sixty-five, he remained president of his vast industrial em-pire until he stepped aside on September 21, 1945, at age eighty-two. Throughout his life he built things which had practical use. Like Benjamin Franklin, he paid tribute to honest labor by asking, "Did you ever see dishonest callouses on a man's hands? Hardly. When a man's hands are calloused and women's hands are worn, you may be sure honesty is there. That's more than you can say about many soft white hands."[22] He often said laziness and idleness caused all the world's troubles.

But excessive manual labor encouraged anti-intellectualism, with its tendency to scoff at things of the mind. Here, too, Ford had rapport with rural America. His contemporary, Frederick Jackson Turner, described frontiersmen as opportunists who regarded care-ful planning as a waste of time. The scholar seemed nonessential, nonfunctional, and at times parasitical. Professional people faced this rural prejudice. Will Rogers, an expert on rural psychology, once urged the formation of an organization to regulate the conduct of lawyers because, "You've got to work on his conscience, and his lack of conscience is what makes him a lawyer."[23] At another time he suggested that if people would refuse to read books there would be more Lindberghs and fewer Leopolds and Loebs.[24] Leo Gurko in *Heroes, Highbrows and the Popular Mind* concluded rural people usually thought intellectual endeavors made men impotent and women sexless, while men of ideas became bookish, nearsighted sticks.[25]

These views were compatible with Ford, who often criticized intellectuals, saying he never had much faith in experts, they were full of theory but lacked practical experience. He believed univer-sity degrees meant nothing; performance alone counted. In 1934 he confessed he had not put a pencil to a piece of paper to work out a problem in years. "I do it in my head." When asked in 1922 about the study of government, he held that such efforts were a waste of time, and when interviewed in 1940 about history, he replied, "Why, it isn't even true."[26] Arthur Pound, writing for *Atlantic Monthly* in 1924, claimed Ford, like the common man, "scoffs at learning that has no earning power, at influence that is based only on affluence, at history, art, and the finer graces of life, which even in a democracy, as yet, mean little to the masses."[27]

Some of Henry Ford's insensitivity to the fine arts is revealed in his experiences with Joseph Duveen, a famous art dealer who made a reputation selling valuable paintings to men of wealth. During the slump in the art market in 1920, Duveen and four other dealers decided to combine their talents to entice Henry Ford to become a substantial buyer of famous masterpieces. Elaborate preparations were made. Reproductions of a hundred great paintings of the world, each accompanied by a scholarly text, were published in three beautiful volumes. These purveyors of art went to Dearborn where they met the Fords in their home. According to the *New Yorker,* the art dealers were astonished at the simplicity of the house furnishings, but they found Mr. Ford delighted with the three illustrated volumes. The visitors presented these catalogues to Mr. and Mrs. Ford as a gift. When they asked the billionaire to buy some of the original paintings, however, Mr. Ford looked up in all innocence and said he did not need any of the originals because he already had the nice pictures in the brochures which had just been given to him.[28]

Such practicality may have astounded the art dealers, but not the average working man who gave little thought to esoteric verities. Those who met at the crossroads country store could understand why Henry Ford shied away from artists but paid tribute to those in science and technology by having carved above the entrance to his laboratory the names of Darwin, Franklin, Fulton, Whitney, Bell, Wright, Burbank, Edison, Burroughs, Diesel, Curie, Newton, Pasteur, and Galileo.

Whether Ford deliberately posed as a plebeian to curry the favor of the common man will probably never be known. But if he did, it took little effort on his part because his outlook on life reflected the midwestern agrarian mind.

Furthermore, Ford's economic thought reinforced the assumptions held by most farmers. He talked like a Populist in attacking Wall Street financiers who maliciously despoiled the public, while he himself had more wealth than any of the accused in New York City and was not adverse to making more. On one occasion, after visiting J. P. Morgan, he stated with a straight face, "It is very interesting to see how the rich live." He constantly identified with the lowly by asking where the bankers got all the money to build such impressive buildings? He knew of nothing in banking that could not be written on a milk stool. He often said interest did not stimulate honest production, that bond holders were parasites, and that it was folly to worship the gold standard. Ford insisted he made his money honestly, while bankers loan out money, collect interest, and let others do the work. A capitalist did not work at all, his money worked for him. Bankers, as a lot, knew nothing about business. Ford gained popularity on Main Street and Mill Street because of his open dislike for Wall Street. Some referred to him as "Wall Street's Shock Absorber."

This was something farmers could understand because they had excoriated bankers, middlemen, and city slickers since colonial days. The Greenbackers, Populists, and Non-Partisan Leaguers fought against eastern money interests. The cartoon featuring an elongated cow with her head eating grass in Kansas but with her udder being milked by New York bankers expressed this protest. The antibank fetish appealed to rural people because they were frequently in debt to money lenders and feared foreclosure of mortgages which would strip them of virtually everything they owned.

The resentment also applied to brokers, insurance executives, real estate dealers, and traveling salesman. One farmer warned that when some dignified devil wearing a plug hat, Prince Albert coat, checkered vest, and spats knocked on the door, he should be spurned because the visitor would invariably turn out to be a book agent, a lightning rod salesman, or a blue sky promoter.[29]

Ford pleased the farmers when he criticized the railroads as self-perpetuating corporations which were managed by inept directors, and who were more interested in securing dividends for the stockholders than in providing services for people at reasonable cost. The sale of stock only increased the prices charged by corporations because the dividends were tacked on the selling price to the consumer. Ford believed stocks should have real value, such as a bushel of potatoes sold at a vegetable market. He insisted stock companies were a curse to business and acted on this premise by buying out his original stockholders and keeping the management of his vast industry within the family. He also purchased the Detroit, Ironton, and Toledo railroad in 1919 to demonstrate that efficient management could improve service and reduce freight rates without losing money.

These pronouncements provided solace for ruralists who believed railroad magnates charged all the traffic would bear, made up the narrowest-gauged crowd in the business world, and resorted to more questionable practices than pawn brokers. Frank Norris in *The Octopus* depicted the Southern Pacific railroad in California as an evil force which exploited the ranchers in the San Joaquin Valley. The editor of the *Southern Cultivator* urged farmers to pull fodder, organize themselves, and protect their interests. If forefathers could fight John Bull for eight years and push his nose in the ground at Yorktown, now thirty million farmers need not stand by and see their labor sold for a song.[30]

Henry Ford personified the dynamic democracy of rural people. He was born on a Michigan farm on July 30, 1863, where he lived until he was sixteen years old. Since he disliked manual labor on the farm, he went to Detroit where he worked as a machinist in three different companies. In 1886, his father lured him back to the country by offering him a farm. But he stayed only two years, during which time he married Clara Bryant in 1887, built an agricultural steam engine of dubious value, and did some threshing for neighbors with a Westinghouse portable engine. He deserted the farm for the second time, returning to Detroit where he built his first quadricycle in 1896, an event which eventually led him into the automotive field.

The eighteen years he spent on a farm, however, made him a product of an agrarian society, and he never fully escaped from this heritage. He often mentioned that he had been "born on a farm and have always believed that the real future of America is in the land." On another occasion he commented that nothing contributed so much to an appreciation of real values as living in the open country or in a small community. When interviewed by Philip Kinsley of the Chicago *Tribune* in 1935 he commented that New York City and Chicago were not typical of this country. "America is out there among the old village sites, the small towns, and the farms."[31]

By stressing the virtues of rural life, Ford embellished the shibboleths of agriculturalists who had always been told that Adam and Eve were farmers, that Washington and Jefferson had praised them as God's chosen people, and that Lincoln had sanctified the log cabin. William Jennings Bryan in his famous Cross of Gold speech, shouted, "Burn down your cities and leave our farms and your cities will spring up again as if by magic, but destroy our farms and the grass will grow in the streets of every city in the country." James Bryce, in a Charter Day address at the University of California at Berkeley in 1909, insisted that living in the country developed better character than living in the city. Large rural populations created good government because the people were more stable than city crowds. He repeated the cliché, "God made the country and man made the town."

In this rural ethos, certain traits were apparent. Farmers tended to be informal in speech, shunned evening dress, despised tipping, and insisted on eating family style. Socially gregarious, they turned up at picnics, county fairs, literary societies, Sunday School meetings, and celebrations on the Fourth of July. They called on neighbors unannounced, talked about children, the crops, and prospects for rain. They minimized class distinctions, ate with the hired help, and picked their teeth with a blade of grass. They had been prejudiced against royalty and foreigners ever since the revolt against George III. The editor of the *American Thresherman* in 1904 noted that a few Americans, who started life driving cows to pasture and pitching manure and later became wealthy, now tried to barter their daughters to some shop-worn nobleman with a title as long as a broom handle and with holes in his socks. No sensible girl should allow herself to be placed on the auction block and be knocked down to a warty looking nobleman in exchange for his title of Senor Spaghetti Au Gratti, or Don Pedro Fernandez. "Talk about blood," he seethed, "Why half the so-called noblemen now on the market are simply apologies for men, while in the United States there are real men, worthy of any woman, who are cutting corn, running threshing machines, and who are better than any foreigner advertised in the herd book as wanting an American wife with a million dollars to sew patches on the seat of his Sunday pants."[32] William Hale "Big Bill" Thompson, mayor of Chicago in 1929, campaigned on the slogan "If George V sets foot here, I'll punch him on the snoot."

At least Henry Ford looked like a rural hero. He disliked high society, possessed simple tastes, and avoided ostentation. He dressed modestly, shunned crowds, and liked to stay at home with his wife. He had a folksy sense of humor, talked like a Chamber of Commerce man, was nonintellectual, and represented a polysymbolic ideal of the anti-corporation, pro-labor, democratic industrial genius and common man, to both rural and urban America. He was beloved throughout most of his career, and he provided a unique integer in the comparative mythology of the American capitalist. The man in the street felt a brotherhood with Ford, and as long as the symbol remained static, their attitude toward him remained constant.

II

The Automobile Alters the Rural Scene

Henry Ford was lucky. He sired the Model T car in 1908, the most propitious time to bring out a practical automobile to meet the needs of rural Americans. By this time most of the initial experimentation in the auto industry in the United States had been completed by the Duryea brothers, Elwood Haynes, R. E. Olds, Alexander Winton, Ford himself, and a host of other inventors. Not only had the automobile come to stay, but future events confirmed Thomas Edison's prediction in 1895, that the cars of the twentieth century would be powered by gasoline rather than steam or electricity.[1]

These early technological achievements opened up a vast market for the auto industry. In 1908 half of the people in the United States lived in towns of less than 2,500 inhabitants or on the six million farms in the country. Since there were only two hundred thousand automobiles in the nation, and less than 2 percent of the farm families owned cars, the Model T arrived at the best moment to ride the wave of the future. Philip Van Doren Stern called it the "right car at the right time at the right price."[2]

Fortunately, the Model T escaped the prejudice focused on the first automobiles by those who believed them inimical to the the welfare of rural people. In contrast, a friendly rather than hostile public greatly enhanced the popularity of the Tin Lizzie. The importance of this advantage can be better understood when contrasted with the stubborn resistance to the early automobiles by a large segment of the population.

Much of the rural opposition stemmed from the farmers who disliked innovation and feared the unconventional. This same rugged individualism had prompted some of their ancestors to wreck the spinning jenny, to insist that iron plows poisoned the soil, to ridicule the early railroads, to object to the first farm steam engines, to decry the advent of bicycles, and now to resent the appearance of automobiles on country roads. As one enlightened farmer lamented, "Its the same old bigotry, the same old prejudice against the new. . . . Mankind is instinctively hostile to change."[3]

Because of this rural conservatism, the first city auto drivers who streamed out onto the country roads were resented. The owners of these "Red Devils" were viewed as undesirable city dudes, devoid of virtue, swarming over the land like a plague of locusts. One farmer called them louts who thought farmers had more tobacco in their mouths than brains in their heads.

In addition, automobiles were playthings of the rich, demonstrating Thorstein Veblen's notion that the wealthy poured money into wasteful luxuries instead of into goods which would raise the standard of living. Honorable men worked, but city automobilists toiled not, neither did they spin. The Minneapolis *Journal* in 1899 reported that the auto craze had hit the fashionable people, like children with new toys.[4] The *Breeder's Gazette* in 1904 stated that the new auto fad smacked of privilege. Metropolitans were racing their cars over country roads without considering the safety of rural people.[5] In similar vein, the Philadelphia *Public Ledger* in 1906 protested the invasion of rural regions by city mobs that turned the highways into a reign of terror. These criminals were no more fit to be at large than so many mad dogs.[6]

Although the rural press exaggerated the dangers in driving the early automobiles, it is interesting to note how vividly these fears were expressed. The rhetoric revealed an anxiety which had reached the level of paranoia. The *Breeder's Gazette* in 1904 insisted that speeding cars roared by with screaming horns, "driven by a reckless, blood thirsty, villianous lot of purse-proud crazy trespassers upon the legitimate avenues of trade. A fear spread, paralyzing men, women and beasts.[7] Farm journals ran editorials under such titles as, "The Murderous Automobile," "The Deadly Auto," and "The Auto Menace." In 1906 the *North American Review* claimed automobiles had killed more people in the United States in the last five months than the number killed in the Spanish American War.[8] Others referred to the lawless, goggled, overbearing, insolent brutes crouching over their machines and enjoying the butchering with ghoulish delight. A farmer near Gas City, Indiana, said he saw a car approaching at a high rate of speed. The driver's face was set, his long hair streaming behind, with the speed mania coursing through his veins obliterating all sanity. As this apparition drew near, the farmer flattened himself against a fence to escape the menace. Some farmers refused to let their wives or children travel on the roads. One suggested intervention by the Humane Society.

During the horse vs. auto debate, some rural people took a legal position, arguing that the squatter's rights principle gave horses the preemptory rights to the roads. An Illinois judge pronounced this as an established common right, thereby branding the auto drivers as enemies of the general public. Some horsemen complained about the absence of democracy. Why should a majority of farmers bow to the will of a few automobilists scorching the country highways? The few should yield to the many. An opinion poll in 1903 showed only 5 percent of the American people favoring automobiles.

Furthermore, farmers insisted that they paid the taxes for road building, that they kept them in repair, that the roads were designed to move agricultural products to market, and that these highways belonged to those who had made them. One protestor remonstrated, "Why should I be run off the road I built and paid for?" If city drivers wanted to drive in the country they should buy land and build their own roads. Failing to do this, they should be forced to limit their driving to Sundays and holidays.

Added hostility came from livestock men who believed the auto detrimental to the horse and mule industry. The fourteen million horses in the United States represented a sizeable economic vested interest. If horses were replaced by automobiles, harness makers, horse breeders, and the publishers of journals such as the *Breeder's Gazette* would be ruined.

In addition, a sentimental affection for horse flesh lent weight to the anti-auto crusade. Intelligent horses were superior to brainless machines. No automobile could compare in beauty to a team of high-stepping trotters with thunder in their manes and fire in their nostrils as they raced along tossing their heads and blowing flecks of foam on their glossy necks. It was more fun to hold the reins over a spanking pair of Morgans than to clean spark plugs, recharge batteries, or handle axle grease. Cars were inanimate. The horse was made for man; what the auto was made for had not yet been found out. Walter Taylor, editor of *The Rider and Driver*, speaking in 1908, said he would paraphrase Mark Antony at the corpse of immortal Caesar and ask whether they had come to bury the horse or to praise him? Answering the rhetorical question, he described heroic steeds which protected their masters on dark roads, faced storms without flinching, and, if required, pulled the drunk driver home safely in his buggy. Lovers need only wrap the lines around the dash post while the carriage traversed pleasant places. Besides, horses never climbed trees or exploded. Warming to his subject, the speaker explained he had no Caesar on the cold slab of his contemplation, but only the lovable companion for which every human heart throbbed with reciprocal love. "Would you have this friend knelled," he pleaded, "and make the garage his tomb? Not I."[9]

For a time it seemed doubtful whether horses and automobiles could co-exist on rural roads. The horse lovers predicted farm horses could not be trained to face the motor juggernaughts on the highways. An Indiana farmer believed the horse never lived which could meet cars on the road with a cool head. When they bolted and ran away, one had as good a chance of stopping the team by grabbing the bridles as one would have trying to stop a railroad locomotive by grabbing the fireman's whiskers. A farmer in Wisconsin challenged anyone to come to his state and break horses to the auto because "every last horse up here is a fool." One car owner suggested that nervous horses that were afraid of automobiles should have their necks broken. Angered by this comment, a farmer explained that when a country boy went to town Saturday night, stayed in a saloon until he felt good, and then emitted a few hollers, he was promptly put in jail, but when auto fiends hit the highways at forty miles an hour, leaving death at every turn, then the old grangers must say nothing, simply break their horses necks.

The more stubborn farmers urged that cars be barred on country roads, and such laws were enacted in several counties in Pennsylvania and West Virginia. Extremists went further, urging vigilantes to take matters into their own hands. Farmers near Sacramento, California, in 1909, dug ditches across several roads to block traffic and actually trapped thirteen cars.[10] At times, logs, chains, broken glass, tacks, and cables were used as deterrents. The Minneapolis *Journal* on August 9, 1902, reported farmers near Lake Minnetonka preparing to fight against automobile drivers. As a result a chauffeur was shot in the back. Citizens in Walxroth County, Wisconsin, talked of carrying shot guns for self-defense.

Many engaged in wishful thinking in opposing the early automobiles. They hoped the new cars would prove too expensive to gain general acceptance. One farmer thought motor cars would become as notorious for conspicuous consumption as the purchase of yachts, living in high society, or sending a daughter to a private school for girls. This sentiment is expressed in a bit of doggerel describing the plight of Farmer Jones:

> He owned a handsome touring car, To ride in it was Heaven
> He ran across a piece of glass. . . . the bill, $14.97.
> He started on a little tour, the finest sort of fun,
> He stopped too quick and stripped the gears. . . . the bill, $99.47
> He took his wife down to shop, to save the horses was great,
> He crashed into a grocery store. . . . the bill, $444.88.
> He spent his pile of cash, and then in anguish cried,
> I'll put a mortgage on the house, and have just one more ride.[11]

Others hopefully believed the unreliability of automobiles would lead to their demise. Break downs were frequent. Sprockets wore out, chains broke, tires blew out, ignition systems failed, electric cars had battery trouble, and winds too easily blew out the boiler flames in steam cars. Mechanical malfunctioning coined the "Get Out and Get Under" maxim, while the bogging down in muddy roads prompted the phrase, "Get a Horse." A poetic indictment appeared in the *Ford Times* on January 15, 1909:

> *Father, dear father, come home with me now,*
> *The clock on the dashboard strikes one.*
> *Don't fuss with the car any longer pupah,*
> *You can't get the old tub to run.*
> *The cylinder's cracked and the timer won't work,*
> *And mother's been waiting since ten.*
> *So tether the car to a post, father dear,*
> *And come home on the trolley with me.*

Naturally, the pro-auto faction defended themselves with vigor. They insisted the fears of the horse crowd were based on unreasonable assumptions. All car drivers were not maniacs who left pedestrians dying by the roadsides or fleeing into the woods. Cautious drivers avoided accidents. An Ohioian, in 1904, reported driving 4,000 miles without killing or paralyzing either man or beast. The calamity howlers were pessimists who tried to blame everything from the boll weevil to housemaid's knee on the arrival of the automobile. The arguments of these croakers were decidedly *sui generis.*

Support for the use of motor vehicles was augmented in 1895

when E. P. Ingersall of New York began publication of *The Horseless Age*. Believing that civilizations rose according to their facilities of locomotion, he stressed the public's growing support for the automobile. He argued that if the auto frightened horses, so did railroad locomotives, street cars, Fourth of July celebrations, and lots of other things. To be sure, horses usually hated autos, but they feared almost anything unusual. On the contrary, an automobile would not shy away from parasols, wheelbarrows, flying newspapers, and strange noises. Besides motor vehicles would reduce the number of injured horses that fell on icy streets or died of sunstroke on hot summer days. The number of runaway teams dashing uncontrolled through crowded streets would be lessened. Furthermore, the roads should be open to all forms of transportation and not remain a monopoly of the king and his fat pony. Farmers should stop grumbling and writing silly letters to the newspapers. They should discontinue reading romances about the days of chivalry and refrain from attending too many horse shows.

As a matter of economics, the auto enthusiasts pointed out that horses were expensive to own. Most farm experts estimated that it took five acres of grain and grass to feed a horse for a year. A Texan, writing to Henry Ford in 1909, explained that the thing that stuck in his gizzard was that on the farm the greatest part of the produce went to feed horses. He added, "Let us use that ground for something we can eat ourselves."[12]

It is a gross misconception, however, to assume all rural people fought the introduction of the automobile. While it has been easy to depict farmers with their pitch forks and corn cob pipes as plodders far behind the times, yet among them were those with extraordinary mechanical ingenuity and technological acumen. These skills were demonstrated long before the advent of the ubiquitous Model T. As early as 1807 Southern planters purchased stationary steam engines to saw wood, gin cotton, thresh rice, and grind sugar cane. Following the Civil War, grain farmers bought binders, seed drills, cultivators, and mowers to reduce manual labor in agriculture. To secure more power, they used portable steam engines for threshing grain and other belt work. After 1875 these engines were self-propelled, enabling farmers to pull threshing machines from one farm to another. Before Americans had ever seen an automobile, approximately seventy-five thousand farm engineers were driving their steam engines across the fields in the major grain-producing regions of the nation. Awake to new ideas, these mechanical pioneers encouraged others to reject the horse and accept the new era of mechanized agriculture. Charles A. Singer, editor of the six volume *History of Technology*, insists that America became a fertile field for improved technology because American workmen liked machinery for its own sake.

Not only had many farmers in the United States been using steam engines for almost a century before the automobile appeared in 1892, but they had also been exposed to the stationary gasoline engine. The internal combustion engine, like the steam engine, had been invented in Europe. Jean Joseph Etienne Lenoir, a Belgian residing in Paris, patented an engine in 1860 which used illuminating gas for fuel. Nikolaus August Otto, of Cologne, Germany, invented a four-cycle engine in 1866 and received a Gold Medal at the Paris Exposition of 1867. During the next thirty years, forty-seven thousand five hundred Otto engines were sold in Europe and America.[13]

Significantly enough, these stationary gasoline engines reached American farms before the advent of the automobile, hence the notion that cars took rural people completely by surprise is fallacious. Why would farmers be awed by gasoline buggies if they were already operating internal combustion engines for farm work? As early as 1895, James A. Hockett of Sterling, Kansas, used a 16-horse-power gasoline engine for threshing grain, grinding feed, and pumping water. In 1900, The *Country Gentleman, Dakota Farmer,* and the *Nebraska Farmer* carried no advertisements for automobiles or tractors, but featured numerous ads for stationary gasoline engines such as the Leffel, the Foos, and the Fairbanks Morse. Before Henry Ford founded his company in 1903, *Wallace's Farmer* published numerous letters from farmers describing their use of gas engines for various types of belt work. A typical letter described the purchase of a six-horsepower engine in 1901. "I used it in grinding feed, shredding corn, and sawing wood. The engine does its work well, is easily kept in order, is always ready to start, and the cost of operating it is slight. . . ."[14] Other farm journals claimed these engines were so easy to operate that even women could run them. One farmer said a gas engine was like getting married; after one had tried it, he wondered why he had put it off so long.

In addition, many farmers were familiar with gasoline tractors before they drove automobiles. In fact the first tractors built in the United States appeared in 1892, the same year that Charles Duryea drove his first auto buggy in Massachusetts. During the 1890s numerous tractor companies manufactured experimental machines. There were approximately six hundred tractors operating on farms in the United States before the emergence of the Model T in 1908. As a result, the technical skills acquired in operating tractors could be transferred to the handling of automobiles. Many farm journals mentioned that when city auto drivers experienced trouble on country roads, they secured help from farmers whose mechanical knowledge surpassed urban competence. The *Motor Age* in 1910 claimed farmers had more skill in repairing autos than 80 percent of city drivers.

At the turn of the century, rural Americans added impetus to the boom in the auto industry because agriculture had been relatively prosperous from 1898 to 1918. The price index for farm products rose 52 percent from 1900 to 1910, a rate of increase that has seldom been duplicated in the nation's history.

With money in their pockets, farmers began buying automobiles until at times the demand exceeded the supply. New garages were built in every small town, while on Saturday night the town square was lined with farmer's cars. In 1910 one half of the automobiles in Iowa were purchased by rural people; in the following year the *American Agriculturist* claimed that farmers were the largest buyers of cars in the country. *Collier's*, in 1909, concluded that in Iowa one farmer in every thirty-four owned an auto, while in New York City the ownership was one to every 190 families.

Most of the early rural autos were sold by farm implement dealers, who added the gas buggies to their line of farm machinery. This was a natural business arrangement because many of the wagon and carriage factories began manufacturing high-wheel auto buggies to straddle the stumps and deeply rutted farm roads. For example, in 1908, M. M. Baker, a farm implement dealer in Peoria, sold farm steam engines, tractors, and six different makes of automobiles. His correspondence reveals scores of letters from farmers wishing to trade their old farm machinery for a new car. With horses selling for $150 to $300, many thought it more economical to exchange them for automobiles.

As auto sales zoomed, some business leaders feared the auto craze would endanger the financial credit of the nation and create tight money at the banks. Motor cars were said to be expensive, unreliable machines that tied up capital, piled up debts, and made money scarce in the market place. Farmers were criticized for spending money for vehicles which snorted, choked, and gurgled like a hog's snout in a trough of buttermilk. Farm implement dealers disliked the farmer's practice of buying farm machinery on three-year credit but paying cash for autos. To secure this money, they often borrowed from banks, sold livestock, or plastered their homes with mortgages. The *Wall Street Journal,* in 1910, reported that one automobile company had acquired $1 million of farm notes given for the purchase of cars. When one dealer was asked if so many people could afford to buy automobiles he replied, "They can't. People should be taught to save their money, but who are we to tell the neighbor that he is keeping an auto on a bicycle income."[15]

Apologists for the car-buying farmers were equally vocal. Most farmers insisted autos were not luxuries or fads, but were essential for business and pleasure. If eastern financiers were worried about public extravagance, they should attack the brewery industry. The editor of the *Gas Review,* in 1910, believed every banker posed as an apostle of the Almighty to guard other people's money. They were telling farmers not to buy automobiles, "but this whole crowd should put a muffler on their exhaust."[16]

The public image of the automobile improved following the San Francisco earthquake and fire of April 18, 1906. During these tragic days, autos were driven through fire, smoke, explosions, and debris to rescue victims and to carry doctors, city officials, and rescue squads. These cars carried food supplies, medicines, sped the wounded to hospitals and transported nurses to aid the victims. Three hours after the shock, the city was under martial law and every automobile put in the service of the militia. Since telephone wires were destroyed, messages were sent by carriers. One car owner ran his machine for forty-eight hours without rest. The so-called devil wagons were now angel wagons. J. C. Cunningham, a pioneer motorist who lived through the holocaust, later wrote that when horses fell from the heat, lack of water, and overwork, the motor car became the best rescue vehicle. These cars often ran on the rims because the hot pavement burned the tires off the wheels. Some frightened people seeking safety offered to pay $100 to any car driver who would carry them to safety.[17]

It was the medical profession, however, that proved the practicality of the automobile in rural areas. Henry Ford recalled that his first enthusiastic customers were country doctors who realized the importance of dependable transportation to a widely scattered practice.[18] A doctor living on the plains of Dakota in 1902 explained he had used an automobile in his practice for two years in a region where there were no other motor vehicles within a radius of fifty miles. In a November storm he made a trip into the country during a fierce blizzard. Snow reached to the hubs, but the car made the ten-mile trip in twenty-two minutes.

Although doctors for centuries had relied on horses, they required constant care, were limited in speed, and were subject to illness, lameness, and accidents. During intense heat waves, livery men refused to let their horses out on the road. One doctor abandoned horses as early as 1898 and drove 24,000 miles a year in a gasoline auto. The *Horseless Age* for Novenber, 1905, printed eighty-nine articles written by doctors describing their experiences with automobiles. A doctor in Illinois bought an auto in 1903 to replace his three horses. The company sent an expert to teach him to drive and make repairs. He raised the car on jacks twice a week to rest the tires and used a stove to heat the motor on cold mornings.

Since most doctors were mechanically minded, they were often as adept with wrenches as with scalpels. One physician spent forty-five minutes before breakfast oiling and tuning the vehicle. This service lasted all day except on long drives when the oil cups needed to be refilled. Every six weeks he had a mechanic clean the motor and tighten loose bolts. He traveled 30 miles per hour, made ten calls a day, covering 100 miles without fatigue, whereas a single forty-mile ride with a horse took all day and left him exhausted. One doctor stretched a canvas under the car to catch the nuts and bolts that shook loose during the days drive. Another advocated thirty minutes a day under the car looking for trouble spots. Some of the doctors thought that the early automobiles required too much cranking and that at times the repair work enroute left the medics looking like round house engineers. As a group, however, they liked to drive motor cars and most of them would probably have agreed with one doctor who swore that all automobiles were like Kentucky whiskeys in that none of them were bad.

As a rule, doctors rushed to farm houses to perform medical services. One doctor found his patient in need of an immediate operation. Since the kitchen lamp threw insufficient light, the doctor detached the acetyline lamps from his car and, piecing out the tubing that connected them with the generator, he proceeded with the operation. After the farmers purchased automobiles, however, they reversed the process by picking up the injured and rushing them to the doctor's office in town. A farmer in Kansas received a telephone call from a neighbor who said that his wife needed immediate medical care. By using a car, the woman was on the operating table in a hospital twenty-four miles away in less than two hours time.

For a vast majority of rural people, the arrival of the automobile gave new hope to those trying to keep young people on the farm. The fear of urbanization sprang from the notion that rural life was more virtuous than city life. Farm parents tended to think of cities as sinks of iniquity where sidewalk loafers hurled obscenities at innocent strollers and tried to lead them down the slippery road to ruin as fast as the wheels of destruction would carry them. The *Knoxville Sentinel*, in 1907, wanted to know why bright young farm lads were rushing to town to become forty-dollar-a-month dry goods clerks?

Now technology seemed the ideal answer for rural contentment. Automobiles and tractors would add a bit of excitement to farming, relieve monotony, and keep the boys on the farm. Farm journals urged farmers to buy cars so that the whole family could go for a spin after a hard days work. This would renew energy and provide new interst in life. The *American Agriculturist*, in 1909, believed all young people on the farm would work harder knowing there was some pleasure at the end of the day. The editor of *Gas Review*, in 1908, stated, "Let boys tinker with machinery. Don't tell them to feed horses, harness the grays, and plow the north forty."[19] A picture on the cover of *The Progressive Farmer* revealed a farm family cruising over beautiful country roads. The caption asked, "Would any boy or girl wish to leave a farm like this?"[20]

On the other hand, the more skeptical refused to believe that motor cars would create a rural Utopia. The frustrations of youth were too complex to be resolved by such simple suggestions as, "Give a farm boy an engine and see the smile on his face," or "The automobile ties the family together," or "The pure country air, fresh eggs, and brisk exercise make people healthy." The plain facts were that the hard physical labor on the farm often broke the health of the workers at middle age. One farm girl described her routine as rising at four, cooking breakfast for the family, milking the cows, getting the vegetables, washing dishes, canning fruit, preparing supper, cleaning the house, and going to bed. A mother, writing to *The Southern Cultivator* in 1913, noted that farm boys slept in unheated rooms in the winter. In the morning they tried to button their shirts with numbed fingers before going downstairs to build a fire, stumble out to the barn to do chores, and spend the day pitching manure. They kept going without any type of recreation and without anything to look forward to but meal time and sleep. Many worked for their parents for years without receiving anything more than room and board and a few clothes.[21]

Now, however, the automobile altered the rural scene by introducing a new dimension to people's mobility. While Americans by tradition were migratory, having crossed the Atlantic by boat and the western plains by covered wagon, steamboat, and railroad, the auto provided the individual with means of travel. Now the common man could strike out for himself, independent of schedules, passenger rates, and commercialized transportation. Earlier, travel had been confined to the upper classes. Rural people in the pre-auto days seldom went over twelve miles from their homes—a round trip a team of horses could make in a day. This explains why railroad towns in farm regions were usually spaced about twenty miles apart. A farmer near Berea, Ohio, writing to Edsel Ford in 1938, recalled that Henry Ford had done more than any man who had ever lived to free farm families from monotony and isolation. He remembered the early days of the Model T when farmers in working clothes could be seen driving down the road with their wives beside them and five or six children in the back seat. With curtains flying, they went along, happy, jolly, and wholesome. "Until your father provided low-cost transportation, the vast majority of these families had scarcely been five miles from home. I can truthfully say that every time such a family group met my eyes, I would reverently say, "God bless Henry Ford. . . ."[22]

This type of emancipation had real significance. Hamlin Garland claimed that isolation, boredom, and loneliness had driven pioneer women in the West insane, and Ole Rolvaag also emphasized this tendency in *Giants in the Earth*. The *Pacific Rural Press*, in 1910, insisted this hazard to mental health had been eliminated by automobiles, which annihilated distance, permitting farm women to get to town, go shopping, attend theaters, or visit neighbors.

The automobile relieved rural ennui by providing a diversion. The editor of *Collier's* in 1909 hailed the auto as the greatest social force in rural America, stronger than university extension work, telephones, rural free delivery, or trolley lines.[23] A little trip to look at the crops, a stop at the mail box, or a spin into town on Saturday were experiences of salutary pleasure. One cynic discounted this emancipation from tedium, saying the typical farm family with eleven children, four dogs and six cats could hardly be said to be living in isolation.

The liberating influence of the automobile seems convincing, however. Motor cars made attendance possible at lectures, religious camp meetings, and political rallies. It was often said that William Jennings Bryan was always good for forty acres of Ford cars at his Chautauqua programs. The attendance at entertainment centers in Hutchinson, Kansas, doubled in 1909 from the previous year, primarily because autos brought in rural folks. One farmer's wife cultivated corn in the forenoon, did the wash in the afternoon, and then took a sixty-mile ride into town to hear a band concert. When the state fair opened in Hutchinson in 1910, two hundred cars were parked on the grounds, most of them farmer's vehicles.

During the early days of the automobile, farmers frequently initiated "sociability runs" which included a group of farm families and which lasted several days. They carried picnic lunches and stayed in hotels. Denver, Colorado Springs, and other resort sites in the Rockies were favorite rendezvous spots. E. A. Knapp, of the United States Department of Agriculture, in 1910, noted that automobiles had increased the restlessness of an already mobile people. It bestowed status on the humblest segments of society. "Never before had any such proportions of the nationals of any land known the lifting spirit that free exercise of power and independence can bring."[24]

This wanderlust seemed to spread among rural folks; a yen to see something of the country. So they poked the radiators of their cars along obscure trails and probed remote terrain. After 1915 the "See America First" crusade thrived. Entire families gypsied along highways in quest of a cool spring, quiet shade, a fishing creek, or a country school yard, all eager to get close to the earth and to see nature with new eyes. Farmers did not feel conspicuous moving down the road with cars piled high with camping supplies, tents, and suitcases lodged between the fenders and the hood, and crates lashed to the running boards. The New York *World* on July 16, 1916, in an article, "Take Your Hotel With You in Your Ford," stated that tourists were camping by the roadsides because hotels were unable to accommodate the crowds. In 1920 approximately ten million people stopped in auto courts, and in 1925 the word "Motel" was coined. The lure of the road had become an obsession. Looking at this era, William F. Ogburn, the noted sociologist, declared that the inventors of the automobile had been more influential than the combined exploits of Napoleon, Genghis Khan, and Julius Caesar.[25]

If any rationale were needed to justify this peripatetic exuberance, it could be justified as a boon to good health. Roadsides dotted with campers represented clean fun, with children getting color in their cheeks, a new spring in their steps, and a renewed burst of energy. Rides in the country had therapeutic value as they banished worry and soothed jumpy nerves. The *Ford Times*, in 1914, claimed campers received motormorphic medicine because of the laws of motion. Babies were put in cradles, children rode rocking horses, savages swayed to sinuous dances, and grandmother rocked ceaselessly in a rocking chair. And now the automobile with its poetry of motion gave its occupants changing scenery, laughter, and an improved appetite. It produced sound sleep which "knit up the raveled sleeve of care." One auto enthusiast claimed a ride into the mountains increased the number of red corpuscles in the blood. An 82-year-old codger in California, in 1916, said he went west in 1891 to die, but later he began driving a Model T which rapidly improved his health and added years to his life. Some simply said, "Trade your doctor bills for an automobile."

The photograph files in the Ford Motor Company Archives in Dearborn portray much of the early history of touring and camping in America. Most of these pictures were taken by proud Model T owners who wanted to share their travel experiences. These scenes usually depict a brass radiator Ford parked under a tree, a camp fire nearby over which hovered a frying pan, sizzling with bacon and eggs. Scattered about were picnic baskets, coffee pots, camp stools, and a folding table. Some had kits resembling a built-in kitchen. One Model T had a box of supplies, a stove, a wash tub, gas can, funnel, and a tow rope all tied to the running board.

Since the tourists camped in remote areas, their supplies had to be substantial. A farm family driving to Lake Tahoe in California in 1915 explained they were all tucked in at night snug as cocoons, with a flash light and Colt revolver under the pillow, and with oil of citronella to ward off mosquitoes and hot rocks to heat the thermos bottles. Supplies included chairs, tables, sleeping bags, cooking utensils, a folding iron stove, a length of stove pipe, lanterns, and boxes of groceries. A New Jersey tourist, after traveling fifteen thousand miles, sent a picture of his Ford touring car with springs and mattresses piled six-feet high in the back seat.

Generally speaking, the cost of camping remained relatively

low. Prior to 1920, it was commonly believed that a family of five could take a month's vacation trip for less than one hundred dollars. Gas, oil, and groceries were the major items. Travelers bragged about the small cost for repairs. One drove from California to Ohio in 1918 with a repair bill of only $3.50, while another farmer from Pennsylvania visited Yellowstone Park with a repair bill of 25 cents. Asked if he were impressed with the sight of geysers he replied "I drove my Model T Ford, and the boiling water in the radiator shot higher than Old Faithful all the way to Altoona."[26]

The most simple camping technique involved sleeping on the ground beside the car wrapped up in a blanket. In the fall, some took oat bundles from adjacent fields to make a softer bed. Others removed the cushions from the car and made a bed on the ground.

Another method consisted of converting the auto into a pullman by putting hinges on the front seat permitting it to fold back to form a bed. One could also hinge the back seat letting it flop back like an endgate on a covered wagon. Again, heavy rods might be run from the top of the back seat to the front seat with a mattress placed on the rods. This method got travelers off the ground away from snakes and under cover of the touring car top.

The use of tents provided yet another type of camping comfort. Half-tents, with the car acting as a pole, provided an eight foot lean-to. Larger tents covered the whole car with sleeping quarters on both sides. Sinclair Lewis drove his Model T from Minnesota to California in 1916. His wife, Gracie, described the camping equipment:

> We also set about collecting a camping kit which included a tent designed by Hal. The five-passenger touring car, with the top up acting as a support, was tightly enclosed on all sides by the canvas, with a piece extended at a slant to form a tent long enough to shelter our air mattresses at night and a folding table and stools when it was not practical to eat outdoors. . . . Once more the town scoffed and we, too, were skeptical until we set it up at Fairy Lake and the darn thing worked. . . .[27]

Still a further method of camping made use of a panel truck built on the standard automobile chassis. The rear seat was removed and plywood or canvas enclosures were constructed to resemble the modern station wagon. A farmer in Montana built a camper large enough to accommodate two families. Another farmer in Illinois took off the deck of his Ford runabout, added a truck bed, and covered the space with a 24-foot tarpaulin. He traveled 3,000 miles through the midwest in 1918, covering 200 miles a day while averaging 16 miles to the gallon.[28]

The first trailers were made by cutting an old car in two and hitching the rear seat and wheels to an ordinary automobile. Others removed only the motor from the second car and thus added two seats to the trailer. An Arkansas farm family in 1919 loaded twenty-seven people into one of these trailer outfits and hauled them to a Farmer's Day celebration.

The thousands of rural Americans roaming the countryside revealed an ambivalence in human nature. After working hard to build comfortable homes, they now took delight in reverting to primitive camping conditons and bragged about the virtues of getting back to nature.

The novelty of travel impelled travelers to share their experiences and these adventures were significant enough to produce a vast literature in letters, articles, and books. From 1910 to 1920 newspapers in small towns carried numerous letters to the editor describing in detail trips to such places as Texas, the Grand Canyon, the northern woods in Minnesota, California, and Yellowstone Park. Some described the scenery in lyric prose, while others recorded mechanical problems or the cost involved in travel. These argonauts referred to narrow passes, hairpin turns, long grades, smoking brake bands, flat tires, sun burned faces, unmarked highways, and the distance between gas stations. Some tried their hand at humor, such as the tourist who, after crossing Death Valley, remarked that this godless place had all the advantages of hell without some of the inconveniences.

Some farmers, however, complained that the "go fever" had encouraged their neighbors to neglect their work at home. If the money going into travel were put into milk cows, money would be coming in rather than going out. They claimed farm lads were beginning to steal farm products, such as wheat, in order to get money for gasoline. A West Virginian in 1923 pointed to the automobile as the greatest curse to mankind, next to the traffic in whiskey.

The farm automobile proved to be more than a luxury, however, it became the most versatile and practical power available to the working man. During the harvest season, if a binder broke down, the operator could dash to town for repairs. Since getting work done on time could make the difference between a profit or loss, the time-saving car became a necessity. A newspaperman in

Kansas in 1910, noticed a threshing outfit suddenly stop. The engineer took a quick look at the separator, then raced to his automobile and started for a town seven miles away. Half an hour later he returned with new cylinder teeth to replace those knocked out when a pitch fork accidentally went through the machine. With a horse, it would have taken four hours to get repairs, while a crew of fourteen men remained idle.

Prior to the automobile, migratory field hands usually rode the box cars on trains to get to the harvest fields. In one evening alone, the trains entering Aberdeen, South Dakota, in 1905, were dotted with 500 transients, including hoboes, Y.M.C.A. boys, city clerks, and college students. These men usually worked like slaves during the summer months, saved a little money and then drifted back to the cities when snow fell. By 1914, these hired hands began to provide their own transportation by purchasing second-hand cars and moving northward with the harvest season from Texas to the Canadian provinces. This added mobility brought a sense of dignity to those who shocked grain and pitched bundles during the harvest season.

In addition, farmers used their cars for hauling all kinds of produce to market. Egg crates, milk cans, and boxes of vegetables were carted to town. A farmer in Iowa who wanted to rush some hogs to market, yanked the tonneau off his car, rigged up a large crate, and hauled the pigs to town. A neighbor, not to be outdone, put a colt in the back seat of his Model T and hauled it to a veterinarian. Stockmen often used cars to ride fence or to pick up newly-born calves to protect them from inclement weather. A tourist in Wyoming saw a girl herding cattle with a racy roadster, while in Cheyenne he saw a man placidly mowing his lawn with one. The owner of a one hundred thousand-acre ranch in New Mexico used five Fords in 1916 to repair windmills and round-up cattle. One man could do the work of three cowboys, and the cost of autos was one-fourth as much as using horses. He explained, "When we find it necessary to rope a steer, we can do it with a car as easily as with a horse."[29]

Few agencies have been more helpful to farmers than the rural free delivery which distributed mail and parcel post packages. By 1905 a number of mail carriers had substituted automobiles for horses. A rural mailman in Kansas served five hundred people on a 30-mile route which took nine hours with horses. After buying a car in 1910, he finished the job in three hours. This type of service aided the mail order houses and made the Sears Roebuck and Montgomery Ward catalogues the Christmas wish books for millions of farm children.

Another contribution of the automobile was in the field of religion. Most people agreed that improved means of transportation helped spread the preaching ministry into isolated areas which had no regular church services. Evangelists affiliated with the American Sunday School Union, like the circuit riders in the days of John Wesley, spoke to scattered groups that met in farmer's homes or rural school houses. If the Word took root, Sunday Schools were organized which often grew large enough to support a church. With a car, and by staggering his schedule, one preacher could preach in three or four different churches each week.

Automobiles increased church attendance because they made it easier for the elderly and shut-ins to get out Sunday morning. Farmers no longer had the excuse that their horses had worked hard all week and needed to rest on the Sabbath. Some families drove as far as 30 miles to attend services. Preachers with cars now rushed long distances to be at the bedside of the dying, conveyed the sick to hospitals, and took invalids out for rides in the fresh air. The pastor of the Christian Church of Baker, Oregon, placed a Model T by the church pulpit one Sunday morning and preached a sermon on "Ford and the Christian."[30]

On the other hand, there were plenty of Jeremiahs who prophesied that the automobile would mean the demise of the rural church. With a car a farm family could drive to town for church services. A minister in Georgia in 1912 attributed the declining membership of rural churches to the automobile and to a new crop of ministers who had lost their thunder and steadfastly refused to explode a little dynamite to soften up the hard pan and let the springs of truth gush forth. Paul Moody, the son of the famous Dwight L. Moody, in 1916 decried the decline of rural churches, while some returning missionaries claimed it easier to convert the heathen in foreign lands than to save souls in rural America. Some church leaders blamed the auto for enticing the flock to stray from the narrow path. Instead of being in church Sunday morning or at Wednesday night prayer meeting, the lost lambs were out joy riding, rushing into town to see movies, or necking in a parked Model T. It seemed uncertain whether it was the devil or technology which had hit the rural churches.

The Model T era likewise produced profound changes in rural education. In 1910 most of the country schools in the Midwest were one room, not unlike those of Edward Eggleston's *The Hoosier Schoolboy*. The teacher conducted all eight grades like a three-ring circus. Usually a picture of George Washington hung on the wall, a water bucket stood in one corner, and a pot-bellied stove provided the heat. But in the 1920s consolidation of schools became more prevalent since buses and private cars made it easier to transport children greater distances. High school attendance increased now that young people could live on the farm and commute to school in town. Since children began driving cars at age nine or ten, driving to high school was not unusual. This writer drove to high school in Faulkton, South Dakota, a distance of 22 miles each day. My brother and I did chores on the farm in the morning, then headed down the dirt roads regardless of weather conditions. On one occasion we hit icy ruts in the road and turned over in the ditch with a crate of chickens tied on the rear deck. These memories of age thirteen remain vivid. One of my letters written to a sister attending school in St. Paul, Minnesota, in 1925, included the following eye-witness account:

> . . . If you were home, you would see us start off to high school each morning. As we tear down the highway, the radiator of the Model T blows off steam, the wind whistles past our ears, and you might hear me yell, "Dave, choke her a little more, now turn the carburetor down, its only hitting on three cylinders, tap the coils, where are my mittens, keep her going or we will be late. . . ."[31]

On the farm the Model T proved extremely versatile. In the fall when sparks from railroad locomotives often set prairie fires, farmers would use a car to pull a walking plow to make a fire guard to control the flames. Model Ts were used as early as 1913 to fight forest fires. In butchering hogs, the power from a car could be utilized to hoist the pig out of the hot water in the scalding barrel. In the fields, Model Ts pulled hay rakes, mowers, grain binders, harrows, and hay loaders. Pick-up trucks stretched woven wire, hauled water to livestock, and distributed supplies where needed. Ford trucks hauled grain to elevators, brought cattle and hogs to market, and returned from town with coal, flour, lumber, and feed.

To secure belt power, farmers attached pulleys to the crankshaft, or bolted them to a rear wheel to utilize the 20-horsepower motor for grinding grain, sawing wood, filling silos, churning butter, shearing sheep, pumping water, elevating grain, shelling corn, turning grindstones, and washing clothes. One ingenious fellow used the spinning rear wheel to knock the shells off walnuts. One farmer said his Model T would do everything except rock the baby to sleep or make love to the hired girl.

Cognizant of the popularity of the Ford car, several companies manufactured attachments to convert the automobile into a tractor. The L. A. Tractor Company of Los Angeles sold an attachment which weighed 800 pounds and cost $150. Tractor wheels replaced the regular rear wheels and were driven by a set of gears. In Minneapolis, two firms, the American Ford-A-Tractor Company and the Handy Hank concern, built similar attachments for less than $225. Their catalogues featured Ford cars plowing, binding grain, and hauling freight. The ads claimed these mechanical units would displace hired men and provide power in the harvest fields for sixteen hours a day. In addition, the top provided shade and spring cushions added comfort.

All these designs had limited value, however, because automobiles were not built to work on full load in the heat and dust of the fields. They usually required special cooling systems, and the motors were damaged by the excessive strain. When the small tractor industry emerged after World War I, these make-shift tractors were ignored as bad investments. But they represented the faith of those who believed the Model T could do everything except talk and climb a tree.

III

The Ford Name Spreads Across Rural America

The rise of Henry Ford from obscurity in 1900 to national fame in 1920 represented a great achievement. If it were true, as stated by a New York *Times* writer in 1919, that Ford became the only man in our history to make farmers happy, then the factors behind this accomplishment become matters of paramount interest.[1] If the Ford mystique embedded itself in the rural mind, what techniques were employed in the process? Was the Motor King a shy, self-effacing person who shunned the limelight, or did he crave attention and become the most hungry publicity hound since P. T. Barnum?

Obviously, the soaring Ford reputation grew out of diverse forces and circumstances. Virtually unknown in 1903, he first attracted national attention in January, 1904, when he and Spider Huff set a new world's speed record for automobiles by streaking across the ice on the St. Clair river, covering a mile in 39⅖ seconds. After the event, seventy newspapers wired for special stories on this dramatic performance.[2]

It was the advent of the Model T, however, which made Ford famous, especially in rural America. The Tin Lizzie was only 100 inches long, could turn within a twelve-foot circle, and had enough power to pull itself out of loose sand and sticky gumbo. It could go almost anywhere. It had better steel than most automobiles and seldom would anything go wrong that could not be repaired by the average driver. Model T drivers usually claimed their cars could be fixed with twine, wire, clothespins, or chewing gum. The only tools

34

needed were a screw driver, a monkey wrench, a hammer, and a pair of pliers.

Yet the sales of the Model T required organization, salesmanship, good public relations techniques, and the wide use of the mass media. In retrospect, it appears that the Ford dealers scattered across the country performed a vital service. Convinced that people wanted to travel, they risked their capital to secure Ford dealerships. From 1908 to 1915, major dealerships embraced one to four counties with sub-dealers established within the district. By 1912 there were thirty-five hundred dealers in the United States, with more salesmen meeting the public than any other organization. This number rose to ten thousand in 1925, with an additional twenty-six thousand authorized service stations.[3] This meant that in the midwestern states farmers were seldom more than 15 miles away from a Ford service man.

Aware of the importance of public relations, the Ford dealers were admonished to keep salesrooms clean, to post "no tipping" signs, to use prescribed advertising in local papers, and to separate the salesroom from the repair department to prevent prospective customers from seeing mechanical failures. All agencies were required to carry one of each of the five thousand Model T parts in stock. Of these, 43 percent sold for 15 cents or less.[4]

During the T days, most dealers received their cars knocked down, in box cars, thus packing seven cars in the space of two assembled ones. A competent mechanic could assemble two cars daily, although at times it took a Houdini to disentangle the sub-assemblies.

Most Ford dealers took seriously the advice given in *Ford Times* in 1911, "Early to bed and early to rise. Work like hell and advertise." To demonstrate the power of the Model T, dealers frequently engaged in hill-climbing contests. In 1912 a Model T defeated four cars in a race to the top of Mount Wilson near Pasadena.[5] Similar contests occurred on Queen Hill in Seattle and Tamalpias near San Francisco. Another dealer-publicity stunt was running the front wheels of the Model T up the front steps of a house to demonstrate the flexibility of the three-point chassis suspension. One dealer drove up the front steps of the Y.M.C.A. building in Columbus, Nebraska; another scaled the steps of Alamo Square in San Francisco; while still another went up two flights of stairs, through a door, and into the hall of the courthouse in Paducah, Kentucky.[6]

For a brief time Ford cars were used to play auto polo as a means of advertising. On an ordinary football field, two stripped down Ts, with little more than a chassis and a protective steel rod above the driver, raced after a large white ball. A polo player rode on the running board of each car ready to drive the ball towards his opponent's goal. During the game the cars slipped, skidded, danced, and bumped about the field. Dealers claimed the Fords were the only cars that could play this game, because the planetary transmission allowed the driver to move forward or backward without shifting gears.[7]

Additional advertising appeared in local newspapers featuring such expressions as: "Ford, the Farmer's Car," "Your Harvest is Incomplete without a Ford," and "Don't Experiment, Just Buy a Ford."

Meanwhile car dealers borrowed many of the advertising gimmicks used by farm implement agencies at state fairs. To illustrate the sensitivity of the clutch on a steam traction engine, one of these fifteen-ton machines would be slowly backed up to a post on which hung a watch with an open back. The engine backed gently until the watch snapped shut without breaking the glass face. At times these steam engines climbed an inclined plane built at 45 degrees. As crowds held their breath fearing the engine would overturn, a steam calliope boomed out incidental music effects to accompany the rhythmic bursts of smoke from the engine. Some of the Ford dealers ran their Model Ts up the same ramp to prove their hill climbing ability. At a fair in Seattle, a dealer placed a Ford on a teeter-totter five feet above the ground. The car moved forward and backward to demonstrate the accurate control over the car.

To seek publicity, a Ford dealer in Houston ran his car ten miles per hour for six days and nights without stopping the motor. A dealer in Litchfield, Minnesota, hauled the entire graduating class of thirteen students; while at St. Hilaire, Minnesota, fifty boys weighing 3,492 pounds climbed into a Ford touring car. In Paducah, three hogshead of tobacco and twenty-six men were piled into a Model T and driven through the town. Another dealer took the entire St. Louis Browns baseball team out for a ride in a Tin Lizzie.

In 1908 a Ford dealer in St. Louis organized "Ford Clubs" to promote sociability and sales. In a spirit of fraternity, Ford owners banded together to attend picnics, band concerts, or to go on excursions. As many as six hundred families joined in these special events.

With more than a million Fords on the road in 1916, many county fair boards decided to set aside "Ford Days" to give these families special recognition. On one of these occasions, a Ford dealer in Las Vegas sponsored a Model T rodeo. As an announcer introduced the exhibition as America's most dangerous sport, a Ford touring car stood outside a corral filled with high strung Mexican steers. When the gates opened, a wild longhorn rushed out across the field with the Model T in pursuit. As the car drew closer, a cowboy leaped from the running board to grab the steer by the horns and wrestle him to the ground, while thousands cheered.

Many of these events took on a typical folksy, rural atmosphere. The Ford Day in Wausau, Wisconsin, in 1914, attracted some five hundred Ford owners. In a local bank, forty five-dollar gold pieces spelled out the word Ford. During the day, prizes were given Ford owners who brought the most people to the event, the one who came from the greatest distance, the one who had the prettiest girl passenger, the one who could make the quickest change of a tire, the one with the noisiest Ford, the best decorated one, the most dilapidated one, and the car with the fattest driver. Free coffee and lemonade were served. A Ford drivers test determined how many could move their car at less than one-half mile an hour in high without killing the engine. Those who guessed the closest to the number of Fords in the parade received awards. In 1914 there were 10,688 registered Ford owners in Wisconsin, with 1,200 of them showing up for the Ford Day at the state fair in Milwaukee. As one reporter noted, "It seemed as though the whole countryside had taken a holiday and gone A-Fording."

For the San Francisco Exposition in 1915, elaborate exhibits were prepared to help celebrate the opening of the Panama Canal. Among these were three prepared by the Ford Motor Company. In the Palace of Mines, an exhibit demonstrated the improved living conditions in Detroit created by the profit-sharing policies of the company. In the Palace of Education, a motion picture showed improved working conditions, while in the Palace of Transportation an assembly line produced eighteen Ford cars each day before the eyes of thousands of spectators. In fact this assembly was the most popular exhibit at the fair. Here an endless chain moved over a narrow-gauge track. First the rear axle unit went on the chain, then the springs, brake rods, fender irons, gas tank, engine, and body parts. Cars run off the line provided rides for dime fares. This exhibit received the Grand Prize, Medal of Honor, and Gold Medal,

the three highest awards in these fields. Thomas Edison and Henry
Ford received bronze medals. Rose Wilder Lane writing for the San
Francisco *Call Bulletin* told how a poor Michigan farm boy rose to
fame but never lost touch with humanity. Edsel Ford joined the
celebration after driving a Model T from Detroit, a 35-day trip re-
pleat with hardships of travel over bad roads and camping in desert
country.

To enhance advertising, the Ford Motor Company Band of
fifty-five members came to San Francisco in July. En route the
musicians traveled by train, stopping in such major cities as Minneapolis, Fargo, Butte, Spokane, and Seattle. Returning by way of
San Diego and Denver, the band played before a crowd of 40,000
in Omaha.

Eager to capture public favor, a Ford Clinic was opened in
New York City in April, 1919, to demonstrate how to repair disabled
cars. The clinic imitated the medical profession with an operating
room built with seats for spectators. Surgical tables held tools of
every description. Several healthy Fords had been vivisected. A
"surgeon" from Detroit operated on the Universal Car. The press described the Ford doctor treating Model Ts for sprained axles, tu-
bercular radiators, rheumatic valves, fractured bearings, and afflic-
tions of the crank case.[8]

In the small towns Ford dealers supplied the local newspapers
with timely information. Pictures were supplied depicting Model
Ts which had hit trees, bridges, fence posts, or ditches. The captions
read, "Bent but not Broken." A grandmother in Pine Creek, Oklahoma, was shown at the wheel of a Model T on her hundredth birthday. An armless dealer was shown cranking his car with his feet. At
Mount Carrol, Illinois, a dealer took a photograph of eleven Model
Ts owned by a father and his ten sons. Another claimed the Ford
handled so easily that a woman could drive with one hand and knit
with the other. In Brockhaven, Mississippi, a dealer rang the bell in
the town whenever he made a sale. In Spartanburg, South Carolina,
in 1923, four mechanics disassembled a Ford roadster and reassem-
bled it inside a local newspaper office in less than two hours. In
Oregon, a weight lifter hoisted a Ford on his back, while some dealers hung the Model T from the ceiling with wires attached to the
fenders to prove its toughness. Cash prizes were offered to school
children for essays explaining why the Ford was the best car on the
market. Essays were limited to forty words, and contestants were
asked to avoid the well-known expressions, "Watch the Fords Go
By," and "You Can Afford a Ford."

Well-known personalities helped spread the Ford name in the press. When President Wilson bought a Model T for his summer home in 1914, the information had national coverage. In the same year, when William Howard Taft visited the Ford factory at Highland Park, he exclaimed, "It's wonderful! Wonderful! I am amazed at the magnitude of the establishment. I can almost hear the wheels buzz, and the machinery hum now."[9] When Eddie Foy left the Ford plant, a reporter asked, "Got a car, Foy?" He replied, "Yes, and it's a Ford." "Why do you like it?" asked the newspaperman. "Because it goes." Ring Lardner quipped, "Henry Ford once said that he would rather be right than president, but I will go him one better and say I would rather have a Ford than be Henry."

The Model T also received attention at various state fairs. Farmers had traditionally supported these fairs because of their interest in livestock, machinery, and entertainment. Horse racing had been a favorite attraction, but after 1900, the automobile began to compete for attention. By 1908 auto races were common during fair week. Some of the excitement could be seen at the fair in Syracuse, New York, in 1911. Here 6,000 people watched Frank Kulick in a Ford race against a Mr. Robertson in a six-cylinder Knox. Robertson took an early lead with Kulick on his heels as they circled the track. Kulick pulled even during the third lap as they raced past the grandstand going 70 miles an hour. Most fans expected Robertson to defeat Kulick, but just as they reached the stands, "Kulick pulled the throttle on his 20-horsepower Ford and the little machine jumped into the lead leaving Robertson in the dust as if his high-powered racer had been spiked to the track. Ex-President Theodore Roosevelt leaned out of the stands as far as he dared, clapped his hand, and yelled again and again, "Marvelous, marvelous, marvelous."[10]

For several years Henry Ford furnished cars for Kulick. In the Mardi Gras races in New Orleans in 1911, he defeated drivers in a 90-horsepower Fiat and a 100-horsepower Buick. At the Michigan State Fair in the same year, he defeated a 200-horsepower Benz, covering a mile in 51 seconds from a standing start. In appreciation, Ford gave Kulick a thousand dollar bill. However, after a subsequent racing accident, Ford withdrew from the racing business because he was now convinced that this sport was too hazardous.

Meantime, Ford dealers participated in stock-car races. A Model T driven in Saskatchewan won thirteen trophies in three years. The Flivver also won its share of reliability runs such as the 191-mile trek from Washington, D.C., to Boston; from Kansas City to St. Louis; from North Platte to Omaha, and the 600-mile run from Jacksonville, Florida, to Asheville, North Carolina.

With attention focused on endurance, a transcontinental race between New York and Seattle took place in 1909, as the grand-daddy of all endurance tests. Thirty-five auto companies promised to send entries but only a Stearns, Acme, Shawmut, Itala, and two Fords showed up at the starting line. President Taft pushed a golden key, Mayor McClelland fired a gold revolver, and they were off, the winner to collect $2,000 in gold. Robert Guggenheim provided the winner's trophy. The drivers encountered deep mud near Toledo, quicksand near Denver, and snow in the mountain passes. After three weeks, the Ford car driven by B. W. Scott and C. J. Smith reached Seattle first, but was later disqualified for the prize because the judges ruled that the drivers had received some outside assistance enroute. This endurance test brought great publicity for the Ford Motor Company and demonstrated the practicality of light cars on poor roads. To capitalize on this achievement, the company published thousands of booklets relating *The Story of the Race.*

To gauge public reaction, the Ford company in 1911 polled two thousand Ford owners asking them why they bought the car. When 85 percent said they took the advice of other Ford car owners, the company emphasized testimonials in its advertising. These appeared in *Ford Times*, a bimonthly illustrated magazine which went to the news desks and nine hundred thousand prospective customers. Laudatory letters were published and human interest items were featured, such as Billy Sunday's opinion of the Model T or the remarks of the Tasha Lama of Urga when he received a Ford car after a 700-mile drive across the Gobi desert.

From foreign lands photographs proved the versatility of the Model T. They were shown as taxis in Egypt, as "warmobiles" in Jan Smut's army at Capetown, as police cars in Perth, Australia, as a substitute for dog sleds in the Klondike, as crossing a swaying suspension bridge in Chile, as a vehicle for a doctor in Tientsin, as a hunter's vehicle for shooting elephants in India, as a car used by matadors in Mexico City, as the first car to cross the Pir-i-zan Pass in central Persia, as a winner in an endurance run in Russia where Czar Nicholas II reviewed the competing cars, as pictured before the temples in Bangkok, and as the first Model T advertised in a Japanese newspaper. Today these negatives and prints are filed in the photographic collection in the Library in Greenfield Village in Dearborn—a graphic pictorial record of automotive transportation.

Ford officials also used motion pictures to embellish the image of company products. David L. Lewis, a public relations expert, claims the Ford Motor Company was the first industrial firm to produce and distribute films. From 1914 to 1924, the company maintained one of the best equipped studios in the motion picture business. Over half a million dollars were spent annually on the project.[11] These 15-minute documentary newsreels were loaned to local theaters free of charge. From 1917 to 1920 they were shown regularly in four thousand theaters and seen by five million people, or one-seventh of the weekly motion picture audience.[12] In these films, the Model T made subtle appearances but without commercials. After 1921 the circulation of the Ford films declined, yet on Saturday nights in many rural communities they were projected by local Ford dealers, some of whom used Ford cars to generate the electricity for the projectors. The reels stressed the need for better roads, the necessity to raise improved livestock, and how to keep boys on the farm. When the ten millionth Model T came off the assembly line in 1924, the company distributed a 30-minute film called "Fording the Lincoln Highway," showing a Model T crossing the continent and being honored by Hollywood celebrities. A second film, entitled the "Ten Millionth Hit for Ford," featured Eddie Plank, the former star baseball pitcher for the Philadelphia Athletics. In October, 1924, over a million people saw the movie. Dealers showed it in schools, churches, civic organizations, while the University of Pennsylvania used it in various classes.

The motion picture industry in Hollywood made use of Ford cars, especially in comedy scenes. Charlie Chaplin and Laurel and Hardy performed all kinds of antics ranging from plunging over cliffs to double-crossing the cops. A spectacular trick showed a Model T meeting a railroad locomotive head on in a tunnel. A few moments later the Ford would emerge, but flattened to a width of two feet and still moving under its own power. The car had been constructed with hinges which permitted this freak appearance. The movie "Tobacco Road" utilized a Ford convertible which ran without adequate water, oil, or tire pressure. It still ran after being hit by a falling tree.

The smashing success of the Ford enterprises created news. Most Americans took pride in the triumph of technology, believing that they, too, were part of the American dream. Each fragment of information added to the Ford stature. Small weekly newspapers seemed to glory in statistics, as if the figures themselves embodied a kind of virtue. Frequently, when a farmer bought a new Tin Lizzie he got his name in the local paper. The arrival of carloads of new Model Ts were mentioned, as well as the fact that they had all been sold before they could be removed from the box cars. The press in 1910 claimed the Ford factories manufactured 2,000 cars a month; two years later the figure reached 26,000 cars every thirty days, or a new car every 45 seconds.

In fact the data seemed inexhaustible. Ford motors weighed 7.95 pounds for every cubic inch of piston displacement; other cars averaged 11.2 pounds. Ford cars used 380 acres of glass in 1924, while it took 400,000 hides to furnish the leather for one year. By 1924, Ford cars sold for 20 cents a pound, with the price of a run-about selling for $260 F.O.B. Detroit. At the time, the company paid one-fourth of a billion dollars in wages, and thirty-one thousand salesmen worked out of thirty-five branches of the company. Ford sold 22.03% of all cars sold in the United States in 1912; 42.24% in 1917; 54.57% in 1920; 61.34% in 1921 and 51.85% in 1923. In 1924 the people of this country bought Ford cars at the rate of 250 an hour, 24 hours a day, for 300 days of the year.[13] Sales in three agricultural states in 1915 were as follows: [14]

KANSAS		MINNESOTA		COLORADO	
Ford	19,411	Ford	19,339	Ford	8,418
Buick	5,430	Buick	5,781	Buick	1,589
Overland	3,987	Overland	4,973	Overland	1,544
Studebaker	3,982	Studebaker	4,001	Studebaker	959
Maxwell	2,180	Maxwell	2,260	Cadillac	758

In the meantime, Henry Ford himself became one of the greatest sources of news to reach Americans in all walks of life. His agrarian background endeared him to most rural people. Here was a poor farm boy who made good—a rags to riches story in Horatio Alger mold. It was said that Henry as a lad rose before dawn to milk the cows before trudging off to school two miles away, often through rain or blinding snow storms. Young Henry stayed home in the evenings, avoiding pool halls and shunning the world of the flesh to repair watches, to tinker with machinery, and to devise ways to get rid of the heavy manual labor on the farm. His mechanical skill and business ability made him the wealthiest American. His cars, trucks, and tractors changed rural life. That his parents had been reasonably well-to-do farmers received little attention in the press, nor was much mention made of the fact that he left school at age fourteen and left home at sixteen to try his luck in the city. Any hint that he might have left home against his parents' wishes was conveniently ignored.

The early description of Henry Ford as a devoted nature lover appealed to those who lived on the land. The papers in 1910 reported an incident in which a man killed a robin and Ford offered to take his car and run down the miscreant. Naturalists applauded when the Fords built five hundred bird houses on their farm to attract martins, thrushes, wrens, chickadees, nuthatches, woodpeckers, and wood pewees. S. S. Marquis, a friend of the family, wrote articles for the North American Newspaper Alliance in which he stressed Ford's interest in the world of nature. Marquis said Ford would frequently spend a whole day in the woods with a ten-year-old boy to teach him something about bird watching. He fed and protected the birds in winter. He imported four hundred birds from England. When a robin built a nest over his front door, he used the back door until the new fledglings were able to fly. On another occasion, the farm hands prepared to harvest a field of oats, but Henry waved them off until the meadow lark eggs had hatched. Mrs. Ford, likewise, took an interest in the deer on the estate, and her gardens held over six hundred varieties of roses. She sponsored the Garden Club of Dearborn and served as president of the National Woman's Farm and Garden Association.

Farm journalists, looking for a story, often visited the Ford farm in Dearborn. Mr. Ford liked to guide his visitors around his 7,000-acre farm and discuss agricultural problems. Andrew S. Wing, editor of *Farm and Fireside* interviewed Ford in September, 1925. His article stressed Ford's virtuous childhood, praised his efforts to mechanize farming, and voiced praise for his desire to rid farms of most of the horses, cows, and sheep. When asked what people would wear if wool were unavailable, Ford said he planned to grow flax on his farms in northern Michigan to provide linen for this purpose. *Successful Farming*, with a circulation of 800,000 families in 1916, described the harvesting of 3,000 acres of wheat on the Ford farm. Clyde L. Herring, writing for *The Farm Journal* in 1924, stressed Ford's love for his boyhood home, all of which added to the growing legend of the auto magnate. Herring claimed that at one time Ford refused to plow a three-acre patch on his farm, because as a boy he had lost a second hand from his watch and still hoped to find it. With meticulous care he restored his parent's farm house and kept the wood box filled, the water bucket repaired, and kept groceries on the pantry shelves. When asked why he had preserved the home for fifteen years, Henry stated that they might come back some day and live there. When old broken dishes were found in the yard, Ford sent all over the country to match the same patterns. He kept his childhood room in its original condition and refused to permit the orchard to be cut down, preferring to let the trees die of old age.[15]

Although this type of publicity was skillfully done and partly true, the press tended to dramatize the nostalgia of the bucolic life. Edgar A. Guest touched the zenith of sacred emotions by writing an article for *The American Magazine* in 1923 entitled, "Henry Ford Talks about His Mother." The journal had a circulation of 1,900,000. Guest listened to Henry explain that his mother believed in work, discipline, and honesty. She never got behind in her work and believed in duty as a rule of life. All bumps, bruises, or burns were lessons rather than accidents. She served wholesome food and washed the clothes on Monday, not Tuesday. "I have tried to live my life as mother would have wished," Ford told Guest, "She taught me as a boy that service is the highest duty in the world."[16] One woman wrote to Ford saying, "I read the article in *The American Magazine* and pray God may prosper you for what you said about your mother. When I read about the old fashioned embroidered slippers, I could not keep back the tears."[17]

Henry Ford alluded to his agrarian origins as though there were virtue in rural living. To pep up a sales meeting in Poughkeepsie, he wired on February 22, 1922; "Having been born and raised a farmer, I know what it means to work long hours for pretty small returns. . . . Farming is and always will be the foundation on which the economic growth of our nation depends."[18]

Cognizant of the value of publicity, Ford fed news to the press constantly, acting as a fountain of wisdom and sounding off on topics ranging from international finance to the question of the best cure for corns. Apparently he believed his financial success qualified him to speak on virtually all issues. The small notebooks which he carried are filled with trial and error attempts to formulate pithy maxims with a punch line containing a significant truth. He scribbled down such comments as, "The world will never go back." "People are here to learn," "Remember many of you tried to get rich at somebody's else's loss," "No one can hurt nature," "i expect to have all the money i can use as long as i live, and so will every one else if they use it for the benefit of others."[19]

Since the news about Ford circulated widely, apocryphal statements were often repeated as the gospel truth. One account claimed that Ford changed his telephone number every day to avoid interference. Another said he once carried a $50,000 check around in his greasy overalls for three weeks because he had forgotten it. It was said some banks refused to accept million dollar deposits from Ford because of the fear that he might withdraw it all at once, thus breaking the bank. Items appeared in papers indicating that Ford planned to buy Standard Oil or that he would sell out to this corporation. Following World War I, newspapers reported Ford turned all his war profits, $29 million, back to the United States Treasury. Ford allegedly stated, "If all the war advocates had done the same the country's war debts would be less staggering and there would be less talk of war profiteers."[20] Andrew Mellon, attempting to verify this story wrote to Henry Ford on March 16, 1922, saying he had checked the Treasury files but had not found such a donation.[21] E. G. Liebold, Ford's secretary, replied saying this statement appeared in Sarah T. Bushnell's book *The Truth about Henry Ford*. Since Ford had never seen this book nor had he authorized its publication, he felt no responsibility for the origin of the story.[22]

The degree to which newspapers embellished the facts can be seen in the treatment of Ford's design of the rear axle for his tractor. The Detroit *Times* on July 6, 1915, merely stated that Ford had solved the rear axle engineering problem while returning in his car from Benton Harbor. The Detroit *Free Press* improved on the account, stating that Edsel was driving the car returning from Benton Harbor when Henry suddenly shouted, "Stop a minute. If I don't say anything to you for awhile, don't think I'm crazy. I am thinking about something." The car stopped and Ford sat in meditation. Not a word was said. At the end of forty minutes, Ford looked up and said, "Drive ahead, I've got it." The axle problem was solved. It was a worm-gear contrivance.[23] The Baltimore *Evening Sun* on September 27, 1915, dressed up the incident by explaining that Ford stood on a crest of a hill on his Dearborn estate and looked across the valley of the Rouge river where in boyhood, with one suspender and barefoot, he had driven a mule to plow a field under a broiling summer sun. All land around him as far as his eye could see was his. He had come back to the soil, where, flushed with wealth accumulated at a rate of $20 million a year, he had selected his home. Ford said he made cars for twelve years, merely to develop a farm tractor. In thinking about the axle of the tractor while riding with his son, he exclaimed, "Stop a minute son, I want to think of something." In the middle of a lonely road, the car halted. Mr. Ford was busy in the back seat with pencil and paper. He tore up pieces of paper. He began drawing others. Paper littered the car. At the end of forty-five minutes, he looked up at his son and said, "Go ahead, I've got it. Got what? The axle on my tractor. Been working on it ten years and I've got it settled."

Although Ford seldom spoke in public, he broadcast his views in the newspapers. The front pages often ran captions citing his accomplishments or projected future plans. News stories such as: Ford buys railroad; Ford urges free trade; Ford will salvage 90 million feet of lumber annually; Ford will replace iron with aluminum; Ford will spend $7 million on advertising; Ford will build the world's biggest radio station; Ford will buy dirigibles; Ford will build ocean airliners; Ford will ship 10,000 tractors to Russia; Ford will manufacture a million cars this year; Ford will drill three oil wells; Ford will send Richard E. Byrd to the South Pole; Ford will pay Edsel $415 a day, and Ford will run for President.

Henry Ford liked to read newspapers. According to his butler, J. D. Thompson, he spent hours reading the local papers and clippings from other newspapers which referred to his life and activities. He also enjoyed the comic strips, especially "Little Orphan Annie." In fact, his curiosity became so intense that at times he would ask his secretary to get in touch with the cartoonist Harold Gray for advance information on what was going to happen to Little Annie. He followed Amos n' Andy on the radio and again got advance notice on the script.

Surprisingly enough, Ford initiated a flood of copy even though he did not have a public relations department during most of his industrial career. At times he gave interviews to individual reporters whom he admired, such as Arthur Brisbane of the Hearst chain and James Swinehart of the Detroit *News*. If he liked a reporter, he would give out information; if he disliked the correspondent, he would turn him away empty handed. At times large press conferences were held with reporters firing all kinds of questions, much like presidential press conferences. These moments were usually a battle of wits. When the Model A came out in 1927, a big press conference was held in New York. A cub reporter from the New York *Mirror* kept asking Ford how much he was worth. After the fourth time, Ford turned to the chap angrily and said, "I don't know and I don't give a damn."[24]

Controversy still exists as to how Ford handled his press conferences. E. G. Liebold and Fred L. Black both worked closely with him for thirty years. Liebold insisted that Ford was so inept and inarticulate that newsmen could not follow his line of thought. "He didn't seem to have the facility of being able to go into much detail to explain his ideas," recalled Liebold, and "We had to feel our way and interpret Ford's views to the Press."[25]

On the contrary, Fred Black remembered Ford as a great press character. He was adept in sidestepping embarrassing questions and often parried tricky queries so cleverly that the newsmen would howl with laughter. He never held grudges against publishers who criticized because he believed in free publicity far more than he did in paid advertising. He was a past master in getting attention. Mr. Black insisted:

> Henry Ford was the top guy for creating top stories. Nobody made Henry Ford from the publicity standpoint except himself. Any Ford legend would start with the boss himself, rather than engineered by any staff member. This idea that Ford was an ignoramus, and had his smartness due to his public relations men who engineered all his stuff is absolutely untrue. It was a strange combination. He was a very shy man with an amazing sense of public value. Henry Ford was the most complex man I have ever known. We generally agreed on that, Cameron, Ben Davidson and the rest of us. . . .[26]

A good example of Ford's flair for a good story occurred in 1936 when Dr. James F. Cooke, editor of *The Etude*, interviewed Mr. and Mrs. Ford. Henry's musical appreciation had been limited to folk music and his ability to play the jew's harp and a few tunes on the violin. His taste ran to such musical gems as "The Old Gray Mare," and "Who Threw the Overalls in Mrs. Murphy's Chowder." At first glance, it would seem that a meeting with the learned Dr. Cooke might be a sterile encounter. Yet the results were superb. The Fords took Dr. Cooke through Greenfield Village where two hundred acres had been set aside to preserve America's cultural heritage. Mr. Ford pointed out rare musical instruments such as an old German street organ and the famous Maud Powell Guarnerius violin. He talked about his love of simple tunes in music and told how he had purchased what he thought had been the birthplace of Stephen Foster and moved the house to Dearborn. While three musicians played "My Old Kentucky Home," on the organ, vibraphone, and dulcimer, Ford gave a detailed account of Foster's life and the furnishings of the home. A perpetual flame burned in the fireplace, lighted by fire sent by Stephen Foster's daughter, Mrs. Marion Welch. Ford suggested everyone would be happier and healthier if they would sing every day. Singing was a mental tonic. "Start the day with a song," he urged. "Singing starts the day right."[27]

The phenomenal financial success of Ford naturally received considerable attention in the press. Estimates were made of his wealth, and there was much speculation on the the reasons for this extraordinary achievement. Even the views of phrenologists were offered.[28]

Every story about the Ford car brought the Ford name more publicity. In the First World War, the Model T carried troops up to the front lines in France. The Marines used them for hauling supplies and ammunition in the battles of Belleau Wood and Chateau Thierry. At times the tires were shot off and the cars pierced with machine gun bullets. The Tin Lizzie was even recommended for the Distinguished Service Cross after the battle of the Argonne. "Hunka Tin" touched a sentimental note in a parody on Kipling's "Gunga Din."

The postcard fad which blanketed the United States prior to 1920 was another means of spreading the fame of the Model T. These comic cartoons went through the mail with one cent postage. The punch lines stressed the smallness of the car, its low price, and its simplicity. Exaggeration became the essence of humor. A sketch of a dog with a miniature Ford tied to its tail carried the explanation, "They used to tie tin cans to my tail, now its Fords." Birds in trees watching the Fords go by chirped, "Cheap, cheep, cheep." When a Model T scampered by a limousine mired in the mud, the caption read, "The big car fumes and throws a fit, but the little Ford don't mind a bit." A goat afflicted with stomach cramps complained, "I ate a Ford and it's still running." One card had the line, "War is Hell and so is riding in a Ford." Another one pictured a Model T parked on top of a mountain while a big car stalled at the hotel in the valley. The caption read, "While the huge car sticks around the beanery, the Ford goes up and views the scenery."

Just as novel were the Ford joke books under such varied titles as *Funny Stories about the Ford* or *Uncanny Stories about a Canny Car.* The Preston Publishing Company of Hamilton, Ohio, sold one of these 60-page joke books for 15 cents. They claimed to be the original publishers, although six other books imitated them. In their prime, 1914–1920, the books featured cartoons and simple humor. These jokes were the staff of life for vaudeville monologists of that period. Even well known figures such as Ring Lardner, Irvin S. Cobb, and Bud Fisher contributed their humor to this type of levity.

The origins of these joke books are obscure. Competitors may have started them to criticize the Ford cars, or maybe the mass production feats of the Ford Motor Company gripped people's imaginations. William P. Young, a Ford dealer, recalled that his critics were so severe that he made exaggerated claims in defence of the Tin Lizzie. He added, "From a shy, shamefaced, bedeviled group of doubters of our own sanity, we gradually worked ourselves into a group of militant crusaders knowing we belonged to a mutual admiration society which would avenge the wounds to our pride and self-esteem."[29]

Whether critical or laudatory, the stories were repeated in a spirit of admiration. Lord Northcliffe, after visiting the United States in 1917 observed that the Ford car was a subject for humor in every newspaper and music hall in the United States. The stories were as popular in the White House as in the press. "The terrible fact remains that every third car is a Ford, not only in the United States, but in Canada, South America, and in the Far East."

Needless to say, the humor in the Ford joke books seems simplistic and outdated today. There seems little levity in such quips as: Junk dealer, "Any old rags, bottles or old Fords today?" Or Policeman: "What is the charge against this fellow?" Second policeman: "Stealing a Ford car." Judge: "Take the prisoner out and search him." A farmer sitting in a tree was asked how he got there. He replied, "Well, I was cranking the Ford and the darned thing slipped out of my hands." "In a woman beauty is only skin deep; in a Ford, only tin deep." "Game laws protect everything except husbands, bedbugs, and Fords."

As a homespun American himself, Henry Ford enjoyed these gags to the point where some accused him of encouraging the jokes in the first place. His own favorite story appeared in the Denver

Express on November 13, 1915, shortly after he visited that city. An old timer in Colorado asked that he be buried with his Ford car. When asked why, he explained, "Oh, because the darned thing pulled me out of every hole I ever got into, and it ought to pull me out of this one."

As might be expected, the Model T evoked a musical response. This rhapsody of song had its limitations as a creative art, yet the flow of sheet music indicated something of the emotional quality of the automotive era. Apparently these lyrics had real meaning for those who enjoyed the speed and mobility which the new technology offered. Most of the themes were light, with some semblance of humor. One of the most memorable ones was "The Little Ford Rambled Right Along" created by C. R. Foster and Byron Gay:

> *Now Henry Jones and a pretty little queen*
> *Took a ride one day in his big limousine,*
> *The car kicked up and the engine wouldn't crank*
> *There wasn't any gas in the gasoline tank.*
> *About that time along came Nord*
> *And he rattled right along in his little old Ford*
> *And he stole that queen as his engine sang a song*
> *And his little Ford rambled right along.*

Even the demise of the Model T created a public reaction. By 1926 the famous model had become obsolete because improved roads led to demands for more luxury in driving. Men wanted more speed and power, while women insisted on more "class." Farmers also complained of having to drive for miles on heavy roads with their feet bearing down on the low pedal. The planetary transmission seemed too noisy, prompting the saying, "Of all the noises there is none worse, than a Model T Ford when it is in reverse."

As the Model T bowed in defeat it received grateful tributes from hundreds of farmers who wrote to Henry Ford extolling the merits of the redoubtable T. Many correspondents said it had been the first car they had ever owned, it had served them well in difficult days, and had been a source of pleasure for the entire family. A farmer in Montana said he wanted to cry when he heard the Model T was going to its grave. For the Tin Lizzie had power, personality, persistency, and pugnacity. "It had pepper coupled with push. It had punch which is horse sense with a kick in it. It dragged me out of tough spots, and I had plenty of them out here on the wild prairies of the West."[30]

Another stream of rhetoric was inspired by the arrival of the Model A cars in 1928. Speculation centered on what Henry Ford would bring out; perhaps a six cylinder car or a V-8 model. The company ran full page ads in 2,000 daily papers at a cost of $1,300,000 announcing the new creation. On December 2, 1928, the Model A was unveiled. Mobs rushed dealers' show rooms, necessitating police protection. In New York city, a million people tried to get into the show rooms.[31]

Ford's involvement in court cases also produced a flood of news and publicity. The Seldon Patent Case, the Sapiro suit, the Dodge Brothers' lawsuit, and the Chicago *Tribune* case all made good copy. These confrontations in the courts tended to create strong feelings among the general public, either in condemnation of the industrialist or more often in solid loyalty for his defense.

The Chicago *Tribune* suit grew out of the controversial war-preparedness movement before the United States entered World War I. The Navy League and all those who favored a rearmament program favored appropriations by Congress to strengthen the military and naval forces of the nation. To those of this persuasion, militarism was equated with Americanism.

Meanwhile, Henry Ford, who had returned from his Peace Ship mission to Europe in late 1915, stood by his convictions, in spite of his critics who called him a buffoon who knew as much about world politics as a street sweeper knew about city government. The *Oscar II*, known as the "good ship nutty" could no more stop the war than a fire department could extinguish a blaze in a Ford factory with a teaspoon.

Sore in spirit, but never faint of heart, Ford laughed at those who predicted foreign invasions of the United States and called everyone hypocrites who mouthed religion on Sunday and then advocated war and bloodshed for the economic gain of a few. He ran full page editorials in newspapers across the country on April 9, 1916, under the heading, "Humanity and Sanity." He insisted that fear had been pounded into the heads of Americans by the press and motion pictures. No enemy was in sight, yet the cry for spending millions on military weapons swept over the land. The American duty was to keep out of war, to limit armaments of all kinds, and to crush the armor plate patriotism with its avarice for gold.

Tensions mounted in June, 1916, when President Wilson called out the National Guard to assist in controlling the raids of Villa along the Texas border. In this crisis, the Chicago *Tribune* erroneously charged that eighty-nine employees of the Ford Motor Company called to the border would lose their jobs in Dearborn. On June 23, the *Tribune* published an editorial entitled, "Ford is an Anarchist," which suggested Ford should move his factories to Mexico. "If Ford allowed this rule of his shop to stand, he will reveal himself not merely as an ignorant idealist, but as an anarchist enemy of a nation which protects him in his wealth."[32] When Colonel McCormick refused to retract or apologize for these personal charges, Ford had his attorney file a libel suit against the Chicago *Tribune* asking one million dollars in damages. Because an impartial jury could not be secured in Chicago or Detroit, the trial was moved to Mount Clemens, a small town in McComb County, Michigan. Here in May, 1919, began one of the most dramatic court cases in American journalism.

In preparation, the McCormick-Patterson-*Tribune* headquarters were established in the Park Hotel, where nine lawyers led by Wemouth Kirkland and Elliott G. Stevenson directed the legal work. Henry Ford occupied the Media and Colonial hotels, bringing sixty-three of his lawyers and executive officers. Alfred Lucking, a former Congressman and a Detroit lawyer, headed the Ford staff. Van loads of office furnishings were moved from Dearborn to Mount Clemens, and special telephone and telegraph lines were installed. Although the town swarmed with newspaper men, Ford knew there were thousands of smaller papers which could not afford to send reporters to Michigan to cover a trial which would probably run for weeks. Therefore he established a special news bureau to distribute first-hand information. This bureau supplied copy and boiler plate mats for 2,507 weekly papers and 260 daily papers with reports of the Ford-*Tribune* trial. "Send out the uncolored truth," Ford declared, convinced he had to counteract the bias against him by most of the large metropolitan papers.

The trial began on May 12, 1919, with a jury of eleven farmers and one road builder. After much haggling, Judge James G. Tucker ruled that anything pertaining to Ford's views could be introduced as evidence, which in effect meant that Henry Ford, not Colonel McCormick was arraigned.

Attorneys for the plaintiff attempted to gain the initiative by trying to prove the Chicago *Tribune* had played into the hands of German leaders by pushing the United States toward war with Mexico. The paper had taken this stand because corporations such as Standard Oil and International Harvester wanted to exploit the natural resources of Mexico. In this sense, the newspaper owners were un-American, not Ford.

The *Tribune* counsel claimed its original editorial was true, and the press had the duty to comment on public issues. The defense criticized Edsel Ford's draft exemption during the war and praised Colonel McCormick's military service in France during World War I.

Since the suit originated in charges that Ford was an anarchist, this word punctuated the testimony throughout the trial. Its definition became crucial. Elliott Stevenson claimed Ford was not a bomb thrower but was an anarchist because the Supreme Court had defined anarchy as the absence or insufficiency of government. With William A. Dunning of Columbia University on the stand, Stevenson said he would prove Ford's pronouncements were similar to those of Emma Goldman and Peter Kropotkin. These were alike because they believed in the violent overthrow of the government. Dunning interrupted the cross examination to taunt, "You would have less trouble showing that Mr. Ford and George Washington were alike." [33] When Stevenson introduced a Ford pamphlet which referred to soldiers, bankers, and munition makers fourteen times in thirteen pages and repeatedly held that war was murder, the plaintiff called Dr. Francis W. Coker, professor of political science at Ohio State University to the stand. Dr. Coker said he had read all of Ford's writing and asserted the "war is murder" phrase had been characteristic of the writings of Victor Hugo, Martin Luther, James Russell Lowell, Voltaire, Washington Gladden, ministers of the Gospel, and members of peace societies. "So you believe that 'war is murder' is not peculiar to anarchists," asked Lucking. "It is not," responded the witness, "The opinion is held by men of all shades of belief and unbelief." [34]

On the issues of patriotism and anarchy, Ford's case looked strong. His booming factories during World War I, producing 190 million dollars worth of war material, did not reflect anarchy, sedition, or un-Americanism. Dr. S. S. Marquis explained that, as head of the welfare department of the Ford Motor Company, he had noted that Ford had bought American flags in 5,000 lots for use in his schools.

Although the Ford attorneys had the better of the anarchy issue, the second phase of the trial dealing with Ford as "an ignorant idealist" was more difficult because Ford himself was the target. Interest in the trial reached its height on July 14, 1919, when Ford was called to the stand for eight days of gruelling examination. Arthur Brisbane, long friendly to Ford, described the witness as tall, thin, wiry, alert, intensely active, intensely nervous, and unmindful of his nervousness. He clasped and unclasped his hands a hundred times and looked like a whale out of the water. He was even-tempered and patient, however, and at times seemed to be more eager to answer questions than his legal advisers wished. He stuck tenaciously to his position that war was immoral because it killed people while others made a profit.

Meanwhile, the defense attorneys attempted to reveal Ford's educational deficiencies, thus proving that he had no right to speak out on social, political, or military matters. On one occasion, he was asked if he ever heard of Benedict Arnold and Ford replied, "He is a writer, I think." Unfriendly reporters played up this faux pas, but the more sympathetic insisted the millionaire was thinking of Matthew Arnold, or Horace L. Arnold who had written a shop manual for workers in his factories. At one point, Henry admitted he was an ignorant idealist, which seemed to concede the whole issue to the defendant.

During the trial, 408 exhibits were placed in evidence and 120 witnesses paraded through the court.[35] As the press spread the news, the "common man" tended to sympathize with Ford in spite of the fact that he was rapidly becoming America's wealthiest person. He now seemed cast in the role of the underdog, suffering persecution from "The World's Greatest Newspaper." When skillful lawyers left him intellectually naked, there were plenty of folks who understood how exposed he must feel.

The avalanche of favorable mail reaching Ford was encouraged by Arthur Brisbane's syndicated columns in the Hearst newspapers. He suggested that all idealists were ignorant in one way or another, and to confess ignorance was the beginning of wisdom. If America had a few more ignorant idealists like Ford, dividing their millions with workmen, it would be a good thing for the country. The newspaper publishers who hated to pay decent wages had tried to belittle Ford. "Write him a line" urged Brisbane, "If busy with your crops, cut this out and mail it with your name signed: "Dear Ford: I am glad to have you for a fellow citizen and I wish we had more of your brand of anarchism, if that is what it is. Yours truly: Sign here ————" [36]

Thousands responded by clipping out the editorial and attaching it to their letters. Some thought Ford's attorneys should take the offensive and force Colonel McCormick to disclose all his business transactions. Others suggested Ford buy up a chain of newspapers to battle the enemies of the republic.

Strong religious sentiments colored some of this correspondence. Ministers sent their prayers for Ford's deliverance from the hands of the Philistines. Others suggested that Jesus Christ was an anarchist and that Ford emulated Him by uplifting humanity.

It was an ironic situation in which those in dire poverty tried to sympathize with a man whose income ran to $100,000 daily. One farmer sent a horseshoe for good luck. Many simply stated they had been reading so much about the trial that they wanted to tell Ford he was right.

Yet not all heaped kind words on Ford. One malcontent thought the lawyers had made a monkey out of Ford, showing him ignorant of history and a traitor to the United States. He was the laughing stock of the country, he was a scoundrel, and the writer would do all in his power to restrict sales of his cars.

After three months the case went to the jury on August 14. After eight hours of deliberation, the jury returned a verdict citing the Chicago *Tribune* as guilty of libel and awarding Ford six cents in damages. Both sides claimed victory. Telegrams reached Ford with one stating, "You should get more than six cents for making the *Tribune* look like thirty cents." The Halifax *Chronicle* viewed the verdict as a vindication for Ford, but what was he going to do with all that money.

During the 1930s, the radio became a more important medium for spreading the Ford name across America. The Ford Motor Company had sponsored concerts by the Detroit Symphony Orchestra at the Century of Progress Fair in Chicago in the summer of 1934. Fred L. Black convinced Edsel Ford that the company should continue the program on a national hookup. According to *Radio Guide*, the program rated high among musical broadcasts. In October, 1936, it rated even with the Lucky Strike "Hit Parade" and ahead of such competing programs as "Cities Service Concert," "Gillette Community Sing," Paul Whiteman, and Fred Waring.

From 1934 to 1942, the "Ford Sunday Evening Hour" was heard over the Columbia Broadcasting system. It featured the Detroit Orchestra, with guest artists such as Eugene Ormandy, Richard Crooks, Robert Casadesus, and Helen Traubel. At times lighter works were presented. For example, the program on September 21, 1941, featured a chorus under Meredith Wilson and the artists Eleanor Steber and Lanny Ross. It was estimated that the broadcasts reached an audience of sixteen to twenty million people.

Undoubtedly the most innovative aspect of this program was the six-minute talk by William J. Cameron, one of Henry Ford's most trusted associates. Listeners could receive a free copy of these talks by writing to the radio station. In 1934, a majority of the talks focused on Henry Ford and the company; others were critical of Franklin D. Roosevelt and the New Deal policies. When listeners criticized the political views expressed by Cameron, however, he judiciously shifted to less controversial themes. John W. Spaulding of the University of Michigan, who made a study of these talks, pointed out that the speaker tended to sermonize, using abstract phrases and tired clichés. His prophets were doleful, his mettle fine, his memories poignant, his salesmen zealous, his faults glaring, his movements ominous, his roots spiritual, and his future challenging. The foundations were the "Noble Forefathers," "Heroes of American Liberty," and "Americanism." [37]

Although Cameron spoke to middle-class America, he denied speaking for Henry Ford. When invited to speak before a sales manager's meeting in St. Louis in 1938, Cameron replied, "I am not a spokesman for Henry Ford; I am not Director of Public Relations for the Ford Motor Company; I am not a clergyman; I am not an orator; . . . . All there is to say about me is that I am sixty years old, have been with Ford for twenty-one years, and occasionally am damphool enough to go about making speeches."[38]

Apparently the common man accepted the Cameron declarations as gospel, for his mail praised him for his eloquence, his intelligence, and as one listener put it, "You are the best horse-sense speaker on the whole network." The critics told Cameron that his speeches were a waste of time, pompous and trite. One called him a "miserable, hypocritical, sanctimonious dog. . . ."[39]

Yet these efforts embellished the Ford image. The programs were educational and far reaching in their scope. In 1938 approximately one hundred fifty thousand Americans, most of them from the working middle class, wrote to Detroit to receive copies of Cameron's talks. When World War II diverted the energies of the Ford Motor Company to war production, this program was dropped. One rural American lamented, "I am sorry to hear of the loss of the Ford Sunday Evening Hour, and to think Fred Allen is taking that hour is nothing short of sacrilege. . . ."[40]

World fairs helped spread the glad tidings about Ford and his works. He believed fairs encouraged the young to have faith in the future. In fact, he claimed his early attendance at fairs started his mind working along mechanical lines. On one occasion at the New York World's Fair in 1939 he pointed to an exhibit and asserted this type of history was not bunk. This was the story of mankind, and it made politics and wars look cheap. Over four million people saw the Ford "Road of Tomorrow" at the New York Fair. A memo sent from the fairgrounds to the Ford offices in Dearborn read, "Today we entertain 70 editors of farm papers at luncheon. Thursday we have 50 county agents from New York and New Jersey to put on tractor demonstrations."[41] The cost to the Ford Motor Company for supporting the World Fairs at Chicago, San Diego, Dallas, New York, and San Francisco from 1934 to 1939 was $7,578,435.93.[42]

Additional publicity came in providing tours of the factories and assembly plants scattered over the country. Thousands went to see the assembly line operate in the new plant in Seattle when it opened in July, 1932. Ford dealers were brought to sales meetings in Dearborn for tours of the River Rouge factory. The guides were instructed to give straight answers and not to "bull anybody."[43] In 1927 one thousand farmers were brought on special trains to see the production of tractors at the Ford plant. In 1960 almost two million tourists went through the Rouge plant, while 900,000 visited Greenfield Village and the Ford Museum. The information center in the Ford Office Building received approximately four thousand letters a month asking for free Ford literature.[44]

Prior to Ford's death in 1947, farmers visiting Dearborn would sometimes ask to see Ford personally. Harold M. Cordell, one of Ford's secretaries, explained that if some chap looked interesting, he would send a note to Mr. Ford. If he took an interest in the visitor, an interview was arranged:

> He really got a kick out of those fellows, because many of them were right down his plane. They were farmers who didn't know any more than he did about generalities. They would really get down and enjoy the conversation. I've seen him bundle them in their own cars, or his, and drive out with them to show them around the country. . . . He took people he never saw before, or had any particular interest in, just on an impulse.[45]

When Henry Ford reached his eightieth birthday in 1943, he received a mountain of congratulations. William Stidger of Boston University wrote an article, "Henry Ford Looks Ahead at Eighty," in which he insisted that the industrialist still had faith in young people, that he believed nothing permanent could be built on hate, and that he thought man could act with some degree of sanity. Stidger said Ford carried a card in his pocket with the well-known lines:

> *For I dipt into the future, far as human eye*
> *could see*
> *Saw a vision of the world, and all the wonders that*
> *could be.*
> *Till the war drum throbbed no longer, and the battle*
> *fangs were furled,*
> *In the Parliament of Man, the Federation of the World.*

On the bottom of the card, Ford had added, "If we get the last part—The Parliament of Man, that will be worth it all. I believe I see it coming."[46]

Evidently Ford knew something about public relations and adopted techniques which were effective. He did come across to people. Louis P. Lockner, who knew him intimately, said in 1925, that Woodrow Wilson and Theodore Roosevelt possessed a keen sense of publicity and were masters of the art, but both men could have learned a thing or two from Henry Ford. The Omaha *World-Herald* on May 5, 1916, commented that Theodore Roosevelt kept himself on the front page, but Henry Ford had a more subtle way of doing it. He took hold of something of general interest, something that millions of people were interested in, and got it into every paper in the United States. The success of Ford and his associates can be seen in results of a survey conducted by the National Association of Manufacturers for *Fortune* magazine in 1937. The opinion poll asked the question: "Will you name one manufacturer or manufacturing company, either in this city or elsewhere, whose policies you approve in the main." The results were:[47]

	Percent
Ford Motor Company	47.2
Procter and Gamble	3.3
General Motors	3.1
Hershey	2.0
General Electric	1.4
Chrysler	1.2

IV

Barnyard Inventors
and the Model T

The famous Model T represented an amazing resistance to change. In fact, Henry Ford's comment in 1909, that his car would stand with "no new models, no new motors, no new bodies, and no new colors," was made evident to the motoring public during the next eighteen years.[1] The Flivvers over the years were not identical, but they retained their fundamental design more consistently than any other American automobile. In the mid-twenties it still appeared with a buggy-like top affixed to a light body mounted on a flimsy chassis. A twenty-horsepower motor provided torque for a planetary transmission, with its three foot pedals to activate a brake, reverse, and a high and low gear. Four coils under the dash broke the electric current flowing from the magneto to the spark plugs. Across the radiator were the letters in script, "Ford."

Although the Model T remained popular, most owners believed it had weak spots and many expressed their dissatisfaction with its performance. In 1912, when the Ford Motor Company announced there would be no changes in the car because it could not be improved, the news seemed unconvincing.[2] When the 1920 model came out, many were surprised to learn that the only innovation was the introduction of demountable rims. For several years the company received about one hundred letters a day from those requesting some mechanical alteration in the Tin Lizzie.

Most suggestions reaching Dearborn had an honest ring, for the average American farmer thought he was an inventor of sorts. After all, his tradition had been one of utilitarianism. Frontiersmen had improvised to survive, and early settlers had shown an affection for machinery. Scion of a long line of tinkering mechanics, the modern farmer became self-reliant because he had no alternative. Short on cash, he repaired worn out implements and solved daily mechanical dilemmas. The arrival of the Model T failed to intimidate these barnyard experts, it only challenged them. They overhauled the motor, changed the transmission bands, took up the shimmy in the front wheels, and ground the valves. Begrimed with crank case oil, these mechanics felt qualified to express their technological views to their families, friends, and to Henry Ford himself.

In addition, many farmers were interested in inventions because they believed they might lead to a fortune. They had heard that inventions could be sold and income received from royalties. Thus there lurked the chance that the lucky might secure sudden riches.

Unfortunately most farmers knew nothing of patent procedures or legislation. In the twenties they were unaware that filing fees cost $40 and that regular patents protected the patentee for seventeen years. Most were ignorant of the doctrine of equivalents, subsidiary patents, interferences, and the two hundred Patent Office regulations.[3]

One prevailing misconception held that Henry Ford would reward anyone making a feasible suggestion on how to improve the Model T. Some believed that if they could demonstrate a way to reduce the cost of the car by ten cents, Ford would pay enough to support the fortunate one for the rest of his life.[4]

Such optimism seems incredible for there is no evidence that the Ford Motor Company paid individuals a dime for suggested improvements in the manufacture of automobiles. It is true that secretaries were instructed to answer letters offering information, and sometimes the company asked to see models or drawings. The archival records in Dearborn, however, fail to reveal payments of this type. On the contrary, W.T. Fishleigh, head of the Experimental Division during the twenties, answered letters stating, "We have so many requests from inventors for financial aid in getting their products on the market, that it is necessary for us to refuse all such requests."[5] E. G. Liebold, Ford's secretary, writing to a correspondent in 1925 declared, "First of all, no statement has ever been published with our authority which stated that we would pay liberally for any suggestions that might be received and adopted that would improve the Ford motor car. This is further corroborated by the fact that no suggestions have ever been adopted that would not follow any ordinary course of manufacture and development. . . ."[6]

Unaware of this policy, and with the jackpot in mind, inventors sought Ford's attention. Many wanted interviews, but these were difficult to arrange because secretaries protected Mr. Ford with various excuses.

When inventive inspiration struck, the mechanical-minded submitted the innovations. Although most farmers hated letter writing and usually preferred "talkin to readin, and readin to writin," the lure of sudden wealth encouraged them to mail a letter to Henry Ford. Laboring men with blunt pencils scribbled their notions with crabbed hand on bits of paper at hand—brown wrapping paper, cheap tablet paper, and sent them to Detroit. Housewives working over the kitchen stove dashed off suggestions on paper splattered with hot grease sprayed from the frying pan.

The motives behind these varied. A farmer's wife in South Dakota explained that her husband had been inventing things for twenty years, but he had not sold any of them. A Michigan farmer awoke at midnight with the construction of a complete machine in his mind. A convict in a Florida jail said he had invented something that would enable a car to pull itself out of a mud hole.

The brash exuded confidence and usually exaggerated the significance of their inventions. A note from Superior, Wisconsin, stated, "I am going to sell this invention because I need the money. The price is $250,000 and it is easy worth it. I would like to have the cash by return mail." A resident of Robbinsdale, Minnesota, would share his patent on a watch for one million dollars spot cash. A mechanic in Galena, Illinois, made a tire gadget which he would sell. Although he knew the governor of the state and hob-nobbed with millionaires, he preferred to "walk up to the rack with Mr. Ford, fodder or no fodder."

Brave souls often tried to bluff their way to success. A designer of a new brake claimed the gadget would stop a car going 60 miles an hour within the space of a yard, without strain on the gears or tires. One thought his invention worth a million dollars, but out of kindness he would give Henry Ford first chance because he was an honorable man. Another had a patent which would do more for civilization and make more money than electricity, the automobile, or the railroads. J. P. Morgan had offered a million dollars for it when patented. In the meantime the writer would accept $300 from

Ford, pending patent approval. Some even claimed to be relatives of the Ford family, and one person insisted he was their adopted son.

Since it was impossible to describe an invention in detail without revealing secrets, writers often withheld vital information, fearing Ford would appropriate the ideas without compensating the donor. Many promised to divulge the secret if Ford would promise to pay for the suggestion; others insisted Ford keep the information in full confidence.

Severe financial crises encouraged mechanical speculation. Farmers facing foreclosure of mortgages tried to conceive of inventions which would bring prompt rewards.

Illness and medical bills impelled some to peddle their plans. During the long hours of convalescence, hospital patients who worried about finances hoped a patent idea would banish this fear. In writing to Henry Ford, they often described their surgery in vivid anatomical detail, before presenting their inventive ideas. An Iowa housewife lamented the exchange of her gall bladder for a $300 doctor bill at the Mayo Clinic in Rochester, Minnesota. Her family still owed $200 for her husband's appendectomy. She hoped the enclosed drawing would prove valuable. She told Ford she would accept a royalty of fifty cents per car, or split the savings resulting from the new invention. A seventy-three-year-old invalid in Ohio, who had not walked for thirty years, wrote, "I know you believe in helping people help themselves. I want to pay my way in the world. I have some debts I want to pay. Inventing is all I can do. I have invented a child's seat for the Model T. Are you interested?

The more sanguine, refusing to take Ford more seriously than themselves, exhibited touches of informality and humor. A motorist from the South asked, "You may think me a nut, but I leave that to you. But why can't a engine run on part air like one of those lamps you pump up. . . ." An Oklahoma farmer asked:

Would the best transmission in the world interest you? Listen Baby, I've got the Deluxe Baby. Now listen boy. I'm no scientist or automotive engineer or yet a master of machines, but listen here, man, I want some pay for all this. If I come to Detroit, will you promise to give me a square deal? I don't know what anything is worth, but I will trust you. I will have to. If I prove to be a blank, I can work off what I owe you in your shops.

The Model T fraternity was a motley crowd, somewhat lower class economically, yet possessing some heroic qualities. Patience in distress, tolerance of the obstinate, optimism in the face of disaster, courage to rough it mechanically, and the fortitude to take it physically, characterized these argonauts of the dusty road.

Yet, during these halcyon days, the T drivers, or at least a good proportion of them, were not above protestation. They criticized poorly designed mechanical features of the Flivver. The inconveniences in driving irked many, and they said so. No doubt they expected perfection, but even Ford could not provide the ultimate in luxurious motoring for a few hundred dollars.

When the Model T failed in its performance, the owners reminded Ford of these unpleasant experiences and suggested he remedy the faults. When a driver on mountain roads in Pennsylvania broke an axle and almost went over a cliff, he demanded that Ford remedy this defect to cut down on the loss of life on highways. From the prairies of Illinois came the complaint that valve stem holes in the rims admitted water which formed rust, which in turn cut the inner tubes, all of which was hell on a hot Sunday afternoon. A malcontent in Texas had advised improving the timer, but his suggestions were ignored. He wrote, "Dear Mr. Ford: If Jesus were as hard to get to as you, I would be out in the cold as far as redemption is concerned. But He ain't and I ain't. . . ."

Anyone who has ridden in the old Ford knows its had weaknesses. For example, the location of the gas tank was an abomination. It hid under the front seat as if to defy observation. When the car, fully loaded, stopped for gas at a service station, a complicated maneuver ensued. To get at the tank required the removal of the front seat cushion. This meant out with the driver, out with the wife, out with the kids, out with blankets, packages, and other paraphernalia. This ritual was necessary in rain, snow, and subzero weather. After unscrewing the cap, a measuring stick was thrust into the tank, a procedure similar to the present checking the oil under the hood. Without a gasoline gauge, the amount of gas in the tank had to be estimated by sight, sound, or intuition.

Needless to say, this inconvenience caused resentment. A South Carolinian had heard the complaint a hundred times, while a garage man in North Branch, Michigan, said he had heard it more than a thousand times. The Ford Motor Company, however, retained this awkward feature until 1926. Hundreds of letters reached Detroit recommending the simple solution of adding a spout to the tank which extended outside the car body. Some submitted ideas for gasoline gauges. One suggested a baffle plate in the middle of the tank. When the gasoline got low, this plate would trap two gallons, which then could be released by turning a petcock. One invented a gadget which whistled when the gas in the tank got too low. Another writer advocated an auxiliary tank as a solution. When one ran out of gas, all one needed to do would be to turn on the reserve tank and go on.

The absence of a door on the driver's side of the open Model Ts proved frustrating. If the sedan had four doors, why only three on the touring? If this were part of the simplicity in design, why not eliminate all doors and let passengers vault over the side? Obese drivers, trying to scale the high side and muscle through the side curtains, lacked dignity. A Georgia housewife complained that though the Ford car could go through impassable roads, every time her husband climbed over to the wheel he mashed the baby and stepped on her toes. A minister traveling for the American Sunday School Union in Nebraska in 1923 said much of his driving occurred in rural areas where there were many gates to open. In the winter with the side curtains on, he admitted it took a great deal of the grace of God to keep him from losing his temper when getting out of the car on the left side.

Actually, the side curtains themselves were an annoyance. Designed to fasten on in sections with small turnbuckles, they often came unfastened, flapped in the wind, tore into shreds, or sagged like hound-dog ears. They were intended to be neatly folded and placed under the rear seat cushion, but this trick, like folding a road map, proved difficult. To remedy this, some urged the company to put zippers in the curtains, or attach them to a spring roll to be drawn down like window shades in a home.

Farmers complained of the limited space in the back seat for hauling egg crates and milk cans. A Minnesota dairyman knew of twenty farmers who refused to buy Ford cars because they could not get a ten-gallon milk can on the floor by the back seat. Some suggested rings at the center post so more boxes could be lashed to the running boards. One disappointed writer thought the foot pedals were too close together for farmers with boots or overshoes.

Only people with small feet could drive a Ford and "most farmers who buy Fords have big feet."

It is significant to note the amount of concern for comfort held by Model T owners, and how long it took automobile companies to comply with these modest requests. In fact, some of the recent innovations advertised by the auto companies were advocated by hundreds of rural Americans forty years ago. For example, a mechanic in Aberdeen, South Dakota, in 1919, urged Ford to introduce an adjustable head rest for the driver. A universal joint would permit adjustment to any position, while padding would absorb road shock. Thus driving down the road could be as comfortable as sitting in a barber's chair.

Interestingly enough, a common invention, mentioned as early as 1910, consisted in placing a set of hinges on the front seat, permitting it to fold back as a reclining chair or bed. People got tired jostling over rough roads and craved a bit of relaxation. Mothers crowded with fretful children wanted a chance to recline the seat like a railroad pullman chair to relieve tension and provide more room. In addition, farmers usually viewed hotel bills as a form of larceny—an imposition to be avoided. Some did cut the seats and add hinges. A New England Yankee boasted he had made a flexible seat for less than one dollar, while a Canadian traveled 2,000 miles sleeping in the car at night. He said he found it better than sleeping in stuffy hotels. He arose in the morning fresh in spirit, listening to singing birds, and "breathing the Lord's free air. . . ."

Concerned with noise, one inventor developed a mute similar to those used with musical instruments. Some suggested that exhaust fumes could be reduced by extending the tail pipe above the car rather than underneath. To dissipate carbon monoxide, a muffler with a charcoal filter would prove effective. This was anticipating the smog problem in the twenties.

Naturally, the heat and cold evoked mechanical suggestions. Nothing could be much colder than clutching an icy steering wheel of a Model T as it moved over the wintry prairies of the Midwest. Hot-air heaters were often attached to the exhaust manifold, but these were inadequate, especially in touring cars. Hands numbed by cold might let a car get out of control. One suggested the steering wheel be hollow so it could be filled like a hot water bottle. Another thought an electric wire running through the wheel might act as a heater. A Dakota farmer wrote, "You know Mr. Ford, when I drive through blizzards on the way home from town, my hands are all bundled up with three pairs of mittens, but they still freeze. Why don't you run the exhaust pipe up the steering column so I can warm my goll-darn hands. . . ."[7]

Intense heat could be equally uncomfortable. On a hot day in Kansas in 1923, a young lady took a ride in a Model T. It was so hot the passengers had to open the doors to cool their feet. When she got home she wrote Henry Ford suggesting the doors on the car be made like the window shutters in some homes. A Texan thought the heat from the motor might be counteracted by having trap doors on the floor to admit a draft. Other ideas included a rear window in closed cars which might be lowered to permit a breeze; a fan driven by electricity generated from a pulley on the rear wheel; air scoops on the cowl; a Frigidaire unit built in the dash to cool milk, butter, and iced tea; a double top, the upper one eight inches above the other to give shade to the main body of the car. One correspondent, in 1926, advocated putting the engine behind the rear seat to eliminate excessive heat.

Since travel involved risks, the question of safety became a vital issue. According to the American Automobile Association, death from auto accidents increased from 400 in 1904 to 11,154 in 1919, and to 39,643 in 1937. These numbers declined to 32,582 in 1938 and 33,411 in 1946. By 1955, the figure reached 36,000 and 52,000 in 1966. It is interesting to note that there were 24 million automobiles on the road in 1937 and 76 million or three times as many, in 1955. Thus on a basis of statistics, it was three times safer to drive a car in 1955 than in 1937. These figures contradict the superficial comments in the press, radio, and television which invariably give the impression that the rate of auto fatalities has increased each year, whereas the opposite has been the recent trend.[8]

During the Model T era, these deaths were high enough to cause concern. To save human life, a Nebraska farmer in 1923 urged Ford to put multicolored electric light bulbs on the front and rear of each car. These would light up according to the speed of the vehicle. Thus policemen and other drivers could tell the speed of any automobile at a glance. Many suggested a large speedometer be fastened to the outside of the car, so the speed could be read by traffic officials. Others recommended a cylinder on the dash with a needle which would record the speed of the car on a permanent record, like a seismograph. This would eliminate arguments between drivers and traffic cops because the proof of speed would be on the cylinder. One ingenious fellow built a speedometer which sounded gongs, indicating the speed of the car. Other gadgets would cut off the ignition when the speed limit was broken or flash danger signals to the driver.

To protect pedestrians, various types of cow-catchers were suggested. Some were similar to those on street cars—a low scoop-like affair. One inventor, believing human life should be spared, devised a huge revolving wire brush attached to the front of the car. He claimed this contraption would not only catch the pedestrian if hit, but the device would hoist the victim up and drop him in the back seat of the car all in one continuous motion.

In order to reduce injuries, automobiles could be built to a sharp point in front. This would eliminate head-on collisions because the cars would merely glance off of each other. No predictions were made as to what would happen should such a spear hit another car broadside. Since most of the deaths resulted from the crumpling of the car itself, some believed in putting a bumper all around the car like the electric bump-car rides found in amusement parks. Another suggestion called for rubber inflated turbans to be worn by all passengers.

The Model T brakes did little to invalidate the law of inertia. Theoretically, the brake pedal should squeeze the brake drum in the planetary transmission. If the brake bands were new they had some influence, but if worn down to the rivets, or out of adjustment, the brake became a ritual, not a function. The driver might reach down with his left hand and pull the emergency lever which activated shoes on the rear wheels, but this, too, was usually ineffective. As a last resort, the driver could step on the reverse pedal to use its braking power. Again farmers were ahead of their times when, in 1919, they asked Henry Ford for four-wheel brakes. One farmer claimed he had perfected the braking system by hanging two logs under the car. By pulling a lever he lowered the logs and skidded to a stop.

Most people agreed that the Model T lighting system was simple in principle, but an aberration in practice. Electricity generated by the magnet ran directly to the headlights, thus the faster the motor rotated, the better the lights. A driver in low gear with a wide open throttle had bright lights, but when he shifted into high, the engine slowed down, causing the light bulbs, like dying campfires, to send out only a feeble yellow glimmer. On dirt roads, drivers tried to avoid rocks and made split-second decisions in selecting the most favorable ruts to follow through mud holes. Since this navigation proved impossible with poor lights, drivers roared along in low to develop more candle power. Even after the Ford Motor Company adopted the battery and generator as standard equipment in 1921, the lights tended to fluctuate as if controlled by a rheostat. A Montana farmer said his Model T lights were so bad that he ran into sheep on the road, while his neighbors were buying Overlands at higher prices for no other reason than to get better lighting.

To promote safety, scores of letters recommended the adoption of dirigible lights which would be synchronized with the steering column. When rounding curves the beam of light would follow the road instead of shooting off at a tangent. Some suggested a third "cyclops" headlight in the middle of the radiator to serve this purpose, a feature incorporated in the experimental "Tucker" car of the 1930s. One invention provided for a flexible cone over each headlight. These could open and close at the driver's command, thus directing the focus of the beam of light. An Oklahoma farmer in 1923 begged Ford to save many a neck and liver by installing a floor button to tilt the lights downward when approaching an on-coming car. Ten years later this idea was adopted by the automobile industry. In addition, there were hundreds of farmers imploring Ford to incorporate directional turning lights in the early 1920s, yet the manufacturers waited until after the World War II to adopt this simple and practical suggestion. After twenty-five years of agitation, the auto companies adopted the idea and then advertised it as a mechanical innovation discovered by their brilliant engineers.

The Ford crank proved to be no respector of persons; a wicked appendage which snapped wrists, sprained thumbs, and broke arms. Small town papers mentioned these fractures with the regularity of weather reports. Theoretically, this doctor's bonanza should never have existed. With the spark lever advanced the motor should start without trouble. But men were fallible and machines deteriorated. The absent minded forgot to advance the spark, while dirty timers shot irregular impulses to the spark plugs causing the motor to backfire. Even with self-starters, cold weather or weak batteries necessitated cranking by hand. Wiseacres said one should never fork the thumb around the crank, because the recoil could not spin out of the fist. To place the thumb with the fingers felt unnatural, however, and most people violated this safety precaution. Successful cranking required the spinning of the engine with one hand and pulling the choke wire extending through the radiator with the other. This ambidextrous effort gave little protection against these premature explosions. Victims asked Ford to add a safety rachet to the crank, but company officials said these accessories could be bought from jobbers.

If the emergency brake was defective, the Model T would creep forward as soon as the motor started. In a garage, the person cranking the car could be pinned against the wall. Max Cooper, a columnist for the Aberdeen *Daily News* in South Dakota recalled that:

> The car advanced on you the instant the first explosion oc-curred and you would hold it back by leaning your weight against it. I can still feel my old Ford nuzzling me at the curb, as though looking for an apple in my pocket. In zero weather, ordinary cranking became impossible, except for giants. The oil thickened and it became necessary to jack up the rear wheel, which for planetary reasons, eased the throw. The lore and legend that governed the Ford were boundless. Owners discussed mutual problems in that wise, infinitely resourceful way old women discuss rheumatism. Exact knowledge was pretty scarce, and often proved less effective than supersti-tion. . . .[9]

The danger of theft also bothered motorists. A resident of Newport, Kentucky, after examining the local police records in 1923, stated that 85 percent of all stolen cars were Fords. He wanted Ford to remedy the situation because poor folks were sustaining too great losses. A hired man near Ivesdale, Illinois, said he had in-tended to buy a Ford coupe, but had refrained because they were so popular that someone would steal it before he got ready to drive it home.

Favorite antitheft schemes included locking the wheels of the car in a fixed position when the ignition switch was removed, a dial lock like those used on bank vaults, and a burglar-proof mechanism which would throw the entire electrical system out of order. A Rhode Island farmer proposed installing a fire-truck gong concealed beneath the car which would spread an alarm. One man suggested encasing a heavy iron bell inside a steel box on the fender. If the car were stolen, the bell would ring, but the thief would be unable to break the steel container to shut off the noise. A lad in Texas claimed he had invented a beartrap which would nab and hold any thief attempting to steal the car. The device also sounded a siren to call police. An elderly man wanted the running boards to recede within the automobile when the doors closed to frustrate robbers who jumped on them with pistol in hand. A woman near Ponder, Georgia, believed the running boards should have hinges, with a rope running to the steering wheel. Then if a robber boarded the car while in motion, the driver could pull the trip cord and dump the miscreant unceremoniously in the dust.

Something of the fertility of the minds of Ford owners can be seen in the suggestions mailed to Dearborn during the 1920s. These included: a dial on the dash to register altitude for mountain driving; a dual-purpose bumper made to serve also as a jack; a fender box to provide sand for icy roads; a tire pump driven by a rear wheel; an air pressure tank to fill flat tires; and electric plug to heat a toaster, coffee percolator, or flatiron; rubber fenders to prevent ugly dents; a collapsible canvas bag in the rear to carry excess baggage; a cigarette ash tray; inflated cushion seats; and a hot plate to fry eggs.

Most T owners took pride in their cars, and over the years virtually every one of its 5,000 parts received suggestions for improvement. For instance, the steering wheel elicited reflective thought. The space between the spokes could be filled to make a businessman's writing desk, or a pad to record oil changes. One woman composed poetry as she drove through scenic terrain. If the steering wheel were a writing desk, she could jot down this verse as she cruised along. Likewise, one could record the license plate numbers of fleeing convicts. The wheel might hinge in the center to accommodate obese drivers, or support a mirror so people could touch themselves up a bit before meeting friends. The windshields on most cars hinged in the center permitting the top half to be folded back to admit a draft. Since windshield wipers were nonexistant on touring cars, the driver usually thrust his head out the side of the auto when frost or ice formed on the windshield. A Connecticut Yankee advised fixing a square piece of glass before the driver's vision fastened in the center by a pivot. If ice obscured vision, the driver could easily reverse the glass inset and clean it off inside the car. To avoid being cut from flying glass in auto accidents, the windshield could be attached to two rods which extended from the windshield to the front bumper. If a crash occurred, the windshield would be pushed above the car, thus removing the glass in front of the passengers. One farmer suggested the windshield be made of bullet proof glass to reduce injuries.

The nasal "beep" of the Model T horn embarrassed some. It was a feeble squawk like a catarrhal duck calling for its mate. One writer said he blew his horn on one occasion, but the driver ahead just took out his fly swatter as a matter of precaution and otherwise ignored the whole thing. A wireless operator, accustomed to hearing signals, thought the Ford horn harsh and unpleasant to the ear. He recommended a buzzer system with a more musical note. Since truck drivers were often unable to hear the horn from behind, a rubber hose should run from the cab to the rear where a huge funnel would pick up the warning blasts. One farmer, with a flare for advertising, claimed he perfected a horn which would pronounce the word, "Ford" as distinctly as any phonograph. Others insisted their horns would warn pedestrians by shouting "Look Out" or "Gangway."

The radiator cap was a cause of trouble when the threads got ruined or the cap worked loose and fell by the wayside. Many ran without them, letting the steam and boiling water seek their own course. Frequently, corn cobs wrapped in burlap or wooden plugs inside a glove would be jammed into the aperture. Some suggested a snap-on cap to replace the threads so it would open like the back of a watch. Since the original cap appeared plain, many urged substitutes in the shape of cougars, Christmas trees, ships, or the Statue of Liberty. One man designed one in the shape of a Ford car, an idea which he would sell for an annual sum of $20,000. A service station attendant near Saginaw, Michigan, offered to sell his old-fashioned sleigh bells bolted to the radiator cap and called, "Auto Tinks."

The radiators on the Model T changed from the brass shell to steel on September, 1916, because World War I created a shortage of brass. The first 2,500 Lizzies manufactured had water pumps, but these were removed in 1909, and the cooling system relied on heat of the engine to circulate the water. Since Model Ts usually ran hot, it was difficult to keep alcohol from boiling out. In winter, therefore, radiators frequently froze, which tended to break the tubes in the radiator core. If radiator compounds failed to stop these leaks, homemade remedies were used such as soap or axle grease.

Since the fan belt ran off a pulley without a flange, the belts often slipped off and, being out of sight of the driver, the radiator would boil out the water leaving the motor smoking hot. Farmers carried buckets for dipping water out of ditches or from stock tanks. A school teacher in South Dakota, driving to school one morning, discovered his motor was so hot it missed and backfired. "I was late and I was mad," he recalled. "I took a can, dipped some snow-melt water out of a ditch and poured it over the hot cylinder head. Old Nellie cooled right down and ran on to school in fine shape. Try that ice-water deal on an over-heated 1967 model; that ordeal would melt down a modern V-8. . . ."

The ignition system could be either simple or complex depending on the luck of the owner. Floyd Cylmer, in *Henry Ford's Wonderful Model T*, explained that an alternating current was generated by 16 V-shaped magnets clamped to the flywheels and rotated past a ring of 16 coils fixed to the inside of the transmission case. Voltages up to 28 could be obtained. This was the magneto. This low-tension current flowed to the commutator or "Timer" located in front of the motor and turned by the cam shaft. From the timer, the current carried to the four vibrator spark coils under the dash, where it was converted into a high-tension current and relayed to the spark plugs. During the twenties, the six-volt battery could be used for electric current as well. The switch on the dash could be turned to "Mag" or "Bat." The electric starter became optional in 1919, and the generator became standard in 1921.[10]

Perhaps the most criticism focused on the timer, located below the fan, where it caught water spilled from the radiator or oil from the motor. This weakened the spark or shorted it out entirely. Frost inside the timer ruined its efficiency and prompted winter drivers to heat it with a torch. Some mechanics found it impossible to get good service out of timers. In some cases the rollers had to be changed three times in a week. Lee Strout and E. B. White in their immortal, "Farewell, My Lovely!" in 1936 gave a classic description of the timer problem:

> Whatever the driver learned of his motor, he learned not through instruments but through sudden developments. I remember that the timer was one of the vital organs about which there was ample doctrine. When everything else had been checked, you "had a look" at the timer. I have had a timer apart on a sick Ford many times, but I never really knew what I was up to—I was just showing off before God. There were many schools of thought as there were timers. Some people, when things went wrong, just clenched their teeth and gave the timer a smart crack with a wrench. Other people opened it up and blew on it. There was a school that held that the timer needed large amounts of oil; they fixed it by frequent baptism. And

there was a school that was positive it was meant to run dry as a bone; these people were continually taking it off and wiping it. I remember once spitting into a timer; not in anger, but in a spirit of research. You see, the Model T driver moved in the realm of metaphysics. He believed his car could be hexed.[11]

The Model T motor has often been called the most famous engine ever manufactured in the United States. Four pistons with a 3¾-inch bore and 4-inch stroke developed 20 horsepower. The engine and transmission weighed 400 pounds, was simple in design and easy to repair. Minor changes were made in the motor over the years, but not enough to change its fundamental design.

When the engine burned too much oil, or developed knocks caused by worn connecting rod bearings, the barnyard mechanics removed fifteen nuts and took out the cylinder head. Next the oil pan was detached, the connecting-rod bolts removed, and the pistons lifted from the block. To grind the valves, a grinding compound was placed on the valve seats, and a small cranking device used to twirl the valves until they were ground down far enough to become well-fitting. "To grind the valves," became a common expression. Well-seated valves improved the compression of the motor and new piston rings reduced oil consumption and the fouling of the spark plugs.

The oil system in the motors worked well under ideal conditions. In the absence of a pump, the oil circulated with a splash system. The connecting rods dipped up the oil in the pan for their lubrication and a pipe carried oil to the main bearings of the crankshaft. On steep hills, however, the front bearing frequently failed to get enough oil and burned out. In addition, the oil pipe could clog, bringing about the same result. A garage owner in Loomis, Nebraska, wrote Henry Ford on June 25, 1923, stating that a large percentage of the Model Ts coming in for repairs had clogged oil pipes. He believed the oil pipe should run through the front of the motor block. Then farmers could unscrew a cap on this pipe and ram a piece of wire back into the motor, thereby opening the pipe without tearing down the engine.

To check the oil, one opened two petcocks on the transmission housing. If oil ran out of both petcocks, there was plenty of oil; if it did not flow from the top cock, the level was getting low; and if none came from the lower cock, the level in the pan was dangerously low. Unfortunately, one had to reach under the car to make this check. A Georgian complained, "Did you ever see people check the oil, Mr. Ford? They get down in the mud on one knee and then reach as far as they can with a pair of pliers, rubbing their necks against the muddy fender. Some lay flat on the ground. Why not run a rod to the side of the car to eliminate all this nonsense?. . . ."

To improve the motor, some advocated making the connecting rods longer to reduce wear on the side of the cylinder walls. One recommended fastening the piston to a ball joint so the piston could rotate within the cylinder to equalize wear. A garage owner claimed his device could be adjusted to increase or decrease the amount of compression at will. Since poor compression destroyed efficiency, one farmer suggested that a tank of compressed air be bolted to the motor and fed into the cylinders. An air pump driven by the engine would keep the tank filled with pressurized air. Others advocated reducing the size of the compression chamber in the cylinder head until the pressure would reach 480 pounds per square inch and the temperature rise to 1,000 degrees. Then no electric spark would be needed because the motor would run on the diesel principle.

Rural people with inventive imaginations envisioned mechanical utopias in which new ways of securing motive power were described. One genius asked Henry Ford if he were interested in an engine which used neither gasoline, steam, nor electricity. A South Dakota farmer claimed his motor would develop a hundred times more power than other engines of the same size. A Methodist minister believed his invention proved the imminence of the millennium because it represented perfection appropriate to the new dispensation. His engine developed power without using fuel. The final resurrection of this motor, however, seemed to depend on Ford's money rather than on celestial entities in a world unseen.

The more articulate hinted at the utilization of new dynamic principles applied to the old laws of physics. Some thought the recoil of springs could be harnessed like the motion in grandfather's clock. Compressed air intrigued many because it would cost nothing. Why not use a battery to compress air and then use the compressed air to recharge the battery? An air-motor enthusiast in Kansas claimed his motor would prevent wars by intimidating the opposition. He wrote, "I have stayed up all night studying motors including your Flivver. If you don't like the idea, France and England will jump at the chance. Kindly wire. Please excuse this bad writing, as I am in a hurry to get to bed. . . ."

Other notions included harnessing ocean tides for power, using electricity generated from windmills, an electric car which generated its own power, motors which exploded on both ends of the cylinder, motors with no crankshafts, motors without valves, and motors with only two moveable parts. One farmer insisted he had replaced the engine in his car with seventy-five electric light bulbs which provided motive power. A woman in Alameda County in California wanted Ford to attach a propeller to the front of the car to lift it over streams. She wished to rise above the traffic and avoid highway accidents. "Would it not be glory on earth to see the heavens filled with these safety machines and people saying, Yes, indeed, why didn't we think of this before. . . ."

Perpetual motion machines were conjured up in the minds of people every day. J. A. Beardsly, chief clerk of the Patent Office in Washington, D.C., stated in 1929 that these ideas had been presented to the agency since its beginning, even though science held that perpetual machines were an impossibility. A mechanic in Rhode Island in 1926 wrote:

> This is gonna be a long letter, but it is worth it. My completed invention is priceless. I challenge with my life to any group of engineers in the entire world that I have the goods and am 100 per cent right. I have invented a perpetual motion machine which can move a machine 24 feet in diameter with unlimited horsepower. The power of my machine is dead weight. If you help me to complete it we will share the glory of this invention. . . .[12]

In almost prophetic terms, E. L. Harding, living in New York, explained to Henry Ford on July 10, 1926, that he had discovered a way to break the atom and use released energy for practical purposes. He believed the new source of energy would ultimately displace coal, oil, and electricity. He added, "Can the importance of this be over estimated. . . .?"

Although the Tin Lizzies were the lowest priced cars in the nation, their owners frequently clamored for greater economy. Perhaps this was because thrift had been one of the factors in the choice of the Model T in the first place. In spite of the unpretentious appearance of the car, caused by the manufacturer's effort to cut production costs, certain customers tried to outdo Ford himself. Noting that the Florida law in 1923 required only one license plate

on an automobile, some one suggested the removal of the front license brackets on all shipments to that state. Ford officials admitted this would save fifteen cents per car, but refused to carry out
the recommendation.

The economizer's fetish, however, was the cost of gasoline.
Since gasoline sold for cash, the expense could be easily seen and
keenly felt. In addition, gasoline prices tended to go up rather than
down. Although prices varied according to locality, farmers reported paying 10 cents a gallon in Nebraska in 1914, and 16 cents
in 1915.[13] By 1917, the price had reached 28 cents in Chinook, Montana, and 51 cents in Edmonton, Canada, in 1922.

A Model T usually made 20 miles on a gallon of gas, but many
believed Henry Ford could improve on this if he put his mind to it.
A common rumor persisted that automobile manufacturers and
petroleum companies were in collusion to keep gas saving inventions off the market. People heard that a certain person had bought
a new car which made 50 miles on a gallon. But shortly afterward
an agent for some firm would arrive and pay a fabulous price to reclaim the carburetor which had gone out by mistake. Of course,
rural people never asked why countries which did not have oil wells
did not favor the use of these secret gas-saving carburetors.

The first deep concern over gasoline prices occurred in 1916,
when petroleum companies in the United States raised their prices
7 cents a gallon above the 1914 price. The oil companies claimed
the European war and mounting demands at home created a shortage of gasoline. The Topeka *Daily Capital* on February 14, 1916,
insisted the oil trusts profiteered, that no shortage existed, and that
the Federal Government should regulate the three-billion-dollar industry. Since autos would burn 720,500,000 gallons of gasoline in
1916, American motorists would pay $240 million for the gasoline for
the three million cars on the road. A farmer near Waynesburg, Pennsylvania, wrote Ford saying the exorbitant price of gasoline would
burden both the maker and owner of automobiles. Thousands of
people were distressed. If a shortage of gasoline existed, why did
oil companies export millions of gallons to Asia and Europe? In fact
the foreign market was sought to get rid of a surplus. "Please expose
this extortion and help us little fellows. Our ability to own a car lies
within your power. . . ."

This crisis seemed to bring forth inventive genius. J. B. Dailey,
a Ford Motor Company secretary, on May 2, 1916, informed a correspondent that "we are in receipt of from 50 to 100 letters a day

relative to gasoline and its substitutes, which makes it impossible for Mr. Ford to give them his personal attention. . . ."

Meanwhile, the claims made for gas-saving devices were impressive. A new invention in Maryland would guarantee 28 miles per gallon; in British Columbia, 30 miles; in Kentucky, 34 miles; in Ohio, 45 miles. Measured in percentages, the performances were equally good, with a Californian saving 12 percent on gas consumption, a Minnesotan claiming 40 percent, and a New Englander boasting 50 percent. Most of these devices were carburetor attachments called vaporizers, vacuum chambers, atomizers, or de-carbonizers. All sold for less than $5.00.

Most Model T drivers noticed that the motor ran better and had more power during rainy weather. Consequently carburetors were designed to add water to the gasoline vapor; others had steam vaporizers to add moisture to the mixture of gas and air. One carburetor called "Flexo" would make a four-cylinder engine sound like six cylinders, according to the inventor. A mechanic near Utica, New York, told Ford to save gasoline by just piping the fumes from the tank to the carburetor instead of the liquid. This would yield 100 miles to a gallon of gas. A minister in Whitefish, Montana, said he had a fuel which was 8 cents a gallon cheaper than gasoline. It was a chemical which could be reactivated by heat, light, and water. A resident of Monhegan, Maine, ran a motorboat on a chemical mixed with water which cost 5 cents a gallon. A mechanic in Missouri wrote to Henry Ford saying he had a patent on a new fuel called "Motorizine," which cost only 4 cents a gallon. In a 5-mile test the fuel actually expanded from 4½ gallons to 5 gallons. An Ohio firm sold "Gas Tonic," advertised to increase gas mileage by 40 percent. A blacksmith in Barberton, Ohio, advocated the abolition of gasoline in motors. He suggested large spools of thread in which, at intervals of one-fourth inch, there would be a small deposit of some high explosive. This thread would then run through the cylinder head, exploding, and driving the pistons. Each spool would carry enough explosives to run a car 1,000 miles.

Early in 1916, Elmer R. Stoll of the Pittsburgh Newspaper Publishers Association carried on a lengthy correspondence with J. B. Dailey, who worked in the office of one of the Ford laboratories in Dearborn. Mr. Stoll asked the Ford Motor Company to evaluate the work of Carl Fisher of Pittsburgh who claimed he could produce gasoline out of water and a secret powder. This self-made scientist called his product "Zoline." Fisher had demonstrated his discovery before automobile manufacturers in Indianapolis, where he produced gasoline at a cost of 3 cents a gallon. He had also made a test before a group of naval officers of the Brooklyn Navy Yard. Here the inventor had been stripped of all his clothing and put in an empty cell. A gallon of sea water was placed in the cell. A few minutes later Fisher emerged with the gallon of sea water and poured it into a marine engine which then started and ran smoothly. It was assumed that the expert concealed enough of the powder in his mouth to produce the gallon of fuel. Mr. Fisher asked $10,000 for a thirty-day option on the process. After a corporation had been formed, the inventor would receive one million dollars and a share of the stock. Again, Mr. Dailey showed interest in the project but claimed Henry Ford was too busy to give it serious consideration.

In more practical matters, Model T owners were distressed by the prevalence of tire trouble. Poor roads, ruts, and rocks played havoc with tires, causing blowouts, rim cuts, stone bruises, and slow leaks for millions of rural travelers. These problems were so common that one of the stock questions asked of one returning from a shopping trip to town was, "Did you have any tire trouble?" Rural drivers prepared for these frequent inconveniences by carrying spare tires, blowout boots, inner-tube patches, and various types of tire pumps. Prior to the introduction of balloon tires in 1924, the high-pressure tires carried 50 to 60 pounds of pressure, a factor which increased the likelihood of tire trouble. A rural minister in Oregon had nine blowouts on one Sunday morning. He returned home on the rims of all four wheels in spite of carrying five spare tires. Some farmers suggested filling the tires with coil springs or sponge rubber instead of air. One farmer said he filled his tires with oats and then added water to expand the grain to the proper pressure.

The simplicity of the Model T was well known. Its functional utility repudiated the bric-a-brac ornamentation of the nineteenth century. Henry Ford never claimed his cars resembled old European coaches with their purple trimmings, hand-carved woodwork, grilled hardware, and fancy coat of arms. Neither did he describe his car as a horseless carriage. It was a twentieth-century vehicle designed to haul passengers from place to place with some sense of economy. J. A. Kouwenhoven in his book *Made in America* described the Model T as "a naked, undisguised machine for transportation, an honest-to-God jeep.[14]

Many flivver drivers, however, were convinced that some embellishments should be added to offset this austerity, and the motoring public made ample suggestions. An inventor of a self-cleaning cuspidor, designed for the dash of a Model T, had blue prints, an attorney, and the patent number 1,453,545 registered with the United States Patent Office. Cigar lighters were advocated, as well as vanity cases and fire extinguishers. After returning from a trip, a family urged Ford to attach a heating unit to the exhaust pipe so passengers could bake potatoes, cook vegetables, heat the baby's bottle, and make coffee. Screens would keep out flies, awnings provide shade, and a pump in the gas tank would force the fuel into the carburetor when climbing steep hills. Seat belts in the back seat would prevent people being tossed into the top of the car. Tilting bars affixed to the side of the auto would prevent the car from tipping over because the bars would swing out and prop the cars in an upright position.

Other suggestions included longer springs, coil springs, or to hang the body on leather straps like the Concord stage coaches. A piece of glass on the front fender would let the driver see the location of the wheel at all times; an iron grate on the running board would let mud fall to the ground instead of being tracked into the car; an adjustable fan would admit air through the radiator as desired; a bottle of compressed air would pump up tires; an automatic jack on the bumpers could raise the car as one drove ahead; better door latches would prevent the slamming of doors to make them stay shut; shorter running boards would leave more clearance for tires and eliminate broken tire chains; and a freeze plug for the radiator would drain the water before it reached the freezing point.

One of the more unusual ideas was attaching ropes to the foot pedals, so that a driver could extricate the car from a mud hold by pushing and manipulating the transmission simultaneously. One suggested that the right wheels be larger in diameter to prevent the tilting of cars when they ran on the slanting graded dirt roads. A collapsible bicycle lashed to the car could be used if the car stalled, or carrier pigeons might be trained to fly for assistance. A small auxiliary motor might be bolted to the regular engine which could function in an emergency. A vacuum cleaner, working off the intake manifold, was invented, while various types of speedometers were designed. One farmer objected, however, saying, "I don't need a speedometer. When I go 5 miles an hour in my Model T, the fenders rattle; when I go 15 miles an hour my false teeth drop out; and when I go 25 miles an hour the transmission drops off."

Since the Model T possessed the bare essentials, most owners sought accessories of some type. In fact, many business firms did a thriving business in providing extra equipment. Catalogues contained such items as: a spindle anti-rattler device for 70 cents, a wheel puller for 19 cents, an oil gauge for 15 cents, an engine-driven tire pump at $5.25, a windshield mirror for 60 cents, a tool box for the running board, $1.25, and a temperature gauge for the radiator cap for $1.00. Various types of shock absorbers were available, the most common being the Hassler which used coil springs. It was advertised in the *Progressive Farmer* as making the Ford ride as smooth as a sleigh.

People using a product are often the first to note the need for improvements. In fact, most of the engineering miracles in the automotive industry were suggested by the common man long before company engineers put the ideas on blueprints. As early as 1901, car owners were asking for a fluid-drive transmission instead of gears. A farmer at Waterstreet, Pennsylvania, in 1923 wrote to Henry Ford stating, "I have a patentable idea by which all autos can be run without changing gears. All gears change automatically when the car goes uphill." Three years later another farmer at Stroud, Oklahoma, tried to interest Ford in a transmission which, "automatically shifted gears as the car picked up speed and when you get in sand, it shifts down again until it spins its wheels." Similarly, a mechanic at Lyle, Minnesota, in 1926 built a fluid drive with a cone coming off the crankshaft enclosing another cone on the drive shaft. Another farmer in Idaho constructed an oil clutch which he tried to sell to Ford Motor Company. To all these petitions, the Experimental Division of the company gave the curt reply, "We are not interested. . . ."

During the twenties and thirties, rural people expected Henry Ford to buy ideas and patents for any machine or device used in farming. Many invented improvements on threshing machines and hoped Ford would help market them. Some wanted Ford to branch out and mass produce all farm implements. Letters included suggestions for air ventilators for barns to promote the health of farm animals; for a self-propelled truck which loaded and unloaded itself; for an improved plowshare; for a gadget to release the foot of one who has fallen from a saddle; for a washing machine to wash white and colored clothes simultaneously; for a parcel-post basket

attached to a mail box; and for an automatic trap for catching fur-
bearing animals. From Esterville, Iowa, a dairyman wrote, "I am a
farmer who invented a cow-tail holder. This holds the cow's tail
while milking so that it cannot switch you in the eye. I believe there
are a lot of eyes hurt from old cows' tails. This device fits any cow's
leg, little or small. You can put it on the cow next to you as well. I
do not know where to send it and get a fair deal. . . ."

Other novel suggestions were that Ford manufacture an electric revolver, a self-ringing bottle to warn people in handling poison,
a machine to locate the wounded on battlefields, a machine to save
the gold and blow out all the sand and gravel, a self-lathering shav-
ing brush, a self-lighting cigarette, collapsible water buckets, anti-
static radios, and a gasoline motor to strap on swimmer's backs to
move them effortlessly through the water.

Since rural people felt that somehow they knew Henry Ford
personally, it seemed quite right for them to write him about their
inventions or proposed inventions of hundreds of things not related
to the Model T. And they did—many thousands of letters. But the
bulk of these communications concerned the Model T—the car they
usually loved, sometimes hated, but always wanted to improve.
These hopes now reside in the 214 boxes of the *Ford Fair Lane
Papers* in the Dearborn archives.

V

Henry Ford's Tractors and Agriculture

Henry Ford's automotive efforts were so fantastically successful that they tended to obscure his efforts to build tractors to furnish power for the American farmer. It is often forgotten that he attempted to make agricultural engines before he turned his attention to automobiles.

Ford had been interested in power farming ever since his boyhood on his father's farm. According to his own testimony, one of the two biggest events in his early life occurred at the age of twelve when he saw a Nichols and Shepard steam traction engine puffing along the road eight miles from Detroit. Since this was the first self-propelled vehicle he had seen, he jumped out of his father's buggy and engaged the farm engineer in conversation. The engine had a chain drive, burned coal, and was used primarily for threshing grain. Ford later insisted this experience had great significance because it encouraged him to think about replacing horses with machines. He had always disliked horses and mules saying they ate their fool heads off six months out of the year.

Ford left the farm to work in the Michigan Car Company in Detroit, and later as a mechanic with the Detroit Drydock Company. In 1882 he returned like the prodigal son to his father's house where he maintained his interest in machinery. He operated a Westinghouse portable steam engine for eighty-three days one fall to do the threshing for the farmers in his neighborhood. In addition, he spent some time as a traveling repair expert for the Westinghouse Company. While still on the farm in 1883, he built a crude self-propelled steam engine for his own use. Although it developed plenty of power, the kerosene-heated boiler required high steam pressure which was dangerous. Since he thought he had nothing else to learn about farm steam engines, he turned his attention to gasoline motors.

It is well to remember that Henry Ford was a farm steam engineer before he became an inventor of automobiles. Contrary to public opinion, he did not jump from the horse age to the gasoline age but from the steam era to the gasoline era. Ford belonged to that group of farm engineers who had worked for a century to supplant horse power with mechanical power. These steam engineers brought power farming to rural America, and Henry Ford was one of this breed. Visitors viewing the Ford Museum in Greenfield Village are often surprised to see that a major part of the main floor is devoted to a display of agricultural steam engines. Because of his early experiences on Michigan farms, he never lost interest in steam power. Even when he was in his seventies, he insisted that his company sponsor an old-fashioned threshing bee each fall at Tecumseh, Michigan, where a Westinghouse farm steam engine, built in the 1880s, provided the power for belt work.

These farm engineers had their heyday during the steam engine boom from 1880 to 1914. Since steam remained the only practical source of mechanical power for general farm use in the nineteenth century, the farmer's demands for it increased. In 1880, a total of 1,200,000 steam horsepower served agricultural purposes, while in 1910 the figure reached 3,600,000 horsepower, an amount equal to the strength of seven million horses. At this time, the Department of Agriculture estimated that a hundred thousand farm engineers were operating self-propelled steam engines for plowing, threshing, grading roads, grinding feed, hauling freight, and sawing wood.[1]

In rural America, the farm engineers staged colorful performances, with engines glistening in bright paint, red wheels, black boilers, green trimmings, and shining brass. Some of the leviathans weighed twenty tons, developed 100 horsepower, consumed 70 barrels of water daily, and cost as much as $6,000. The Best and Hott engines on the Pacific Coast had driving wheels 12 feet in diameter and could out-pull 40 mules. With a grain combine they could harvest 100 acres daily. After 1900, steam traction engines pulling ten to fourteen breaker bottoms ripped up much of the sod lying from the Canadian provinces to the Rio Grande.[2]

Meanwhile, the gasoline tractor emerged slowly because it had to wait for the discovery of petroleum in the Pennsylvania oil fields in 1859. Without gasoline or suitable lubricating oil, the tractor was impossible. In addition, tractors needed electricity for ignition, which meant waiting for the development of batteries, magnetos, and electrical systems which came in the 1890s.

The first tractor to perform work successfully in the United States was built by John Froehlich of Iowa in 1892. It completed fifty days of threshing in the fall of that year and pulled the grain separator from one field to another. The Hart-Parr engines, built at Charles City, Iowa, in 1902 and 1903, were the first successful tractors built in the United States and sold on a successful commercial basis. The first Hart-Parr tractor provided power for an Iowa farmer for seventeen years, while five manufactured in 1903 were still in operation in 1930. In 1906 these engines were used for plowing, and in 1907, in order to distinguish gasoline engines from steam engines, Hart and Parr adopted the name "Tractor"—a name subsequently accepted by the general public.[3]

By 1907 there were 600 tractors in use in the nation, one-third of which were Hart-Parrs, with the rest divided among the Kinnard-Haines Company of Minneapolis, the International Harvester Company of Chicago, and several smaller firms.[4] E. W. Hamilton, editor of the *Canadian Thresherman*, in 1908 said that five years earlier there were only two tractor models on the American market, but that now there were thirty. W. C. Allen of the *Dakota Farmer* observed in 1909 that steam engines had given good service, but "now the gasoline tractors seem to be more popular."

In the meantime, Henry Ford maintained an interest in farm tractors. In 1908, he told Joseph Galamb and C. J. Smith to build a tractor in three days by attaching drive wheels to a Model B Ford engine of 24 horsepower. Galamb recalled that Henry Ford had come to him saying he needed a light tractor to pull a binder in one of his wheat fields. He suggested using a Model B motor and a Model T axle.[5] It took a week to put together an awkward machine which had wagon wheels in front and grain binder wheels in the rear. The gas tank was placed in front of the radiator to prevent the engine from lifting the front wheels off the ground. This machine did some work, but the motor lacked power and overheated too easily.

Ford's intentions were serious, however. He had applied for certain tractor patents in 1910, and when the Highland Park plant opened he hoped to manufacture tractors along with the Model Ts.

But the preoccupation with automotive production and the refusal of stockholders to sanction tractor production stalled his plans.

In the interim, he purchased several tractors on the market for observation. He noted that most of them had automatic intake valves, hit-and-miss governors, and make-and-break ignition systems. Electric current from dry batteries was used to start the tractors, while a low-voltage, direct-current magneto provided current for running the motor. Frames were of channel iron, selective transmissions were used, and the large drive wheels turned on a "dead" or floating axle. Unfortunately most of the tractors in 1910 were modeled after steam-traction engines, and thus were too heavy and clumsy. Many weighed 20,000 to 50,000 pounds. Some of the behemoths had fly-wheels weighing over a ton, with drive wheels eight feet in diameter and tanks holding 110 gallons of water, 70 gallons of fuel, and 5 gallons of oil. Some were so hard to start that owners let them run all night rather than face this baffling problem in the morning. The instruction manual for the Hart-Parr tractor listed nineteen rules for starting and thirteen rules for stopping the engine.[6]

Since tractors pulled a full load, they created more strain on working parts than automobiles cruising over the highways. As a result too many tractors had broken crankshafts, warped clutches, broken gears, dead magnetos, burned out bearings, and faulty spark plugs. An Illinois farmer in 1908 despaired, saying he had run his tractor less than 30 days but his repair bills were so great he was ashamed to meet the public. Some farmers spent as much as $1,500 for repairs in one year, while many discarded theirs in junk piles.[7] Bankers often refused credit to farmers sinking $3,000 in a new tractor.

Henry Ford attended the Winnipeg plowing trials in 1910, where his observations influenced his subsequent decisions. These plowing contests were sponsored by the Winnipeg Industrial Exhibition Association to draw attention to the opportunities for using more mechanical power on the plains of Canada. Since Winnipeg stood as a gateway to a vast agricultural empire, the contests took on international importance. All manufacturers of steam and gasoline engines were invited to enter the competition to determine the best farm engines. Aware of the advertising value, manufacturers bent every effort to win the judges decision.

During the trials, mammoth engines surged across the sod pulling breaking plows to a flag marker a mile distant. As the engineers struck their furrows, turning over 160 acres in a day, a corps of college professors of engineering jotted down the data. Results were telegraphed to the major news centers of the Western Hemisphere. Edward A. Rumely, president of his company, described the scene as one in which clouds of smoke and hissing steam floated for miles across the prairies. Huge engines pulled breakers cleaving the grass land, while mechanics guarded their machines throughout the night. Throngs of spectators lined the fields, "ears alert to the sound of vibrant steel and the cracking roots of age old sod. . . ."[8]

At the contest in 1910, Ford noticed that the heavy engines mired hopelessly in the mud, while the lighter tractors kept moving. The smaller tractors were easier to handle, were more maneuverable, and could be put immediately to work without wasting time in firing a steam boiler. Edward Rumley met Ford at this contest and they discussed the future of power farming in America. Ford thought only 10 percent of the power needs of farmers were being met by mechanical means. He was now convinced that gasoline tractors would replace steam power in agriculture.

Returning to Michigan, Ford decided he would manufacture tractors on the same principle he had used in building automobiles, namely, machines which were simple in construction, light in weight, and low in cost. In 1913 he experimented with a Model T tractor. By placing his auto motor on a heavy frame, he used these tractors on his Dearborn farms for plowing, discing, and harrowing. Philip S. Rose, Professor of Agricultural Engineering at North Dakota State College, wrote a description of the Ford tractor in 1915, saying he retained the Model T engine, front axle, steering gear, and transmission, but used a worm gear to drive the rear axle. The machine was nimble, easily handled, and traveled two to five miles per hour. The tractor could not pull a 15-inch plow four inches deep, however, without wheel slippage. In many ways this was no tractor at all; a team of horses could do more work than this machine. A writer for the Chicago *American* thought many believed Henry Ford had invented something new, but all he had done was put different wheels on a Tin Lizzie and called it a tractor. It was just another Ford joke created for cheap publicity.

By this time farmers were increasing their demands for smaller tractors which would be less costly and which could replace horses in the 100-degree heat of the harvest fields. As many as fifty thousand farmers attended tractor demonstrations held in several midwestern cities. In field tests near Enid, Oklahoma, in 1915, they watched thirty tractor companies demonstrate their engines. Hundreds of sales were made on the spot. Farmers pulled out their checkbooks and dropped down on their knees in the plowed dirt to write their checks. A businessman writing to Henry Ford stated, "There are over two million farmers in the United States and Canada, every one of whom is a legitimate prospect for a small tractor. You never saw the farmers so ripe for anything and plucking should not be long delayed."[9]

Anticipating this trend, the Bull Tractor Company of Minneapolis in 1913 introduced a 4,650-pound tractor advertised as the "Bull with a Pull." Selling for only $645, the model became the forerunner of the small power units to which most of the tractor manufacturers were turning at the time. In 1915 Henry Ford announced his entrance into the light tractor field with an automotive system of mass production.

To avoid objections of stockholders, Ford incorporated a subsidiary called the Henry Ford and Son Tractor Division. Experimental work began in a small shop south of the Michigan Central Railroad in Dearborn. Authority was invested in Charles E. Sorensen, a handsome Dane who joined Ford in 1905 and who, by his hard, driving methods gained the reputation as a good engineer, skillful metallurgist, and above all as a man who could get things done. His chief assistants were Gene Farkas, Seyburn Livingston, and Marvin Bryant.

Most of the tractors manufactured by the one hundred twenty-one companies in 1915 had motors mounted on steel frames. Gene Farkas believed the motor could be bolted directly to the transmission and this in turn bolted to a rear axle assembly. This made for neatness of design and simplicity of construction. It also made it possible to assemble three units—the front wheels, the motor and transmission, and the rear drive wheels—and bring them together in a final production technique similar to that of the auto industry. All gears were enclosed in an oil bath, thus preventing dirt from getting into the gears. Engineers also eliminated vanadium steel, so highly advertised in the Model T, and substituted chrome carbon steel which they regarded as superior in tensile strength. The first tractor from the new factory appeared early in 1916.

The Ford Motor Company's Fordson tractor was born in a fusillade of publicity. The Toledo *Blade* on May 18, 1915, announced that Ford would build a farm tractor for $200 which would do the work of six horses and thus revolutionize agriculture. The Grand Rapids *Herald* predicted the tractor would place Ford alongside Edison as a creative wizard. After thirty years of effort Ford had perfected a tractor capable of reducing the cost of farming by one third. His company would hire twenty thousand men to manufacture a million tractors. Anyone else attempting this would be thought insane, but Ford was different. He had already done more with American opportunity than any other man in history, and no one would begrudge him a billion dollars because his achievements made for social betterment.[10]

Ford himself was not reticent. He sent a motion picture of his tractor to President Wilson, while at the same time he asked the Federal Government to deepen the Rouge River to facilitate shipping. He also announced he would extend the $5.00 a day wage to all workers in the tractor plant. He hinted that he would build a rubber factory to make his own tires and would neither deny nor affirm a plan to buy thirty acres near Chicago to construct another tractor factory. In October word came that he planned to sell his tractors through a mail-order arrangement. In November the New York *Call* blazed the headlines, FORD'S TRACTOR WILL MAKE WORK OF SOIL TILLER ONE GRAND SWEET SONG. These tractors would double productivity on American farms. Another New York paper carried a story by John Reed who described Ford as a miracle worker because he would now sell his tractors at ten cents a pound, the going rate for scrap iron. Ford could destroy monopoly, free farmers from debt, and let them take possession of the land. When asked about a possible depression after the European war, Ford had boasted, "Oh that's all right. I can use all the unemployed making tractors. . . . I am going to plow up the Australian bush and the steppes of Siberia and Mesopotamia."

Late in July, 1916, Henry Ford stopped off in Kansas City where he proclaimed there was a demand for 10 million tractors. He said he was going to make a Ford car, truck, and tractor and sell all three for $600. He added, "I am going to do it, if I don't croak first." The Topeka *Daily Capital* observed that the only people who lacked faith in Ford were those who feared his power to create miracles.

In August the Ford Motor Company entered a tractor in the Fremont, Nebraska, plowing demonstration. Here sixty-five tractors worked in a 1,000-acre field. The Omaha *Daily Bee* estimated Ford's personal appearance during the five days increased the attendance by 10,000 farmers. In the evenings, the people could view a movie or listen to a Hawaiian quartet provided by the Ford advertising officials. The Kansas City *Post* thought Ford proved a bigger attraction than his tractors.

It was the First World War, however, which brought on a crisis in industry and agriculture and focused attention on the production of farm commodities. The stalemate on the Western Front, with its staggering losses in men and materiel seemed to indicate that victory would go to the side best prepared for total war. When German submarines attacked Allied shipping, the situation became desperate.

The crisis in food production was apparent to the British long before the United States entered the war. The London *Times* in May of 1915 reported 80,000 farm hands had gone off to war, leaving the operators of steam cable-plowing outfits short on manpower. "All my men have enlisted," moaned one farmer, and "Some of my land is going out of cultivation."[11] Some members of the British press feared starvation. If farmers failed to produce enough, the State should commandeer the farms to defeat the U-Boats.

Faced with this shortage of farm labor, Britain hoped for a rapid conversion to mechanized farming. Tractors would release men and horses for the battle field. Yet to motorize British agriculture would be difficult because of the conservative nature of most farmers. The *Mark Lane Express* believed farmers hated tractors because they reduced the value of horses. Besides the average farmer knew nothing about spark plugs, short circuits, faulty valves, and the loss of compression. An implement dealer, in jest, said the only way he could get farmers to read machinery catalogues was to put ten pound notes between the pages.

Aware of the necessity to secure greater sinews of war, Lord Northcliffe headed a British War Mission to the United States in 1916, where he visited numerous corporation executives. Impressed with the Ford tractor plant, he returned to Britain convinced that his country needed tractors to win the war. He consulted Lord Perry, head of the British Ford Motor Company. Perry cabled Henry Ford requesting a tractor to be used in field trials; a plea which was promptly granted.

On April 7, 1917, the day following America's entry into the war, Lord Perry cabled Edsel Ford: "Would you be willing to send Sorenson and others with tractor drawings of everything necessary, loaning them to the British government so that parts can be manufactured over here. . . . The matter is very urgent. . . . National necessity entirely dependent Mr. Ford's decision."[12] The following day, Henry Ford pledged full support to save Britain. He promised to comply with every request and would work night and day. A full organization would be sent to England.

Charles Sorensen went into action. He filled an express car with tractor parts, patterns, and farm implements and took a train for Halifax accompanied by five engineers. Henry Ford went to see them embark on the *Justicia* on May 3. By July 1, they were ready to start production of Fordson parts in England.

These moves were met with considerable opposition in Great Britian, however. Many regarded the Peace Ship venture as the work of idealistic faddists who were honest but unrealistic. Others remembered Ford's pacifism which led him to criticize the granting of a British loan of 100 million pounds at 5 percent interest. The *Times* claimed Ford had threatened to withdraw his accounts from banks participating in the loan. He had said that if Britain needed cash why didn't she sell her securities in the United States. Ford was quoted as saying, "If I had my way I would tie a tin can on the joint Anglo-French Commission and chase it back to Europe. The best thing would be for all Europe to go bankrupt, then the fighting would stop."[13] When the Ford Motor Company received permission to build a tractor factory at Cork, Ireland, on March 6, 1917, many called this unwise, because Ford would flood the British market with cheap goods. Besides the factory would not get into production until after the war had terminated, and since British firms were tied up in war contracts, this would give outside competitors a chance to get a strangle hold on the British market.

In the midst of this controversey, the German air raid on London on July 23, 1917, complicated matters. Lord Milner of the Minister of Munitions Board called in Charles Sorensen and explained that the German attacks meant that all Britain's productive capacity would now be geared to the manufacture of airplanes. Therefore the plans to build Fordson tractors in British factories had to be abandoned. Could these tractors be secured in the United States? Sorensen believed they could if Britain would furnish the shipping. Besides they could be built faster in Dearborn than in Britain. To this Milner agreed. When asked how many tractors Ford could produce, Sorensen thought fifty could be built within 90 days with rapid increases later. "Splendid," said Milner, "How about 5,000 tractors and at what price?" Sorensen thought the cost of production plus $50 would suit Mr. Ford. It did. In November, 1917, David Lloyd George announced his government had ordered 8,000 American tractors for use in British agriculture.[14]

There has been a tendency to exaggerate the Ford Motor Company's technical assistance to British agriculture during the World War I years. Henry Ford is often pictured as the hero with a heart of gold, rushing in to save the starving Englishmen from the clutches of the marauding Huns. The mission accomplished, the benefactor received the undying gratitude of the terror-stricken English populace.

Actually, the program of aid never ran smoothly. The newspaper files in the British archives and the farm journals in the Whitehall Library in London reflect the hostility of large numbers of Britons toward Ford and the tractor transactions. The *Implement and Machinery Review*, a London journal, in July, 1917, scored the Government's partiality for the Fordson. Was it the best tractor on the market? Why had the Minister of Munitions Board put so much faith in it? Why had the Fordson been chosen, when the War Agricultural Committee, watching the plowing demonstrations at Middlesex, thought the Bull tractor superior? Was it not true that qualified engineers had been hired by the Government to make recommendations, which were then promptly disregarded? Furthermore, M.O.M. officials knew Fordsons could not be secured for plowing in the fall of 1917, then why did the Board refuse to purchase other makes of tractors? A large consignment of tractors not manufactured by Ford were lying idle in London meanwhile, when it would be six months before Fordsons arrived from Michigan.

Several British manufacturing executives insisted that the Government tractor program should have been left to private enterprise. This would have avoided bureaucracy, divided councils, delays, and an incredible waste of money. Evidence cited for this protest included the effort to use twenty-one tractors to plow 187,000 acres in Stafford County. Here most of the tractors were laid up for repairs which could be secured only by appealing to a London committee. In the House of Commons, a representative from South Melton charged that tractor supervisors were drawing five guineas a week and expenses, while five tractors near Devonshire plowed less than an acre per day per tractor, all at a cost of ten pounds an acre. *The Implement and Machinery Review* on December 1, 1917, called the program wasteful, inefficient, and costly. In 1918 privately owned steam plowing outfits turned over a million acres, while government tractors plowed only 611,000 acres.

As might be expected, efforts were made to silence the criticism. Lord Northcliffe, who had visited Ford in Dearborn on October 17, 1917, praised him as a mechanical genius, with a tractor which would revolutionize farming as his car had altered transit. He loved the land, admired Tennyson, quoted *Locksley Hall,* and resembled the Bishop of London and Sir John Hare.[15]

There is some justification for criticism, however, since only 3,600 Fordsons reached Britain by March 1, 1918, and the entire consignment of 6,000 did not arrive until the war was almost over. The Cork factory in Ireland did not go into production until July, 1919. Some of the frustrations involved in getting the tractors to Britain can be seen in Henry Ford's cablegram to Lord Northcliffe on February 28, 1918, which stated, "We have shipped to date, 1,800 assembled tractors and parts for another 1,800 knocked down. Only 10 percent of this has been loaded on ship." The memorandum added that 3,000 tractors were lying on the docks in Baltimore and Philadelphia. These machines should have shipping priority over food. If the tractors were not handled in thirty days, they would be sold in Canada and in the United States.

On the home front, the Fordson publicity became widespread. A people conditioned to heatless Mondays, meatless Tuesdays, and wheatless Wednesdays were told that food would win the war and the "Man with the Hoe" must go. The New York *Times* on April 22, 1917, ran the banner "A Girl on a Tractor is Worth Two Men Behind the Plow and Two Horses in Front of It." The Bridgeport *Standard* admonished, "Buy Tractors and Win the War," while the Newark *Star-Eagle* predicted, "Detroit will Defeat Essen: Ford will Triumph over Krupp." Henry Ford said motorized farming could solve the food problem because one tractor would produce fifty times its weight in food annually. Therefore, one ship carrying tractors to Europe would equal fifty ships carrying food the next year. Fifteen thousand men in his factories could produce 1,000 tractors a day. Bookkeeping in the cities did not grow crops, but better machinery in rural America would do the job.

When the first Fordson for domestic use came off the assembly line on April 23, 1918, Ford gave it to his old friend Luther Burbank. When the engine rambled into his yard at Santa Rosa, California, the botanist exclaimed, "Just like Ford, all motor and no frame." Thomas Edison received the number two Fordson. Production increased at the River Rouge Tractor Plant until 26,817 tractors had left the factory by Armistice Day, and 91,346 by the end of 1919.

To advertise these tractors, Ford dealers conducted plowing demonstrations in many sections of the country. Several thousand people witnessed a Fordson exhibition in East Oakland, California, on October 6, 1918, where a local scribe explained, "They came, they saw, and were convinced. The horse is now the most extravagant motor known."[16] Special training courses were held to teach women the fundamentals of tractor operations. One farmerette stated she began the training with reservations, not knowing if she could stand the monotony of driving a tractor six days a week for three months. Yet, after the harvest season she said, "To work out in the open air on a farm, knowing that we are having a direct part in supplying food for our fellowmen, was one of the most satisfying things I have ever experienced."[17]

Since tractors were scarce during the war years, the Ford Motor Company announced in March, 1918, that Fordsons would be distributed to American farmers through permits granted by County War Boards. To secure a permit for purchase, farmers must promise to keep the tractor working on the land, while county agents were to see that the machines were given maximum use. The cost was $750 f.o.b. Detroit, but no profits were to go to middlemen as distributors. Most of the leading agricultural states were given a quota of 1,000 tractors.

As with most wartime ration programs, complaints arose on all sides. Some farmers begged for tractors, but were denied permits for their purchase. Unable to get Fordsons, they complained that too many were going to Britain.

Meanwhile, farm implement dealers accused Ford of a clever scheme to unload his tractors on war boards under the guise of patriotism. Thus civilian agencies in the states distributed millions of dollars worth of Fordsons, but the dealers received nothing for making deliveries. Ford got the cash and the dealers got the exercise. The *Farm Machinery Power* magazine in August, 1918, claimed Henry Ford had promised to sell his tractors for $250, hence farmers declined to purchase from other firms, waiting for the Fordsons to hit the market. When they finally arrived they cost $750, proving that Ford's publicity department outran the cost department. In addition, Ford gave the impression that he sold his engines at cost, as a contribution to the war effort. Yet his business records show that the total cost of manufacturing a Fordson, including labor, materials, and overhead was $567.14, leaving a tidy profit of $182.86 on each unit.[18]

Following the war, the Fordsons infested the land like grasshoppers, for mass production techniques produced 350 tractors daily in 1921, and 750 a day in 1924. It took 30 hours and 40 minutes to convert raw materials into the 4,000 parts going into the tractor assembly. Some wags said they reached the farmers before they had cooled from the furnace heat. At any rate, the Fordson production figures reached 486,822 in 1925 and 650,000 by May, 1927.[19] Officials of the company boasted they had manufactured more than half of all tractors built in the United States up to this time. Sales had been made to most foreign countries, with 10,000 Fordsons shipped to the Soviet Union by January 27, 1926.[20]

The original Fordson manufactured from 1917 to 1927, like its predecessor the Model T car, featured compactness and simplicity. A 20-horsepower, 4-cylinder motor was bolted directly to the transmission housing. The tractor weighed 2,500 pounds, was less than 5 feet high, had a wheelbase of 63 inches, and could turn in a 21-foot circle. Like the Model T, the electricity came off a low-tension magneto bolted to the flywheel, while a thermo-syphon water system cooled the motor. The three forward speeds ranged from 2¼ to 6¼ miles per hour. Like many of its contemporaries, the engine burned either kerosene or gasoline, an economy feature which appealed to farmers.

To help farm lads learn more about the operation and repair of tractors, The Ford Motor Company in 1919 established a policy of loaning Fordsons to educational institutions with vocational training programs. Agricultural colleges could use a Fordson for six months and then exchange it for a new one. Under this arrangement, 42 tractors were loaned to such universities as Cornell, Idaho, Michigan, Maryland, and Prairie View State Normal in Texas. Others went to the orphanage at Nacoochee Institute in Georgia, the Berry School at Rome, Georgia, and Camp Dix at Hutchinson, Kansas. Hearing that Sergeant York of World War I fame had opened an industrial school for the youth of Jamestown, Tennessee, Ford sent two Fordsons to his school.

Although the Fordson sold well, it never duplicated the success of the famous Model T because it possessed several disadvantages. In the first place, it arrived too late. Had it appeared ten years earlier, it doubtless would have swept the farming communities like a winter blizzard, but by 1917 scores of other companies had preempted the light tractor field. This spoiled any claims to uniqueness. Second, the tractor was too light and not powerful enough to meet the needs of large farms where the minimum requirements were three- and four-plow tractors. The Fordson thus was limited to small farms, or was used as an auxiliary tractor for lighter work to supplement a large tractor. In the third place, Fordson had weaknesses which reduced its popularity. The small, 45-inch-drive wheels permitted the engine to mire down too easily in muddy soil. Some farmers complained that the tractor ran so close to the ground that corn stalks punched holes in the radiator. The temperamental ignition system made the engine difficult to start, while the absence of a water pump caused the motor to overheat. An erratic governor permitted too great fluctuation in the speed of the motor, and on some, the shifting lever failed to stay in position.

Although the Fordson was quick in its responses and had a high gear which gave it more speed on the roads than most of its competitors, the machine had a tendency to run up repair bills. Most tractors were vulnerable on this score, but the Fordson seemed to demand considerable attention. A farmer near Atlanta in 1921 listed the cost of his Fordson repairs for the year as $1,246. He recorded his problems in his diary; "Jan. 4, could not start motor. Jan. 19, working on tractor. Jan. 22, broke tractor wheel. Jan. 25, engine failed to run. Jan. 26, tractor broke down. Feb. 10, worked on tractor. Feb. 19, had engine trouble. Feb. 28, had to work on engine. Mar. 4, put in new engine. April 21, tractor broke down, put in new bearings, rear end burst. Repairs needed. Total cost; $1,301.13 for 620 hours of work."[21]

A Colorado farmer telephoned his dealer three times a day to tell him what he thought of his Fordson. The dealer added, "I have been with Ford for seven years, but I never had to take the abuse from any of my customers as I did from this fellow."[22] Another farmer at Paris, Illinois, said he had cussed the Fordson for ten of the best years of his life. The most negative feature, however, was the Fordson's tendency to rear up in front and flip over backwards if sudden resistance on the drawbar created excessive torque in the transmission. The first Fordsons had the worm gear above the main drive pinion, but this caused too much heat for the driver's seat. When the worm gear was placed below the big pinion, this increased the lift on the front wheels. One Indiana farmer believed such a dangerous machine should be banned by law. The *Eastern Implement Dealer* claimed Fordsons killed thirty-six drivers in 1918, while *Pipp's Weekly* insisted the tractor had snuffed out the lives of 136 men prior to August, 1922. These publications carried headlines screaming, "Fordson Tractor Proved Man Killer," "Fordson Tractor is Bad Medicine for Farmer's Ills," and "Fordsons are Huns of the Field." Irate journalists believed press agents had made Henry

Ford a benefactor, whereas he was a public nuisance. When two brothers invented an attachment which would cut off the ignition when the tractor began to rear, one editor thought they should be given the Carnegie Medal for saving human life.

In response, Ford spokesmen maintained the accidents resulted from inexperienced and ignorant drivers who had no more knowledge of tractors than Chinese laundry checks. Any tractor could be dangerous if improperly handled. Those printing unsupported accusations were guilty of libel.

Satisfied customers, on the other hand, praised the Fordson, saying it made farm work easier, it performed ideally in orchards and truck farms, it helped keep the boys on the farm, and it was so versatile it could do everything except milk cows. A Mississippi farmer testified it defeated all competition in that region and would do anything any sensible fool wanted done. Some expressed their admiration for the iron horse in poetic lines such as:

> The Fordson on the farm arose
> Before the dawn at four.
> It drove the cows and washed the clothes
> And finished every chore.
> Then forth it went into the fields
> Just at the break of day.
> It reaped and threshed the golden yield
> And hauled it all away.[23]

Although this outburst of sentimentality may not reflect the greatest poetry, the unusual thing about it is that it appeared at all. One would look far to find similar odes dedicated to tractors assembled by International Harvester, Caterpillar, Advance Rumely, Emerson Brantingham, or the Dayton-Dick Company of Quincy, Illinois.

In spite of reasonable success, the Fordson faced tough opposition in the 1920s. The farm depression of 1920–23 created sales resistance, and dealers reported that farmers lacked money to buy machinery. Sales managers blamed the local dealers for being more interested in selling automobiles than farm tractors. Charles E. Sorensen later insisted that the obligation to sell both cars and tractors had proved too much for the dealers. The Ford Motor Company, however, was the only automotive firm to sell cars, trucks, and tractors simultaneously from 1917 to 1927. General Motors produced the Sampson tractor but gave it up after two years. The farm implement companies that tried to build automobiles experienced the same fate, such as the J. I. Case company of Racine, Wisconsin, and the International Harvester Company of Chicago. Neither of them kept up dual production more than three years.

During the 1920s, the success of the McCormick Deering 10–20 and 15–30 tractors gave the Fordson added competition. The advent of the Farmall in 1924, with its ability to farm row crops, made the Fordson less practical. The success of such companies as John Deere, J. I. Case, International Harvester, and Minneapolis encouraged Ford officials in 1927 to discontinue the manufacture of the Fordson in the United States. Tractor production, however, continued at plants in Cork, Ireland, and Dagenham, England. Not until the late 1930s did Ford again begin to manufacture tractors in the United States.

In more recent years, innovations have improved the efficiency of farm tractors. After the introduction of the power takeoff in 1919, starters and lights in the early 1920s, the arrival of rubber tires in 1932 increased the power of tractors by 25 percent, and increased the speed of most field operations from 25 to 50 percent. In the late 1930s, various hydraulic lifting attachments were available, which could manipulate loaders, control tillage implements, activate power steering, and operate removal scoops. An improved three-point hydraulic hitch, developed by Harry Ferguson of Ireland and brought to this country in 1939, strongly influenced the design of tractor hitches. These gave fingertip control over powerful hydraulic activating mechanism. Since 1954, more versatile transmissions permit the operator to shift gears while on the move, while the Ford tractor in 1959 had a ten-speed, fully selective, power-shift unit which let the driver shift gears without the use of a clutch pedal.

Looking back at this period of agricultural history, the important factor is not the degree of success of the Fordson tractors, but rather the role that Henry Ford played in the entire technological revolution in American agriculture. The mechanization of farming became a liberating force among rural people. Henry Ford participated in the movement which permitted farmers to get their hands on mechanical power, either in automobiles, trucks, or tractors. For example, in 1910 there were only 1,000 tractors, 50,000 autos, and no trucks among the farm families in the United States; in 1920 there were 246,000 tractors, 2,146,000 automobiles, and 139,000 trucks.[24] Prior to 1910, a few experts owned steam-traction engines to do the work for ten to twenty neighbors; now the individual farmer was an owner of his own power machines.

These were exciting days because of the speed of change and the controversial issues which the innovations invoked. In the first place, the steam engine enthusiasts had no intention of surrendering to the advocates of gasoline tractors. Those preoccupied with steam loved their engines. They responded to such sensations as the smell of live steam passing over an oily boiler, the sizzle of the injector, the curt barks from the stack, the gyrating governor balls, and the blasts from the steam whistle. To accept the tractor proved difficult, as difficult as for railroad engineers to accept diesel trains. They resented seeing their once proud prairie leviathans reduced to scrap iron or shunted off to rust out along fence lines. The manufacturing companies, not certain which way the contest would go, advertised steam engines and tractors in the same catalogues. F. Lee Norton, vice-president of the J. I. Case Company, the leading manufacturer of farm steam engines, in addressing a dealer's meeting in 1908 stated, "Any salesman heard praising the gasoline tractor will be fired on the spot."[25] Yet, within two years, his own company was selling gasoline tractors. Mechanical evolution and progress welcomed the new and said goodbye to the old.

Another hot issue concerned the debate of horses versus the tractor. Farm journals were filled with opinions pro and con, and rural literary societies debated the question before divided audiences. In many ways this was just a repetition of the earlier controversy over the automobile and the horse and buggy. Now most questions were economic, the key issue being whether it was more economical to drive horses or tractors for field work.

The horse faction argued that farmers did not control the price of what they sold, but they did have something to say about the cost of production. They believed horses were cheaper because they reproduced themselves and consumed hay and feed which were grown on the farm. To buy tractors and gasoline would send money out of the community.

Refuting these arguments, the tractor people cited studies proving that it cost $107 annually to keep one work horse. The Rumely Company claimed the twenty-five million horses in the country cost Americans two-and-a-half billion dollars annually. For every day a horse worked he required 27 minutes of some man's care. Hired men could be eliminated if farmers bought tractors. The Ford

Motor Company in 1919 claimed the wages of hired hands had risen 70 percent during the past decade, therefore both horses and hired men should leave the farm.

Since most farm families did not keep financial records, they were unable to determine their cost of operation. They watched their neighbors buy tractors, speculated on the wisdom of these decisions, and frequently bent with the times. The young people particularly were eager to embrace mechanical power. Farm boys disliked feeding horses three times daily, crowding into stalls to throw on the harnesses, adjust hame straps, fasten up nose baskets to keep out the flies, and fend off the shedding hair. On hot summer days the horses dripped with sweat, while collars blistered their shoulders, leaving ugly sores. Yet the pressure of work drove man and beast beyond any semblance of the humane. At times horses died from sun stroke, or stood out in the pasture worn out, emaciated, and with ribs standing in sharp relief. If tractors did nothing else, they stopped one of the most inhumane enterprises on the rural scene. Henry Ford was right—the horse should go.

No account of the social impact of the farm tractor has ever been written. Such an account would have to include the thoughts and feelings of those horny-handed sons of the sod who saw the profound changes in technology. No one has recorded the view of thousands of farmers who attended the South Dakota Tractor Show near Aberdeen in the summer of 1918. Some came from a distance of 150 miles. Here thirty acres housed exhibits under canvas, while a motley array of tractors roared across fields, plowing, harrowing, seeding, and demonstrating all kinds of farm implements. Of the sixty-eight different makes of tractors on the grounds, which one was the best? If one wanted a large tractor to pull 10 plow bottoms, he might choose a big Avery, rated at 40 horsepower on the drawbar and 80 horsepower on the belt. The Twin City weighed 28,000 pounds, was 21-feet long, with drive wheels 30-inches wide. The Rumely 30–60 Oil Pull had two cylinders 10 inches in diameter and a rear axle which was 5½ inches in diameter. The C. L. Best Gas Traction Company of San Leandro, California, built a caterpillar-type tractor weighing 32,000 pounds, developed 90 horsepower, and was advertised to pull 20 plow bottoms. There were indeed giants in the land.

On the other extreme were the baby tractors—the Fordson weighing 2,500 pounds, the Kansas City "Prairie Dog" at 4,000 pounds, and the Minneapolis "Tom Thumb" weighing 5,000 pounds.

To make the transition from horses to tractors easier, some companies built engines which were operated by lines or reins. The driver sat on the implement and manipulated the tractor like a team of horses. Other oddities included a four-wheel Olmstead tractor, and the Square Turn tractor manufactured in Norfolk, Nebraska, which had two wheels in front and one behind thus permitting it to turn on a dime. The Gray tractor had no drive wheels, but propelled itself on a six-foot drum.

Occasionally promoters bilked the public. They would rent a building, make a demonstration model tractor, print a prospectus, and sell stock in the company. After collecting the money, they would declare bankruptcy, fold, and get out of town. In Minneapolis such a group found a man with the name of Ford. They made him an official of the firm, built one clumsy machine, and then peddled stock in the Ford Tractor Company. This venture was exposed, but not until many innocent people were hurt.

In the early tractor days many farmers insisted on doing their own repair work. If they could overhaul the Model T, they believed they could do the same with tractor motors. Both success and failure ensued. Although the literature on this subject is sparse, a few written comments have survived. One farmer near Groton, South Dakota, in 1921 wrote to Henry Ford stating:

> Did you ever try to adjust the crankshaft bearings in a tractor? You crawled under the engine to take off the pan, found a pipe in the way, drained out two gallons of oil, then fished around in the dark with a socket wrench and took out 15 screws while you held the pan up with your back or feet. About this time you discover a bolt in the way and take part of the frame off to get at the bolt. Just then the pan slips and the oil that is left hits you in the eye, and what misses your eye goes down your neck. You drop the pan and kick it away. Then you are ready to get at the bearings, but your pliers are on the platform so you crawl after them. You put your hand in a pool of oil and wipe it on your overalls. You have a young fight with six cotter pins, you lose four and break two. You take off six nuts, three caps and a bunch of shims and they scatter all over the country; you gather them in, wipe them off, sort them out, and put them back by guess. Then you crawl out, twist her horns and find out you have tightened the wrong connecting rod. So you do it all over again. When tightening the nuts, the holes always come out in the wrong places; you start to hunt up some wire to take the place of the cotter pins and wish your girl friend

would come by and lend you a few hair pins. By this time you have put the pan back and your language is disgraceful. Then you take a half pound of tobacco to put you back in good humor again.[26]

Another farm engineer recalled moving an old tractor in North Dakota in 1919:

> When I saw the tractor, I raised a kick, it was so nearly falling to pieces it was a wonder a good wind hadn't taken it away. However, I tacked it together, stole a chunk of bailing wire and started out. First the feed pipe broke, then the magneto worked loose. Then the cooling oil tank laid a beautiful black mark all along the road. But when I saw a gulley 600-feet deep, I got worried. Just as I started down, there was a cracking sound and the tractor started to break all speed limits between there and Mexico. Just then the roof fell on my head and when I awoke the engine was standing on its head in three feet of mud. I learned later it cost $800 to fix it up again. . . .[27]

One must conclude that Henry Ford became part of the rural scene. His half a million Fordsons did not determine the course of mechanization in agriculture but they did tend to enhance the popularity of small tractors. In addition, they gave Henry Ford an excellent opportunity to propagandize his crusade for power farming. Certainly the Fordson helped prove that light, versatile tractors could replace horses in work where they had been thought to be indispensable. While this model was no better or worse than it contemporaries, the Fordson provided Mr. Ford with a sounding board. Now he could point to his 7,000-acre farms in Michigan in 1921 to demonstrate that tractors did all the field work in twenty-one days without the aid of a single horse. Naturally, he urged others to simplify their farm work in similar fashion. Many looked upon him as a seer, a precursor of things to come, the great White Father of Fair Lane, whose dedication to improved farm machinery carried conviction. Henry A. Wallace believed Ford possessed profound insights in these matters, while the Governor of North Dakota, R. A. Nestos, wanted Ford to apply mass production methods to the construction of all farm implements.

Henry Ford fervently preached the doctrine of faith in the machine. He often said, "Man minus the machine is a slave. Man plus the machine is a free man." He believed machinery spoke a likely language and that technology led to progress. Tractors, trucks, and automobiles would change rural life by easing the burden of labor. He was a leader in the movement to eliminate drudgery from farm work. Although mechanization failed to solve the problem of agricultural surpluses in this country, his efforts did remove much of the misery formerly associated with producing them. American farmers stand as the most technologically advanced agriculturists in the Western Hemisphere, and Ford helped provide the impetus for this significant achievement.

VI

Farmers' Faith in Henry Ford

"Since you are the richest man in the world and I am the poorest man in the world, it looks like we should get together and make some kind of a deal." So wrote a Dakota farmer to Henry Ford in the fall of 1922.[1] The comment had a touch of irony because of the juxtaposition of the characters. Here was a destitute farmer plastered with mortgages, plagued with poor crops, and harried by creditors, addressing a person described by the Associated Press in that year as being worth a billion dollars with a daily income of $264,026.41—one of the wealthiest men in the universe.[2] But in the early 1920s there were millions of rural Americans facing hard times who searched for a solution.

Financial panics always produce ugly consequences, and the depression of the early twenties was no exception. Although businessmen felt the shock of this slump, it was the farmer who suffered most severely. After the prices of farm crops soared to a high point in January, 1920, the market weakened, then plunged downward during the next seventeen months. By November, 1920, market prices were 33 percent lower than the previous year, and by July, 1921, they were down 85 percent. Robert La Follette announced in 1924 that six hundred thousand farmers had gone bankrupt and farm values had declined thirteen billion dollars over the past three years.

The damage resulting from the depression of 1920–23 cannot be measured in statistics alone, for beyond this data were those who suffered adversity—persons caught in bewildered frustration. To these, the crisis became a grim experience. The tear-jerking picture of the sheriff foreclosing on the old homestead was not just a fantasy of the novelist. Too many farm families in real life, however, failed to be rescued by the timely arrival of a beneficent hero. Most of those in economic distress accepted their fate stoically, but others lost courage, and some became bitter.

Angry letters reached the White House and spilled over to the offices of cabinet members. The files of the Secretary of Agriculture in the National Archives contain thousands of pages of lamentations. Henry A. Wallace, Secretary of Agriculture, wrote to President Harding in August, 1921, saying he had received stacks of letters from farmers in all sections of the country. He wanted the chief executive to read some of them so he could get a better picture of rural conditions.

Much of this correspondence showed deep despair. From Iowa came word that corn was selling at 25 cents a bushel and people were unable to pay their taxes. Senator George W. Norris, Chairman of the Committee on Agriculture, received scores of letters from farmers who were burning their corn for fuel rather than buy coal at $21 a ton. A South Dakota farmer wrote President Harding saying people were restless, that Congressmen failed to realize the seriousness of the situation, and that country folks were tired of rosy newspaper editorials and verbose speeches given by windy politicians. A Wisconsin dairyman thought it heartbreaking to get less than $20 for a cow, while a Texas cotton farmer, receiving seven cents a pound for his cotton, said he lived like a slave, unable to pay for groceries, doctor bills, and life insurance. A tenant farmer near Cedar Springs, Georgia, with nine children, confessed his inability to feed and clothe them. "I asked the landlord for $57 for my share of the crop, but he wouldn't give it to me. Please give me information, because my children are barefooted and naked. It is not because I did not work hard. If I could get a square deal, I could feed my family. . . ."[3] An unhappy Californian said he worked sixteen hours a day on his farm but, due to hard times, he had lived on nothing but corn bread and bacon until "I have actually got bristles growing on my back. . . ."

Officials in the nation's capitol offered little consolation. Warren G. Harding suggested farmers quit talking calamity and make the best of a bad situation. Henry A. Wallace admitted farm prices were low, but he believed it easier to diagnose trouble than to find a remedy. If farmers worked harder they might dig out of the morass. William M. Jardine, Wallace's successor in the Coolidge cabinet, took a cold-blooded attitude, saying he saw no solution for the farm problem and had no panacea for the ills of agriculture. At times he merely referred his correspondents to his published annual report.

Since governmental officials seemed indifferent, many rural Americans turned to men of wealth for assistance. As Henry Ford was well known, he became a symbol of hope to thousands of farmers in distress. Although it is difficult to measure this faith, if one may judge from information gleaned from agricultural journals, the National Archives, and the Ford Motor Company, there is ample evidence to prove that the average farmer had considerable respect for Ford and that a remarkably large number of them expected him to aid those in financial trouble.

That destitute people should ask a millionaire for help is not surprising, and Henry Ford received his share of requests for direct aid. A farmer's frantic wife living near Davis, South Dakota, entreated, "Our house burned down. We are in debt. My husband is worrying himself to death and times are hard in Dakota. Can you help us. . . ."[4] Many who were short on cash signed promissory notes and mailed them to Dearborn. A wheat farmer in Montana in 1921 pleaded for $4,000 from Ford so that he might retain his home and get back on his feet.

Many conceived schemes by which Ford might assist rural people. A common request suggested that he go into the wheat pits and buy grain, thus creating a bull market that would force prices upward. No mention was made as to what the buyer would do with this surplus grain, but apparently he was expected to hold it until prices improved. An Iowa farmer, noting that oats sold at 18 cents a bushel, urged Ford to buy eighteen million bushels to bolster the market. The Aberdeen *Daily News* in South Dakota hopefully printed the headlines, "Ford to Bid on Dakota Wheat," and "Ford Plans to Rent Elevators in Duluth and Chicago."

In the South, when cotton prices dropped from 40 to 14 cents a pound, thousands looked to Ford for some kind of relief. An Alabama planter implored him to purchase 300,000 bales of cotton to boost prices. Senator N. B. Deal of South Carolina wired Ford on May 8, 1923, explaining that if he did nothing more than make a statement to the press about cotton being too low, this would frighten the bears and stop depressing the market. Another cotton grower wanted Ford to lead three million planters as one man. "George Washington, Napoleon, and Foch led men to fight with guns, while our battle will be fought with brain force. Since South

Carolina was the first to secede in 1860, now South Carolina will secede from Wall Street."[5]

Livestock men likewise sought assistance. The Highland Ranching Company, with offices in Edmonton, Alberta, asked Ford to finance the raising of 6,000 cattle in three western provinces. A similar petition from a Michigan farmer begged for five million dollars to stock his farms in the state. The officials of several midwestern banks, who wanted to remain solvent and still loan money to ranchers, wrote to Henry Ford asking for loans.

Farmers complained about the scarcity of money and the absence of credit. Caught short on cash, they showed a weakness for greenbackism and soft money panaceas. They believed "Eastern International Bankers" dominated the financial system, charged excessive interest rates, and carelessly permitted bank failures to wipe out life savings. Even the Federal Reserve System was suspected of hoarding money. Others thought the banks insistence on the maintenance of the gold standard accentuated financial panics. The intensity of these feelings was reflected by a cattleman in Washington writing to Henry Ford in 1922:

> Just as a butcher skins a steer with a knife, so do the banks skin the public. The banker holds the purse strings of the nation. He is the State. Mr. Ford, you have the confidence of the common people. You command publicity. You have the money. You can accomplish the abolition of the gold standard. Do it Henry. The way to do it is to do it. The time is now. . . .

Ford gave the impression that he sympathized with those favoring inflationary monetary policies. He permitted stories to circulate to the effect that he thought it folly to worship the gold standard, and that collecting interest failed to stimulate honest production. When he faced a financial crisis in 1921 and it appeared he must borrow 75 million dollars from Wall Street, he raised the money within his own organization. He was reported as saying he would tear down his factories brick by brick with his own hands before he would deal with Wall Street bankers.

The most significant crusade which renewed farmer's faith in Henry Ford occurred on July 8, 1921, when the "Midas of Michigan Avenue," at the invitation of the United States government, offered to pay $5 million for a 99-year lease on the installations at Muscle Shoals, Tennessee. There was hope that this action would benefit all rural Americans and help alleviate the hard times on the farm.

The belief spread that Ford's use of water power would break the British-Chilean nitrate monopoly and produce cheap fertilizers for agricultural purposes. The new source of electric power would industrialize the South, banish unemployment, and restore prosperity to the nation. All could be done without additional taxation or the meddling of bankers.

The Muscle Shoals controversy focused on the valley of the Tennessee river with its major tributaries—the Powell, the Holston, the Clinch, the French Broad, the Little Tennessee, and the Hiwasse. The area contained about 42,000 square miles, with a population of four million people—most of them farmers. This river system drained the Southern Appalachian mountains where the annual rainfall measured 80 inches. The river valley from Knoxville, Tennessee, to Paducah, Kentucky, a distance of 650 miles, frequently flooded. The Muscle Shoals was a 37-mile stretch of the river which dropped 134 feet in elevation. This cantankerous stream came down yellow with mud, washing away the soil until, by 1933, seven million out of 26 million acres in the valley suffered from erosion. In many areas half the topsoil had been lost. As a result, most of the farmers were in poverty, unable to support good schools, hospitals, or roads. Only 2 percent of the farms had electricity, while most of the people lived in overcrowded, unsanitary houses, and lacked proper food and clothing.[6]

Although the economic conditions were deplorable, little had been done about it. President Theodore Roosevelt in 1905 vetoed a bill granting a charter to a company for building a dam at Muscle Shoals on the grounds it would give excessive benefits to a few individuals. The National Waterways Commission in 1907 concluded that the Tennessee River was too powerful to be tamed by private companies because the river with its tributaries needed to be managed as a unit.

The advent of World War I focused new interest in this region. For national defense, the United States relied on the importation of Chilean nitrates for the manufacture of explosives. Since our security seemed jeopardized by German submarines, the National Defense Act of June, 1916, provided for the production of synthetic nitrogen in the United States. Consequently the War Department built a nitrate plant at Sheffield, Alabama, which cost $12 million, but proved a complete failure. A second plant costing $68 million was built at Muscle Shoals, but the installation did not get into production before the end of the war. In addition, a steam electric-gen-

erating plant at Gorgas, Alabama, had been completed at a cost of
$5 million. Thus the Federal Government had invested over $85
million in the Tennessee River project for which it had no immediate use following the Armistice in November, 1918. Worse yet, it
cost $300,000 annually just to maintain the idle installations.

Obviously, Congress had a white elephant, with all alternatives
equally unpleasant. They could let the costly plants stand idle.
They could complete the dams and produce fertilizers, but this
would compete with private enterprise, a concept which was ana-
thema to the conservatives in the Harding administration. The third
option lay in selling the installations to private corporations. This
required special Congressional action, however, because the National Defense Act of 1916 prohibited sale to private investors.

The political arguments were intensified in 1919 when Senator
James W. Wadsworth and Representative Julius H. Kahn introduced a bill authorizing the Federal Government to establish a
government corporation to manage Muscle Shoals. This corporation
would operate the plants and sell electricity and fertilizer. The
House and Senate hearings on this bill were filled with contradictory
evidence. Newton D. Baker, Secretary of War, favored the Wadsworth-Kahn bill because the nation needed Muscle Shoals for national defense. In addition, the project would discover cheaper
ways to manufacture fertilizers, thus aiding private companies
rather than destroying them. It would be unwise to scrap installations costing millions. This view drew support from leading Southern Congressmen and the Farm Bureau. Bernard Baruch believed
that even if Muscle Shoals had not aided the war effort, the money
had been well spent, because this action had forced down the price
of Chilean nitrates, with huge savings to the American people. Senator Oscar Underwood of Alabama argued that they should not let
the special interests dominate Washington, turning the clock on all
progressive legislation.

Opponents, led by Republican William J. Graham of Illinois,
claimed the Democrats had created another Credit Mobiliér; a
fiasco shot through with graft, waste, and scandal. He insisted that
President Wilson sponsored this project, knowing it could not be
completed before the end of the war. The argument that German
submarines would cut off our supply of Chilean nitrates had been
a hoax. Most conservatives believed the Southern states did not
need additional electric power, while officials of the American
Cyanamid Company and the Alabama Power Company screamed

Top left: Tintype of Henry Ford at age three. *Top right:* Ford as a machine shop apprentice at eighteen. *Middle left:* In his forties, Ford wears a jaunty derby in 1909. *Middle right:* Ford in his Highland Park office in 1914. *Bottom left:* Candid picture of Ford in 1919. *Bottom right:* A 1940 portrait of Henry Ford at age seventy-seven.

Top left: Ford with Charles A. Lindbergh, the pilot of Ford's first airplane ride in August, 1927. *Top right:* Ford and his close friend Thomas A. Edison in 1929 at Greenfield Village. *Bottom:* Henry Ford delivering one of his rare radio addresses at the Dearborn Henry Ford Wireless Station (WWI) which pioneered in interplant communications and public broadcasting.

Mr. and Mrs. Henry Ford in their golden years at their Fair Lane home.
The portrait was taken in 1943 when Mr. Ford was eighty, some four years
before his death on April 7, 1947. Mrs. Ford, the former Clara Bryant,
passed away in 1950.

Left to right: Thomas A. Edison, John Burroughs, Henry Ford, and Harvey Firestone, Sr., on one of their celebrated excursions.

Henry Ford, dressed in his Sunday finest, at the wheel of his first car, the famed "quadricycle," in 1896.

Ford at the wheel of his first "automobile plow," equipped with a four-cylinder
Model B engine and parts from a six-cylinder Model K and the rear wheels
from an old binder. In 1907 Henry Ford began experimental work
on the tractor, one of his early dreams.

Accessory equipment converted the Model T into a snowmobile.

The Ford could pull a wagonload of hay on Saturday and take the family to church on Sunday.

At the end of the
day, the Ford is
ready for the
demands of
pleasure.

A wool and hide
dealer in Montana
loads his Ford with pelts.

A Model T furnishes power to grind grain.

One ingenious owner used his old Ford as a trailer.

An early Model T camper used in 1922.

The camper body attached to a Model T chassis was an early attempt
to provide sleeping quarters.

The
"TOURISTS
CAMP BODY"

Early Model T passenger trailer made by joining two car bodies.

When not used for touring purposes, the Model T was rapidly changed into a traveling sawmill.

The Ford fit naturally into a camping environment in 1916.

Postman makes
rural delivery
in a Model T.

Ford examines
a steam
road roller.

Henry Ford in 1941,
viewing the product
of the soil he loved
so much, epitomizes
his lifelong
conviction of the
mutual dependence
of industry and
agriculture.

Ford watches the threshing operation on one of his farms.

Henry Ford and a
Westinghouse portable
farm steam engine, 1938.

Ford, in tie and
coveralls, inspects
the work of a
Fordson tractor.

A Model T carrying milk to the market.

Henry Ford
observing a
Fordson tractor
mired in the mud.

Ford with Robert Boyer,
chief of Ford's experimental
soybean laboratory.

Ford on a Ford-Ferguson tractor.

Henry Ford observing farming conditions on a Michigan farm, 1929.

Two views of the "Motor King" driving a team of horses.

A Model T spattered with
mud and ready to go.

The Model T greatly increased family mobility.

*Under the shelter of their own tent, Mr.
Jacobs and wife made their
home wherever nightfall
overtook them on their
journey*

In the days of
bad roads, one
Ford owner
helps another
car owner.

A Model T traverses a rough prairie road.

A well-traveled
Ford returns to
the Dearborn
Plant.

John Burroughs, the naturalist, poses in his new Model T,
a gift from Henry Ford.

A Model T makes way
for a steam
traction engine.

Ford owners get together for a holiday.

After serving its owner for over 15,000 miles, this 1909 Ford touring car is as good as ever.

Thomas A. Edison on a southern sightseeing trip pauses in a small town near Fort Myers, Florida.

A Model T wins a unique contest by balancing on a teeter.

Henry Ford changes the barnyard scene.

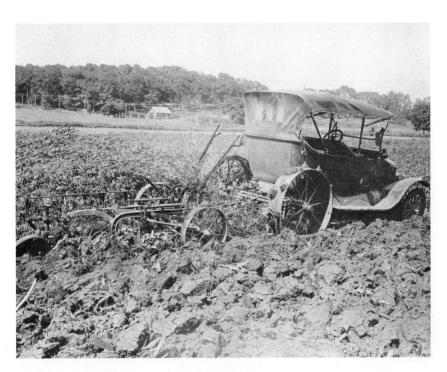

Conversion kits put the Ford to work in the field.

Road, wood, and stream—and a Ford.

A Ford roadster rests in a farmer's yard.

socialism. Although the Senate passed the Wadsworth-Kahn bill, it was killed in the House where it died in committee in March, 1921. Other measures to appropriate money to continue work on Muscle Shoals were likewise defeated.

At this juncture, John W. Weeks, Secretary of War, announced that if any private corporation were willing to lease Muscle Shoals and render the Federal Government a fair return on its investment, he would recommend that Congress complete the Wilson Dam to provide the electrical power. When the Southern power companies failed to respond with definite proposals, the entire Muscle Shoals project appeared dead.

Before the dust settled, however, Henry Ford stirred up a greater storm by submitting a written bid for Muscle Shoals on July 8, 1921. This offer grew out of many factors. He had always been interested in water power ever since he made a water paddle wheel as a youngster on his father's farm. On his vacation trips with Thomas Edison, John Burroughs, and Harvey Firestone, the party often visited old water mills to examine their construction and watch their performance. When Ford visited the Berry School near Rome, Georgia, to observe the institution which he supported financially, he often spent time watching the overshot water wheel operating in a mountain stream. He believed in harnessing the power of nature for constructive purposes.

This early bent undoubtedly turned him sympathetically toward the suggestions of influential people. Major General Lansing H. Beach, the chief of Army engineers, hoped the Federal Government would sell Muscle Shoals to Henry Ford. He asked J. W. Worthington, executive secretary of the Tennessee River Improvement Association to interest Ford in the project. After a meeting in Dearborn on June 6, 1921, Ford and his staff of assistants drafted the original offer for Muscle Shoals.

The Ford bid for Muscle Shoals was a complicated proposal. In fact, the initial offer of July 8, 1921, was revised January 25, 1922, and again on May 31, 1922. First, Ford offered to pay $5 million for the two nitrate plants and the adjacent land at Muscle Shoals. This also included the steam plant at Gorgas, Alabama. Second, if the government completed the dams and installed hydroelectric equipment, Ford would lease the installations for one hundred years. He would pay 6 percent interest on the amount of money required by the government to complete the dams—this amount not to exceed $28 million. To pay for the installations of

power machinery, a fund would be established. Ford would pay
$46,547 into this fund annually. This amount when invested at 4
percent interest over the 100-year span would amortize the cost of
the power installations. In addition, Ford offered to pay the government $55,000 annually for maintenance of the property. Third, Ford
agreed to manufacture 110,000 tons of ammonium nitrate a year for
fertilizers, with profits not to exceed 8 percent. The package deal
added up to approximately $1,700,000 as the annual cost to the Ford
Motor Company. A representative board composed of members of
farm organizations and officials of the Department of Agriculture
would act as a watchdog on business procedures and profits. Disputes were to be referred to the Federal Trade Commission.

Strong support greeted the Ford proposal, especially from the
farm regions in the South and Midwest. Eleven senators and 46
representatives gave their immediate approval. The Oklahoma and
Alabama state legislature passed resolutions urging Congress to
adopt the measure, while the Nebraska legislature asked Ford to
develop hydroelectric power in that state. Scores of Chamber of
Commerce groups requested that Congress give Ford the green
light at Muscle Shoals. The American Federation of Labor sanc-
tioned the plan, as did the National Grange, the Farmer's Union,
and the Farm Bureau Federation.

Most newspapers, at least initially, joined the pro-Ford crowd.
The Southern papers favored the plan because it would utilize
water power to produce fertilizers and open up navigation on rivers.
Editors believed that no other person could make a more liberal
offer, or one in which the people would receive greater benefits.
Ford had great executive ability and financial resources which
would be used to create unprecedented development of the whole
territory. In the midwest, the St. Joseph *News Press* pointed out
that if the Ford bid were rejected, the Federal government would
have to operate the plants and "this makes us doubt that the leopard
is going to change its spots." The Wichita *Eagle* claimed Ford had
nerve and, even though he was an idealist, he had learned how to
make a mint of money without gouging anybody else. In the East,
the Cleveland *Plain Dealer* called Ford's plan the best in sight,
while the Philadelphia *Bulletin* exclaimed, "If Henry Ford wants
to get the Muscle Shoals project out of the congressional trenches
by Christmas, let him try it."

The farm journals in turn supported the Ford crusade. The
Kansas Farmer urged Congress to accept the Ford offer imme-

diately, while the *Michigan Farmer* thought Ford would save
farmers $100 million a year by cutting the cost of fertilizers. The
Prairie Farmer believed Ford wished to develop these plants as a
public service to farmers and a monument to his love for humanity.
An editorial in the *Rural New Yorker*, on March 11, 1922, no doubt
exaggerated somewhat by saying "Thousands of resolutions and
literally millions of letters have been written by farmers in favor of
acceptance."

Meantime, interest soared and excitement was contagious. A
crowd of three thousand jammed into the city auditorium in Atlanta
to endorse a resolution calling on Congress to adopt the Ford proposal. In a poll by the Nashville *Banner*, fifty thousand readers
voted for Ford's program with only three hundred in opposition.
The Tennessee Federation of Women's Clubs announced a Ford
Day on April 1, 1922. They invited Ford to attend and sent out
literature saying this was a people's fight in which Congress and the
whole world must be told that, "We want Ford and Ford only."
They sold nine hundred buttons in Cleveland, Tennessee, at ten
cents each bearing the slogan, "I want Ford to Get Muscle Shoals."

These sentiments flooded the mail of officials in Washington,
D.C. A Georgia farmer, writing to President Warren G. Harding on
September 2, 1921, insisted the Ford proposal remained of highest
importance to citizens of the South. "I need not argue," he added
"that he is one of the few men who have acquired great wealth
without lining his pathway to success with the wrecked hopes of
his less fortunate competitors. He has been willing to live and let
live."[7] John W. Weeks, Secretary of War, also started hearing from
the grass roots. A farmer near Morgan, Kentucky, chided Weeks for
stalling on the Ford deal. The government engineers should stop
quibbling over figures and settle the matter. "If you can't get
together on this why not let Mr. Ford have it at his figures and go
ahead and complete the work. Who would be the loser, the government or Mr. Ford? Wouldn't it be Mr. Ford? Then why not proceed
this way. If Mr. Ford can do just half of what he promised, it would
pay the government to give it to him free gratis."[8] In similar vein,
the St. Louis Chamber of Commerce, after adopting a series of
resolutions, urged Weeks to press Congress for adoption of the plan.
The Kiwanis Club of Talladega, Alabama, and the County Com-
missioners of Lauderdale County concurred. The Central Trades
and Labor Council of Joliet, Illinois, deplored the low wages paid
by large corporations and urged adoption of the Ford program with

its enlightened position on wages. Idle people would have jobs and confidence would be restored. Individual farmers also pleaded with the Secretary of War to accept the Ford proposal.

Henry Ford himself stood in the center of the controversy, a powerful figure who, according to Congressman J. C. Mc Kenzie, had gained the title of "friend to the great agricultural and labor interests of the country, the people who toil from morning till night."[9] The Flivver King played his role skillfully, using the press and his own officials to bolster his campaign. In interviews he spoke glowingly of Muscle Shoals where he would build a city seventy-five miles long, reaching from Florence on the west to Huntsville on the east. The city would be fifteen miles in width, with development so rapid it would surpass Detroit in a few years. Ford described it as one of the greatest undertakings of industrial America. The water power would be harnessed to run manufacturing plants, light homes, and power machinery on farms. This would lead to development of the entire Mississippi River Valley, a valley which could furnish power for the entire nation if the water going to waste were fully utilized. The New York *Times* reported that Ford and his Aladdin lamp had created a rush to the Tennessee valley similar to the gold rushes to California and the Klondike. Real estate changed hands hourly, with old estates, held intact since the Civil War, now put on the market. Orchards were planted, truck farms laid out, and farms stocked with cattle and hogs to supply the needs of the new Ford city. Investors pressured Congressmen to honor the Ford proposal.

In interviews with the press, Henry Ford often took a low voltage approach, saying he did not need Muscle Shoals because his company had done well without it. Various parties, both in and out of government, came to Detroit urging Ford to make a bid for it. Various spokesmen appealed to his sense of duty to the American people. Now he was obligated to serve the public by salvaging a project which had cost taxpayers millions and now faced the junk pile. Ford hoped to demonstrate the value of water power to the American people.

At the same time he chaffed over dilatory action of government officials, such as Secretary Weeks, who kept asking irrelevant questions and postponing decisions which a private businessman would make in twenty-four hours. Along with these delays, Congress was deluged by misrepresentations, distortions, and lies, emanating from the vested interests of money brokers on Wall Street.

Throughout the negotiations in Washington, D.C., the Ford camp insisted they did not seek profits, only a humanitarian program to aid the farmer, the laborer, and the little people. The enemies were bankers, chemical trusts, electric power corporations, and do-nothing conservatives in Washington, D.C. It must have seemed odd to hear Ford identify himself with the poor against the rich, when he himself was the wealthiest man in the country with a virtual monopoly on the production of low-priced automobiles. But this was the Ford genius.

To dramatize his case, he visited Muscle Shoals in December, 1921, where he met enthusiastic crowds. Encouraged by his welcome, he stated that the Government had paid $100 million to prepare for war but had not paid a nickel to foster peace. He would attempt to abolish war by producing nitrates for peaceful purposes. Since wars were caused by a greed for gold, he favored the abolishment of the gold standard. He took the opportunity to apply much of the theory of money which had appeared in twenty-five articles in the *Dearborn Independent,* which claimed international bankers exploited the public. Gold had no value aside from its legal value. The issuance of bonds resulted in interest payments to people who did not work. Ford suggested that the Federal Government should fund the cost of Muscle Shoals by issuing new paper currency against the property. Later the annual income from the sale of electricity would be used to retire the paper money. This would obviate the necessity of paying interest, the property would be clear of debt in twenty years, and it would be unnecessary to expend one cent of Federal funds or to raise taxes. Congress could amend Section 5845 of the Federal Currency Law to provide for the new currency. This would not constitute the issuance of fiat money, as had occurred in Germany after the war, because the issuing would be limited to a specific project which was self-amortizing.

Unfortunately, Thomas Edison confused the issue by injecting his own theories on money. His interview with a correspondent from the New York *Times* on December 6, 1921, was published in a pamphlet entitled, *The Edison Interview on the Money Question.* Here, Edison argued for an "Energy Dollar" meaning that the government should issue new currency based upon the amount of work needed to produce a given commodity. While Ford and Edison both violated Gladstone's dictum that "The surest way to get into the insane asylum is to study the money question," the average American let the theory whistle over his head, but accepted the notion that since he was in poverty there must be something basically wrong with the money system.

This campaign to reform the currency brought congratulations from all parts of the country. A fan in Santa Rosa, California, sent copies of Ford's plan to finance Muscle Shoals to the president of the Civic Club, the Superintendent of Schools, the Public Library, the presidents of two colleges, and the judge of the Superior Court. A testimonial from Decorah, Iowa, thought Ford on the right track because high interest retarded progress by raising the cost of all improvements in the community. If Ford would eliminate interest, his name would go down in history with Solon, Justinian, Lycurgus, and Moses. A bookstore in Sioux Falls, South Dakota, ordered 5,000 copies of the *Edison Interview on the Money Question* and the *Ford Interview on Muscle Shoals*. Someone in the Bronx thought Ford should be careful because half the paper money in circulation had been counterfeited in Russia.

In early discussions, the friends of Ford gained converts by attacking the fertilizer trusts, accusing them of bilking farmers through exhorbitant prices. Now Henry Ford would cut these costs in half. Ford gave credence to these sanguine hopes by saying he would activate the nitrate plants within a few hours after Congress accepted his bid. Next he announced he had a secret method of manufacturing fertilizers which would revolutionize the industry. When William B. Mayo, chief engineer of the Ford Motor Company, admitted before the House Committee on Military Affairs that no secret process existed, Ford explained that Thomas Edison would do it because he was working on these problems in his laboratories in East Orange, and he was the greatest electrochemist in the world. "Why, if he can't make a good, cheap fertilizer down there," fumed Ford, "why is the fertilizer trust telling Congress that if we get Muscle Shoals, we'll wreck their monopoly?"[10]

Later, Edison confessed he had discovered no new tricks in producing nitrates. In fact the whole subject remained clouded in mystery, as it had been for years. Most people knew that nitrogen was essential for plant and animal life. In its free state it remained colorless, tasteless, odorless, gaseous, and inert. It made up four-fifths of the air in the atmosphere. The reduction of nitrogen for organic purposes had limitations. It could be extracted from the air by electricity, and it could be fixed in minute quantities in certain leguminous plants such as alfalfa. Another source was obtained from ammonium sulfate, derived from the distillation of coal tars in the making of coke. In its native state, it was found in a nitrate of soda on the high plains between the Andes and the coastal hills of Chile. This nitrate was crystalline salt, created from leeching of sedimentary rocks. The deposits may have been formed by the decomposition of fish and sea weeds in the ocean bed before the upheaval of the land mass, or they may have come from bacterial organisms.

The Ford proponents claimed that studies by the United States Geological Society and the Department of Agriculture proved that domestic production of nitrates, plus imports from Chile, would still leave a shortage of two hundred thousand tons a year. Therefore, fertilizer prices would skyrocket rather than decrease. The rural press correctly predicted that Ford's promises of low-cost fertilizers would please southern farmers. The Commercial Club of Cedar Grove, Louisiana, commended Ford's fight against the chemical corporations. The president of the Alabama Farmer's Union wired President Coolidge begging for his support of the Ford offer because farmers needed more economical fertilizers in spite of the arguments to the contrary by the American Fertilizer Association. Senator Arthur Capper of Kansas thought farmers favored Ford's proposal. The principal of Tuskegee Institute wrote Ford stating that thousands of Blacks from the South had gone to Detroit to work in his factories. Now conditions in the South were worse than those following the Civil War. He believed most Blacks had faith in Ford's Muscle Shoals project to save them from their present plight. After comparing Ford to Abraham Lincoln on the grounds that both had faith in the common man, the principal told of his conference with President Coolidge in which he had said:

> My people in the South who work on the cotton farms can not buy Ford cars and can not buy Ford tractors. Their cotton crops failed because they were unable to purchase fertilizers and they cannot fight the boll weevil because they have no money to buy calcium arsenate. The cotton crop in Alabama was cut in half, and Georgia suffered even more. . . .[11]

A Black sharecropper in Tennessee mailed $10 to Ford, saying he wished he could donate $100 to further the Ford cause.

The Ford forces invariably linked their opposition with the nefarious financiers of Wall Street. J. W. Worthington, executive officer of the Tennessee River Improvement Association claimed a $90 million chemical trust, financed by J. P. Morgan and Kuen-Loeb and Company, were now trying to defeat the acceptance of the Ford offer. "They are a lot of cowards," said Worthington, "and not one of them will make an offer on Muscle Shoals because they know Congress and the farmers will defeat them and they know it. . . ."[12] In Detroit, Henry Ford promised that Wall Street would have no part in financing Muscle Shoals if he could help it.

Supporters formed a national organization called "Give Henry Ford an Opportunity Club," with headquarters in Atlanta, Georgia. The purpose was to hold mass meetings from Seattle to Boston, led by the foremost orators in America, to pose the question to every free-born American—Which side are you on, Wall Street or Henry Ford? Pamphlets featured a cartoon depicting Wall Street as a fat ogre wearing a brilliant stick pin, puffing on a big cigar and saying, "Money rules this country, I'll keep the key." At a distance stood Henry Ford before a crowd of farmers, saying, "I'd like to help you folks." Banner lines carried the message, employ one million more men at Ford wages? Wall Street says No; reduce hours of labor? Wall Street says No; cut costs of production on the farm? Wall Street says No; secure cheap water power and nitrates? Wall Street says No. Membership in the club was a dollar, but $5.00 merited a silver star; $10 meant a gold star, and $25 earned a red, white, and blue star.[13]

This doctrine spread across the plains like a prairie fire, and it enlivened the conversations in country stores and meeting places everywhere. Five thousand people met in a Ford mass assembly in Mobile, Alabama, on March 1, 1922. The Tulsa *Tribune* on November 15, 1922, insisted Wall Street banking houses were filled with an odd lot, a group of plutocrats who thought they were the financial engine of the nation. They did not know what a laughable group of puppets they were. The real bankers were out in the great open fields. "Call the Ford a flivver, label it a tin can, collect all the jests, jokes, and joshes about the "Henry" and still the sum total of the story is success."

Yet the Ford steam roller, after a strong start, ran into stubborn opposition, led by tenacious men who could not stomach the likes of Ford and his cohorts. From the start of negotiations, the conservative leadership in the Harding-Coolidge era tended to recoil from decisions involving drastic change. A wait-and-see policy prevailed. Respectability meant not shaking the foundations of the Republic. As the *Nation* sadly observed after the election of Warren G. Harding, "It appears that idealism will have to wait for awhile."[14]

In fact, at one stage of the debate, Harding, like Pontius Pilate of old, washed his hands of the whole affair, saying Congress, not the White House, was the place for consideration of Muscle Shoals. John W. Weeks, as Secretary of War and prime mover in initiating policy, never publicly favored the Ford proposal. Andrew J. Mellon, Secretary of the Treasury, opposed the development of Muscle Shoals because it would threaten his vested interests in aluminum. Herbert Hoover, of the Commerce Department straddled the fence, unable to make up his mind. Attorney General Harry Daugherty vacillated in his decisions, first opposing the sale of the Gorgas plant to the Alabama Power Company, then reversing himself and favoring the concession.

The Muscle Shoals project provided more benefits destined to go to the South and the Midwest, with less accruing to New England and the Far Western states. Consequently, Congressional support from these regions lagged, permitting reservations to appear in public speeches and in the press asking, in effect, what is there in this project for us?

As might be expected, a dog-in-the-manger spirit emerged among vested interests. The electric power companies and chemical corporations found the leasing of Muscle Shoals to Ford intolerable because this appeared to be giving one businessman too great advantage. Competition had long been the credo of the defenders of free private enterprise, but monopoly always tasted sweeter than competition. As the debates over the issue dragged out almost four years, the animosity between factions of the business world became more intense. The Alabama Power Company, jealous over the hydroelectric power in the Tennessee Valley, led the opposition to the Ford interests. Various manufacturer's associations and Chamber of Commerce groups which had initially favored Ford now defected. The Tennessee Manufacturer's Association in March, 1924, circulated the pamphlets of 280 newspaper editorials hostile to Ford. By 1923 the *Manufacturer's Record*, representing big business, sided with the private power companies. The National Fertilizer Association circulated a pamphlet, "Cost to Taxpayers of Ford Muscle Shoals Offer," which claimed the Muscle Shoals nitrate plants, if put in operation, would raise the price of fertilizer from $48 to $68.37 a ton. The secretary of the organization, with offices at 1010 Arch Street, Philadelphia, broadcast newsletters predicting that government aid to Ford would be a subsidy from the public treasury to make up Ford's losses in order that he might compete with the fertilizer industry. The suggested limitation of Ford's profits to 8 percent was pure nonsense because these companies prior to 1914 were only making 6 percent interest on invested capital. The plan was pure socialism, designed to destroy a great private industry. This propaganda must be met as a matter of self-preservation. "Will you do your part in this?"[15]

As the antagonists probed the Ford armor, they spotted a vulnerable point. His offer, hastily drawn up in thirty days, incorporated provisions which were extremely vague. Experts were unable to determine from the documents whether the hundred-year lease was renewable when it expired. Neither was it certain that Ford was obligated to produce farm fertilizers if his costs were prohibitive. Could Ford harness all the power of the Tennessee River and sell the electricity over transmission lines? Did Ford secure the mineral rights in the region, such as coal, potash, and aluminum? Who owned the timber on the land? *Pipp's Weekly* on July 15, 1922, warned that Ford was a slippery fellow who needed to be bound by strong legal language. "If you make a contract with Henry Ford make it horse high, hog tight, and bull strong, so high he can't jump over it, so tight he can't crawl under it, and so strong he can't break through it. . . ."[16]

Undoubtedly the most lethal blow at Ford centered in the notion that he would get too good a deal—that the Government in playing Santa Claus had delivered Christmas gifts which were too lavish. Critics estimated the installations and property at Muscle Shoals to be worth up to $16 million if sold as junk. Therefore, if Ford did nothing but salvage the material and scrap, the value alone would treble his offer of $5 million for the installations. Vast accumulations of material were in storage. These included piles of lumber, locomotive cranes, buggies, phonographs, stocks of structural iron, machine castings, an electricity-driven dairy milking machine, moving picture outfits, an automatic telephone system, automobiles, a photographic studio filled with equipment including high-priced lenses and cameras, collections of surgical instruments, bathtubs, office furniture. Everything was there, outside of foodstuffs and clothing, to equip a complete industrial city of twenty thousand when the Armistice closed the plant. In addition, 4,000 acres of land went with the property, together with 1,700 tons of aluminum nitrate and $500,000 worth of platinum gauze.

These give-away protests varied, depending on the figures used to tote up the Government's concessions. Robert L. Duffus of the New York *Times* believed the United States agreed to accept $5 million from Ford in exchange for property in which the Government had invested $90 million. The Seattle *Times* claimed the sum exceeded $100 million, while George W. Norris, the fiery Nebraskan senator put the figure at $106 million. Arthur Vandenburg, editor of the Grand Rapids *Herald*, decried the gullibility of Americans who were willing to give the Ford interests $117 million worth of government property.

Additional benefits included the Government's promise to complete construction of the dams and install power facilities at costs estimated from $28 to $70 million. On this money Ford would pay 6 percent interest over the century. Some critics prophesied Ford would sell the electricity in seven states at a profit of $10 to $30 million a year, bringing in one to three billion dollars profit to Ford and his heirs during the span of the contract. Others said if Ford secured these concessions, he could turn around the next day and sell his holdings for $200 million. In these terms Nicholas Longworth denounced the whole deal as a conspiracy of pelf, and pleaded, "Let us throttle this plunderbund." There were possibilities in the situation, according to Representative Burton of Ohio, "which will make Teapot Dome look like a mere bagatelle."[17]

The Teapot Dome scandals had pointed to the tragedy of permitting greedy men to exploit the nation's natural resources. As a result, the voices of those defending public ownership of these assets began to be heard. Governor Gifford Pinchot, the conservationist, thought the Ford offer violated the Federal Water Power Act of 1920, which limited the leasing of Federal property to individuals to fifty years and provided strict supervision of the licensee's operations.

It was George W. Norris, the fighting liberal, however, who emerged as champion of the public ownership of the power and resources of the Tennessee River valley. Born on a small farm near Clyde, Ohio, on July 11, 1861, he grew up among poverty and insecurity. At age twenty-three he traveled to Nebraska where he opened a law office in Beatrice, then moved on to Beaver City where he sold real estate, practiced law, and entered politics. He served as prosecuting attorney and judge of the Fourteenth Judicial District, and then spent forty years in the Congress of the United States. During the hearings on the Ford bid for Muscle Shoals,

Norris, as Chairman of the Committee on Agriculture, used his influence first to delay action on the proposal, then to oppose it vehemently.

As a member of the Senate Public Lands Committee in 1913, Norris had watched the struggle over the resources of the Hetch Hetchy watershed of the Tuolumne River in California. The Raker Act provided that the grantee of power developed at Hetch Hetchy would be prohibited from ever selling the water or electric energy to any private person, corporation, or association. This meant that the city of San Francisco would have a monopoly of the water and power rights from this source. The private utilities companies, however, continually attempted to get their hands on these resources through new legislation and action of the courts. Hetch Hetchy became an object lesson to Norris both as to the blessing which could flow from public ownership and control of the country's water supply and the sinister designs of vested interests who would put personal profit above the common weal.[18]

Wise to the tricks of both businessmen and politicians, Norris ripped into the Ford case like a fox in a crowded chicken coop. He respected the Motor King of Detroit, but decried the crazy people who exaggerated the Ford mystique. It disturbed him to hear land sharks saying Muscle Shoals would outgrow New York City, or to hear Southern farmers repeating "When Ford comes. . . . When Ford comes," as if they were expecting the second coming of Jesus Christ.

George Norris often said that 99 percent of the propaganda reaching him favored Ford, but this would not influence his opinions. In one of the Senate hearings, Thomas Heflin berated those who permitted the trusts to demand their pound of flesh. He exhorted, "I am asking you to deliver the farmers now—not in the sweet bye and bye. I hope Ford will stretch out his healing rod and give farmers a deliverance from the clutches of these trusts."[19] Senator Norris replied that he saw no trusts and took little stock in the talk about power trusts, fertilizer trusts, aluminum trusts, coal trusts, oil trusts, gas trusts, or Guggenheim trusts. If any existed they should be investigated. Furthermore, Ford could never protect the national interest at Muscle Shoals because he could not develop the water resources of the entire Tennessee River valley. His influence would be limited to ten miles from the dam sites, while government-owned installations would carry electricity three hundred miles. He opposed giving a one-hundred-year contract to anybody and resisted giving any corporation or any person what had cost the tax-payers over $100 million. If Rockefeller, International Harvester, or the United States Steel Corporation made such a proposition, there would be an outcry. The scheme to turn over Muscle Shoals to Ford was no different. A grant should not be made to any man of a heritage of untold value to generations unborn. If Ford got Muscle Shoals this would be "the greatest gift bestowed on mortal man since salvation was made free to the human race."[20]

Late in 1923 Ford's chances looked good. The Congressional hearings had not crippled him seriously and he still received staunch support from most rural Americans who refused to believe the government was giving him a second Niagara Falls. Neither were they convinced by the National Fertilizer Association's accusation that the new "Detroit of the South" would cost the taxpayers a billion dollars during the next century. Then, too, Ford could be admired for the enemies he had made. The malice of the Chicago *Tribune* could be attributed to revenge for losing its libel suit against him in 1919, while the criticisms of the *Wall Street Journal* merely reflected the venom of cruel bankers. The general contempt for the little man was illustrated in a story coming out of Washington, D.C. Allegedly, John W. Weeks had told his banker friends at a Cosmos Club dinner that Ford, his engineers, advisers, and friends were all "hayseeds."

A sensational newspaper story broke on April 28, 1924, which shocked the public and hurt the Ford cause. James Martin Miller, a Washington correspondent and a former paid contributor to the *Dearborn Independent,* announced that he had interviewed President Coolidge on October 12, 1923. During the meeting, Coolidge stated that, "I am friendly to Ford, but I wish someone would convey to him that it is my hope that Mr. Ford will not do or say anything that will make it difficult for me to deliver Muscle Shoals to him, which I am trying to do."[21] Twenty-five minutes after the conference, Miller wired E. G. Liebold, Ford's secretary, repeating this information. In the light of the national political situation, the implications were perfectly clear. If Miller had told the truth, then it seemed obvious that Calvin Coolidge and Henry Ford had made a deal—Coolidge would turn Muscle Shoals over to Ford if he in return would remove himself from the presidential race in 1924.

Such a political fix seemed plausible on several counts. During the summer of 1923, Henry Ford appeared as the strongest candidate for the presidency of the United States. The *Collier's* national poll on July 14, 1923, showed Ford with a substantial lead over the rest of the field, including such prominent figures as Warren G. Harding, William McAdoo, Herbert Hoover, Hiram Johnson, William Borah, Robert La Follette, John Davis, and William Jennings Bryan. After Harding's death on August 2, 1923, Calvin Coolidge assumed office. The uproar over the Teapot Dome scandals and his own inexperience as President undoubtedly gave him a sense of insecurity. In addition, the Ford-for-President boom had been linked to Muscle Shoals. Arthur Brisbane and others frequently asserted that if the Ford bid for Muscle Shoals were rejected, the enraged farmers would demand the election of Ford as President. Of course if he got Muscle Shoals and then failed to produce low-cost fertilizers, the farmers in disappointment would kill his bid for the White House. It might be said here that this was the only time in American history in which the handling of fertilizer could determine the presidency of the nation.

Meanwhile, two meetings between Ford and Coolidge in the fall of 1923 had been publicized. The New York *Times* described Ford as being "well pleased with his audience with the President," on December 3 when the two discussed Muscle Shoals. After emerging from the conference, however, he refused to say he was still in the presidential race. On December 20, Ford announced his support for Coolidge in the coming election. Subsequently, Coolidge denied James M. Miller's charge that he had promised to deliver Muscle Shoals to Ford. E. G. Liebold testifying before the George Norris Agricultural Committee in May, 1924, also denied the Ford-Coolidge conspiracy. On the other hand, Norris pointed to Ford's withdrawal from the presidential race a few days after his meeting with Coolidge in December, a move which "was considered by everybody in the country as a remarkable coincidence."[22]

Regardless of what the true facts behind these maneuvers might have been, events took a dramatic turn. Six months after the James Miller disclosure, Ford wrote President Coolidge on October 15, 1924, stating that since Congress had failed to act on his offer submitted in July, 1921, he requested the offer be withdrawn. Three days later, Coolidge replied saying "I can understand how you may feel justified in not keeping your offer open for a longer period. I trust, however, that should Congress conclude that it is best to restore this property to private ownership, you will at that time renew your interest in the project."[23]

This exchange of notes closed formal negotiations, but not the polemics. Dejected farmers still urged Ford to submit another offer and to continue his struggle against the monied power of Wall Street. One writer entreated, "Say, Henry, don't quit. Are you going to stand up and fight or quit cold, surrender and give yourself up without firing a shot. Now Henry don't lay down. . . ."[24] A woman in Sheffield, Alabama, lamented, "We know you don't need Muscle Shoals, but Muscle Shoals needs you."[25] Others called the attacks on Ford the most bitter ever revealed in Congress. Still others in contumacious mood said too many people were eager to dam Ford instead of the Tennessee River, while Eastern aristocrats still bellowed that to grant the Ford bid would have been the biggest real estate swindle since Adam and Eve were euchred out of the Garden of Eden.

Yet things simmered down. With Ford out of the running, debates in Congress shifted to the clash between the advocates of the government development of the Tennessee Valley and the private power combines. Under the relentless leadership of George Norris, Congress passed public ownership bills only to see them killed by the short-sighted vetoes of Calvin Coolidge and Herbert Hoover. Not until the advent of the New Deal under Franklin D. Roosevelt were these basic issues resolved in the Tennessee Valley Authority Act of May, 1933.

In reflection on these events, it is significant to note that the farmer's supplications to Ford during the 1920s did not suggest a change in the structure of government. As a rule, farmers were too conservative to harbor radical ideas. Rural people merely demanded that the trickle-down theory of money be accentuated. When it came to proposals such as state ownership of banks and grain elevators or price fixing by the Federal government, the farmers lacked unity. Such farm organizations as the Farm Bureau Federation, the Farmer's Union, the Grange, and the Non-Partisan League could never get together in a common cause.

A conservative press also may have encouraged the moderation of farmer's views on political action. The local newspapers and farm journals did not incite one to riot. On the contrary, Herbert Myrick, editor of *Farm and Home*, wrote Henry Ford on January 9, 1924, saying farmers would not be helped by doles or weak paternalism, but they should be inspired to work out their own salvation. Readers of *The Farmer* were told that they should rely on self-help instead of government help, self-control rather than government control, self-reliance rather than socialism.[26]

In retrospect, it appears that while Henry Ford received wide publicity during the twenties, his actual contribution to rural people seems rather limited. He failed to get Muscle Shoals, he failed to provide low-cost fertilizers, he failed to reform farm cooperatives, and he failed to provide specific aid to those suffering hard times.

Obviously, the farmers who expected Ford to give them immediate assistance suffered disappointment. This was not because Ford lacked interest in farmers or that he did not hold positive ideas, but rather that rural folks, in a financial squeeze, wanted relief at once, while Ford offered long-range proposals. When the underdog sought help, Ford recommended the bootstrap formula of self-help. Farmers begging for charity received good advice. Ford's tips for the day smacked too much of the general palaver cluttering up the farm journals. Those in distress found little consolation in the auto maker's admonition to be more progressive, to breed better livestock, to utilize more mechanical power in farming, to be efficient, to avoid waste, and above all to be self-reliant.

Basically, rural people misunderstood the real intentions of the "Millionaire." Estimates of him were confused because the publicity appearing in the *Dearborn Independent* and other newspapers often contradicted the information sent out to individuals by the secretaries answering the avalanche of letters arriving at the factory offices. Stories in the press presented Ford as a crusader for social justice. Many were convinced that he intended to enter the public arena and lead the fight in person. The replies to personal letters, however, reveal that Ford had no intention of divorcing himself from his business activities and devoting his life to the distribution of alms among the poor. This is abundantly clear in the outgoing letters from Ford's secretaries. These responses stated repeatedly, "Ford does not invest any money outside his own business. We have no specialist in our employ who has made a study of these farm problems."[27] He shunned meetings with farm leaders or members of the Department of Agriculture in Washington, D.C. Even during the hearings on Muscle Shoals, there is no record that he ever attended a Congressional hearing to discuss it. He tended to be unresponsive to the dreams of others and followed instead Emerson's dictum—Trust Thyself.

Although farmers eventually turned to the Federal Government for direct subsidies, the publicity associated with Ford's career during these years may have possessed some value. The provocative press releases from Dearborn dramatized the plight of the underprivileged; they injected a liberal tone into current controversies; they gave dignity to the work of reform; and they created a more militant spirit among those concerned with the welfare of the common man.

But the Ford myth persisted. Since he could build a low-cost car, truck, and tractor, it was assumed he could solve economic problems of rural Americans. A correspondent in Alabama expressed this faith in a letter to Ford in 1926. This letter, multiplied by thousands, reflected a widespread and simple faith in Ford and the fixed belief that an understanding bond existed between the writers and this man of immense wealth:

Dear Henry Ford:

We of the South affectionately acclaim you, instead of Lincoln, as the Great Liberator. Lincoln has freed his thousands, you have freed your ten thousands. The rutted roads on mountain sides and water sogged wheel tracks on low lands have been smoothed, that the wheels of Fords may pass. The sagged barbed wire gates of barren cotton patches and blighted corn fields have been thrown open that brainblinded and soulblinded recluses might ride joyously into the world with their families in Fords. An army of white clad serfs on small Southern farms in Ford cars and trucks are pushing onward and upward into a conscious heirship in the nations of civilized living. . . ."[28]

VII

Ford and the Farm Cooperative Movement

In the 1920s, one of the cures for the ills of agriculture centered in a renewed interest in cooperative marketing organizations for farm commodities. These agencies were designed to give the farmer more control over the sale of his products and thus limit the power of middlemen. Cooperative enterprise began in modest fashion in colonial days and developed slowly, until by 1915 there were over five thousand cooperative associations doing a business of $635 million.[1] Following World War I, the movement grew rapidly with the formation of regional type organizations such as the California Fruit Growers Exchange and the California Associated Raisin Growers. By 1921 cooperatives were handling over one billion dollars worth of business.[2]

The Coolidge administration encouraged farm cooperatives because they provided a program of action without involving the Federal Government. Cooperatives made the farmers responsible for reform, not the do-nothing Congressmen in Washington, D.C. Politicians, therefore, adopted cooperatives as a gimmick to be trotted out on all occasions and embellished with rhetoric until it all sounded like the coming of the millennium. President Coolidge often referred to cooperatives in his innocuous speeches on the farm problem. Herbert Hoover, as Secretary of Commerce, followed the same line. William M. Jardine, Secretary of Agriculture, addressed farm groups, saying their interest in cooperatives was indicative of their desire to deal with their problems in their own way. Left alone, rural people were capable of taking care of themselves. "The government should keep hands off the farmer," said Jardine. "He doesn't want to be babied or pitied by other people. He doesn't want the government constantly monkeying around with his business. He doesn't seek legislation to fix prices. What we all need is less tommyrot and fewer wrenches thrown into other people's machinery."[3]

Needless to say, these Jardinian clichés were frequently resented. An Illinois farmer wrote him in 1926 saying he objected to the advice that farmers market their crops in more orderly fashion, while the speculators in the wheat pits of Chicago had just dumped 67 million bushels on the market in one day, depressing the price 7 cents a bushel. If orderly marketing was desirable, why not force the grain exchanges to do likewise. Furthermore, if farmers should go it alone, why then were tariffs imposed to aid United States Steel? A speaker at the Iowa State Fair in 1925 assailed Jardine, claiming he had violated the trust of his office in saying farmers were prosperous and did not need help. The Secretary should be working for farmers, not against them. Another malcontent angrily charged that:

> You say you were raised on a farm and know all about it, is bunk and makes me sick. What you say in the papers gets my goat. You tell the farmers to pull themselves up by the boot straps. Well, 99 per cent of the experts in Washington left the farm because it looked like hard work, long hours and little pay. They flunked out and kissed the old farm good bye. Ever since the Republicans got into office, they have used the farmer as a football to be kicked about by gamblers, speculators, grafters and crooks, and relief is not in sight. . . .[4]

The cooperative movement appealed to rural people as an escape from the agricultural depression of the twenties. If business and commerce thrived, why did agriculture remain in the doldrums? Business and labor had learned to organize on a national scale to protect their interests while farmers remained isolated and disorganized. Collective action might rescue the farmer from those who profited at his expense.

For the most part, farmers believed they were being victimized. When a grain grower hauled his wheat into a local elevator, he accepted the market price made by someone else; when he entered a grocery store, he paid prices set by others. Thus he concluded the economic system separated him from his legitimate profits. Manufacturers overcharged him, railroads took all the traffic would bear, and bankers loaded him with high interest rates. Grain exchanges manipulated prices against him, while merchants squeezed him by collusive buying.

The main issue was the price-cost squeeze; the disparity between the price farmers received for their commodities and the price they paid for the things they bought. Senator Tom Walsh insisted farmers received only 25 cents out of the dollar paid for farm products. A cornbelt farmer wanted to know why he had to pay 400 bushels of corn for a wagon which formerly cost 150 bushels. Senator Shipstead of Minnesota in 1923 reported farmers who had shipped sheep to the stockyards in Chicago received bills for the freight charges because the sheep failed to cover the cost of transportation.[5] One farmer answered the commission firm by saying he did not have any more money, but he did have some more sheep. A distraught woman in Maryland, writing to Secretary Jardine in 1925, pleaded:

> My dentist charged me a ton of tomatoes to work on my daughter's teeth for 20 minutes. A lawyer charged me 150 bushels of corn to prepare a paper giving me permission to put a mortgage on my home. The thing for you to do, Mr. Secretary, is to arrange with the price fixers to give us a price that will keep us in business. . . .[6]

The awareness of the disadvantage of the farmer in the market place was an impetus to the cooperative movement. By 1922, there were ten thousand cooperative organizations in rural America, with memberships of three million and a total business of two billion dollars. Nearly three-fourths of these associations were in twelve North Central states. The American Farm Bureau in 1924 estimated that 20 percent of the cotton crop was marketed through cooperatives; 66 percent of the tobacco crop, and 75 percent of the citrus fruit.[7]

A sensational chapter in this history occurred when Henry Ford and a prominent cooperative leader, Aaron Sapiro, clashed over the management of farmers' cooperatives. This bitter encounter, lasting from 1922 to 1927, involved a million dollar lawsuit and revealed the complexity and growing pains associated with these marketing ventures. When the two powerful men locked horns, farmers were caught up in a dilemma of mixed loyalties.

Aaron Sapiro could have stepped out of a Horatio Alger novel. He was raised in the slums of Oakland until he was placed in an orphanage for six miserable years. He managed to graduate from school with honors and entered Hebrew Union College in Cincinnati where he studied to be a rabbi. However, after eight years he left and returned to San Francisco where he graduated from Hastings Law School in 1911.[8]

Having conquered adversity, he went on to better things. In 1915 he did legal work for Harris Weinstock, director of the California Marketing Commission. This gave him an opportunity to study the legal history of cooperatives. In addition, he often acted as lawyer for various California cooperatives for fees which could total as much as $80,000 annually.

Since he knew the technical aspects of the marketing business, he assisted in organizing new cooperatives in the state. He traveled widely, acquired an acquaintance with farm leaders, and enveloped his work with an evangelical zeal which gave it the appearance of a righteous crusade. In speaking to farm folks he would declare that above all he wanted them to have shoes for their children, good educations, and bathtubs. Dr. Grace H. Larsen, in her study of Sapiro, quotes observers as saying he could "make the marketing of a barrel of apples more exciting than a tale from Boccaccio, and the signing of a cooperative agreement seem as vital to social justice and progress as the Magna Charta."[9]

The Sapiro genius lay in his ability to refine the business methods used in certain California fruit grower's marketing associations and to add some of his own ideas to create the structure of a cooperative system. This formula, usually called the "California Plan," or the "Sapiro Plan," could be adapted to any group of farmers producing a specific crop. The system hung together by use of legal contractual arrangements between the farmers and the cooperative association.

The fundamental features of the Sapiro plan were: (1) Farm cooperatives would utilize modern business methods comparable to those of large corporations. The leadership would be highly trained and well paid; (2) they would be organized by commodity not community; (3) they would pool the farm commodities to spread sales over the year and avoid dumping crops on the market with resulting lower prices; (4) farmers would sign long-term contracts, promising to deliver their entire crop to the cooperative for the following five years; (5) they would receive part of the value of the crop at time of delivery, the remainder to be paid by the association during the year; (6) the cooperatives would be financed by the use of warehouse receipts, which in turn would become collateral for loans from the banks; (7) farmer's commodities would move directly from the local market to the miller, manufacturer, or exporter, with expenses limited to storage, transportation, and handling charges, thus cutting out the middlemen.

Theoretically the plan had great appeal. Collective action would be a boon to the farmer, who traditionally plowed in hope, lived in faith, and marketed by accident. Henceforth, organized farmers would control the market, not the market control them. No longer would they sell their grain at threshing time when prices were low; orderly marketing would banish this obsolete system. At last producers on the farm would have something to say about supply and demand, like the leaders of national labor unions, and the directors of United States Steel. Producers of pigs would now be on a par with the producers of pig iron. In essence, the Sapiro dream envisioned farmers having something to say about their own destiny.

Aaron Sapiro popularized his program on a national scale. As an attorney for fourteen of the largest marketing associations on the West Coast in 1919, he promoted the cause with such zeal that the movement spread like wildfire throughout the country. Like William Jennings Bryan, he delivered his own Cross of Gold speech in Chicago on July 23, 1920. In an address which ran to thirty-six published pages, he pointed to the California farmers who had prospered after joining cooperatives for marketing fruit. Now farmers could concentrate on growing crops while experts handled sales. If a cooperative needed to pay an expert $200,000 to secure the best talent, this should be done. "In California," enthused Sapiro, "we pay for brains, we don't monkey with amateurs." He added, "Give this thing one year and it will be good night for the Board of Trade."[10]

Statistically the Sapiro gains were impressive. By 1925 the Sapiro plan had been incorporated by 90 associations in 32 states and Canada with membership of 890,000 farmers.[11] The value of farm products handled reached $600 million. Meanwhile Sapiro's income had risen from $10,000 in 1916 to $61,531 in 1922. His total income from 1916 to 1926 was $398,922.68.[12]

Sensational as had been the rise of the Sapiro cooperatives, their descent like a falling meteorite occurred with almost equal suddenness. By 1926 many of these marketing associations had failed, leaving the movement in confusion and the leaders in disrepute. As might be expected, the causes for the cataclysmic turn of events were legion, some of them rather obvious and others quite obscure.

The marketing problems, understandably, were accentuated by the persistence of the postwar agricultural depression. Although the prevailing hard times initially had driven farmers into the cooperative movement, the general unhealthy condition of the farm economy drove many of the co-ops into bankruptcy. Sapiro discovered that a deflated rural economy could cripple new business ventures, including his own.

Furthermore, a long tradition of rugged individualism had conditioned farmers for independent action rather than cooperation. Too many joined marketing associations with little genuine philosophical conviction. When they ran into obstacles, they became disenchanted with the system and turned traitor to the crusade. Lacking patience, they often deserted their cooperative if someone outside the organization appeared to be getting a better deal. They were accustomed to delivering their commodities to a dealer and getting paid in cash. When they delivered to the cooperative and received partial payment, then waited months for the next check, the delay seemed unnecessarily irksome.

Most farmers, in addition, were not prepared to accept the ethics of high finance in the world of big business. The iron-clad contracts in the Sapiro plan were reinforced by the power of law backed up by injunctions and court actions. If a member sold outside the cooperative, he broke a written contract, making him subject to a fine up to $500. In the Tri-State Tobacco Growers Cooperative there were thousands of lawsuits against individual tobacco farmers for breach of contracts. While it might sound professional to endow cooperatives with modern business procedures, the constant threat of litigation did not coincide with the average farmer's concept of the American way.

The feud between Aaron Sapiro and Henry Ford came when both men were at the height of their influence; unfortunately, their confrontation reduced the prestige of both. In 1923 Sapiro had a staff of lawyers occupying offices in San Francisco, Dallas, Chicago, New York, and Washington, D.C. He sat in the councils of the American Farm Bureau Federation and worked on plans to federalize all cooperatives in the United States and Canada. Henry Ford, likewise sat on Mount Olympus, selling approximately three-fourths of the cars in the low-price field, owning mines, forests, railroad lines, and leading the pack in the race for the presidency of the United States.

For several years Ford had kept an eye on the farm cooperative movement because of his life-long interest in agriculture, his own ownership of farm land, and, above all, because farmers were his best customers for Model Ts, Fordsons, and trucks. The farmers prosperity affected his own profits. J. R. Howard, president of the American Farm Bureau, on September 20, 1921, wrote to Henry Ford saying he had heard from many sources of his interest in cooperative marketing. He was sending William G. Eckhardt to Detroit to confer with Ford on this matter.

But the Motor Mogul had deep reservations about the value of farm cooperatives. As head of a family-owned industry which bought out the other stockholders, Ford failed to see any benefits in cooperation in management because he believed it divided authority and led to mismanagement of business. When Andrew S. Wing, editor of *Farm and Fireside*, interviewed Ford in 1924, Ford said:

> I don't believe in cooperation. What can cooperation do for farmers? All it amounts to is an attempt to raise the price of farm products. It defeats its own purpose because if prices go too high people won't buy. Farmers had better reduce the cost of production by using more efficient methods rather than increase prices artificially.[13]

When Wing suggested cooperative marketing might cut the cost of distribution, Ford replied, "Distribution is nothing but transportation. You can't reduce the cost of transportation very materially by cooperative marketing."[14]

It seems likely that Ford's criticism of cooperatives would have occurred even if Aaron Sapiro had never appeared on the scene. The Californian became an ideal whipping boy, however, because he had never been a dirt farmer, and besides, lawyers as a class had never appealed to Ford's midwestern Populist mind.

Ford's attack on Sapiro appeared in the *Dearborn Independent*, edited by William J. Cameron. Since Ford owned the magazine, it must be assumed that he had something to say about its contents. On April 12, 1924, Robert Morgan published the first of a series of articles entitled, "Jewish Exploitation of Farmer's Organizations: Monopoly Traps Operate Under Guise of Marketing Associations." His opening sentence announced, "A band of Jews—bankers, lawyers, moneylenders, advertising agencies, fruit-packers, produce buyers, professional office managers and bookkeeping experts—is on the back of the American farmer."[15] The author explained that the new organization, using Gentile fronts, operated across the nation, threatening to extract tribute from virtually every farmer. All local, state, and national cooperative associations would be combined into an international monopoly dominated by Jews. The method employed consisted of first creating dissatisfaction with the local cooperative, and then suggesting that super-salesmen, who were not farmers, should market the commodities. When debts mounted, the cooperative would reorganize with Jewish leaders in control. This had occurred among the deciduous fruit growers in California, the tobacco growers in Kentucky, and the cotton planters in the South.

Morgan insisted the Sapiro managers cheated the farmers to line their own pockets. Ruthless as crocodiles, they filled offices with pseudo-experts paid high rents, and provided salaries ranging from $10,000 to $30,000 for managers of regional associations. Rather than project salaries on a commission basis, they chose flat salary rates.

Subsequent articles attacked Sapiro and his agents for malpractices in the handling of wool, cotton, fruit, wheat, and tobacco. Although subject to exaggeration, and at times to distortion of facts, these muckraking issues did probe weaknesses in the Sapiro system which were now becoming more apparent to farmers. For example, the much publicized "standard contract" in these cooperatives bound the farmer to turn over his entire crop to the association and accept such payments as the association was able to make for him. Yet nothing in the contract held the association responsible for limiting the cost of marketing operations nor for meeting the prices paid by independent buyers. Nothing in the contract stipulated when the farmer would get his check. There were no limitations on the actions of the marketing agent who could sell commodities, when, where, to whom, and at what prices he might choose. The contract was binding on the farmer but not on cooperative officials. Robert Morgan claimed this added up to a skin game which fleeced the wool growers, destroyed the value of more cotton than the boll weevil, and in the end farmed the farmer.

The *Dearborn Independent* attacked at the very time the Sapiro forces were trying to control the rising dissension within their own membership. It appeared evident that Sapiro had over-sold his program, promising more than he could deliver. He had claimed he would control enough of a given commodity to secure better prices for his organization, yet outsiders often did better in the market place. His efforts to organize the industry from the top down failed to gain the confidence of rural people who tended to regard these so-called experts as city slickers with evil intentions. In this sense, Sapiro had merely substituted a new class of middlemen for the old without guaranteeing any improvement in personal integrity.

Sapiro's aggressive promotional schemes left him vulnerable to censure by the alienated. In his efforts to organize Canadian wheat farmers he tried to secure the backing of Mackenzie King, the Prime Minister. On November 12, 1922, he wrote to Joseph Passoneau, his director of marketing in Colorado, saying he had met the Prime Minister and worked out a plan of putting over the cooperative plan in Canada without arousing suspicion as to its political significance. He added, "I told the blamed Canadians that I had the ideal man; that they could not do it themselves. . . . and that you and I between us could actually put it over for them."[16] Later, in promoting his program in Alberta and Saskatchewan, he bragged about the success of his Burley Tobacco Growers Cooperative in Kentucky where Passoneau had assisted in organizational work.

Passoneau broke with Sapiro in 1923, however, and sent a bitter letter to Frank O. Lowden, Chairman of the Wheat Marketing Advisory Committee in Washington, D.C., explaining the reasons for this rift. He described Sapiro's conduct in directing the Burley Tobacco Growers Cooperative as positively dishonest. He claimed Sapiro received $30,000 for making eight speeches in a three-week campaign to sign up tobacco growers. In addition, he collected $16,000 as fees in the purchase of tobacco warehouses, without the knowledge and consent of directors of the cooperative. His fees for enforcing the tobacco contracts during an eight-month span were $22,845. Exorbitant salaries were authorized ranging from $7,000 to $25,000, annually.[17]

When en route to Wenatche, Washington, to organize apple growers, Passoneau refused to put Sapiro on the payroll because he was already receiving money from the Wenatche apple packers, and thus he would be collecting funds from both sides of the fence. Passoneau believed this to be bad ethics; Sapiro thought he was capable of determining his own ethics.

These Passoneau charges appeared in the Regina *Leader* and Saskatoon *Star* on February 18, 1924. Enraged, Sapiro filed a

$100,000 libel suit against the Canadian newspapers. After two days of testimony in Regina, Judge H. Y. Mc Donald threw the case out of court, congratulated the press for publishing vital information, and slapped Sapiro with the court costs. Ignominiously, Sapiro and his fourteen associates retreated to Chicago.[18]

Now the disintegration of the Sapiro empire accelerated, with bickering among leaders, mounting disaffection of farmers, and the increased rate of cooperative bankruptcies. What happened in Kansas became typical of the whole movement. The Sapiro organizers had told wheat growers that pooling their grain with the Kansas Wheat Growers Association would yield higher prices at threshing time. Even with the backing of Arthur Capper and Frank O. Lowden, they managed to sign only 4 percent of the farmers. In the fall of 1924, fifteen hundred of the members petitioned to dissolve the cooperative because the association had spent $242,000 on overhead costs in marketing 4,400,000 bushels of wheat. The cooperative spent $94,000 in one year for promotional expenses alone. Businessmen were encouraged to go out and coerce farmers to join the pool. This created ill will and hastened the demise of the cooperative. Noting this trend, the United States Department of Agriculture in 1925 warned farmers about joining cooperatives because, of the two hundred forty-three organized since 1913, two hundred had collapsed from lack of capital, over-extension of credit, or bad management.

Harried by these pressures, Aaron Sapiro became more extreme. He relied more heavily on legal weapons to keep the members of his associations in line. He filed more suits against members who sold their commodities outside the pool. He sued the Kansas City *Packer* for libel and filed a $100,000 suit against the Jones Mercantile Company of Canton, Georgia, for publishing alleged malicious articles against the Georgia Cotton Growers Association. When President Coolidge appointed an agricultural commission to investigate the cooperative movement, Sapiro labeled "the whole thing as the biggest piece of folly ever attempted by a government investigating committee.[19]

To defend his interests and to humiliate his opposition, Aaron Sapiro filed his one million dollar suit against Henry Ford for defamation of character. The suit came to trial in the Federal District Court in Detroit in March, 1927, under Judge F. S. Raymond. Senator James A. Reed of Missouri headed Ford's staff of lawyers, while William H. Gallagher led the Sapiro legal counsel.

The declaration in the Sapiro case stated that the defendant had acted to "harass, oppress, impoverish and wholly ruin the said plaintiff in his said profession and did otherwise falsely, wickedly and maliciously compose and publish. . . . certain false, scandalous, malicious and defamatory libel. . . ."[20] The plaintiff's case contained 141 indictments against Henry Ford and the Dearborn Publishing Company.

Since these charges were first made in 1925, the attorneys for the defense had two years in which to prepare their case. A corps of lawyers and investigators scoured the country for evidence. They retraced the steps of Sapiro since 1915, secured 40,000 pages of depositions, and received signed affidavits from 125 witnesses. The transcript of the trial contained approximately 5,000 pages, including one speech of Sapiro which contained 25,000 words.[21]

Meanwhile, the grass roots opposition to Sapiro flourished. Those in financial distress sent thousands of letters to Henry Ford in which they gave vent to their grievances, fears, and anger. Ford became identified with a virtuous cause; his enemies with the forces of evil.

Wheat growers in Nebraska resented the invasion of a self-styled Moses from California who claimed marketing was too complex to be trusted to dirt farmers. The big guns pressured them into signing on the dotted line, while the agents collected thousands of dollars in fees. A farmer near Wecota, South Dakota, in September, 1925, wrote Ford saying he had heard about the Sapiro suit, but he believed the *Dearborn Independent* presented only half the truth. Sapiro should be fined a million dollars for robbing the wheat farmers of Dakota and fleecing them with deceiving contracts.

Tobacco growers charged that Sapiro had promised his cooperative would triple farmer's prices. He had spoken over the radio in a persuasive manner, exaggerating the numbers joining in order to favorably influence the unwary. By securing the backing of prominent business leaders, he had made it a blasphemy to criticize Sapiro and a misdemeanor to oppose the movement. The Sapiro officials graded tobacco two grades lower than normal. When the directors were elected, they set their own salaries and refused to reveal the amounts, saying this was a private matter. Another farmer, hospitalized with tuberculosis and unable to feed his family, wrote the cooperative asking for an advance on his tobacco held in storage. He got a firm "no" in reply. The Sapiro contract had tied him up for six years, making him a slave to the system. A South

Carolinian, writing to Henry Ford on March 21, 1927, presented a view which was typical of these protestations:

> Sapiro is more than you accuse him of being. He put the country on the bum. He broke farmers right and left. He used Russian methods to turn father against son and son against father. He tore the country assunder. He caused fathers and mothers to lie awake nights planning how they could get their neighbor to secretly haul some of their tobacco to the auction floor so the family might have something to eat. The contract looked like the farmer was to be the party of the first part, but he turned out to be party of the fourth part. Now farmers are hog tied hand and foot. They are forced to steal from themselves to beat the contract. . . . I can prove that Sapiro is worse than you accuse him of being. Annanias on one of his best days could not have out-lied Sapiro. . . .[22]

In the Ford Archives in Dearborn, the accession number 48 is filled with a huge collection of letters written by farmers who believed Sapiro's cooperatives were detrimental to their welfare. Although it would be redundant to quote them at length, a few sentences gleaned from the correspondence convey some of the bitterness residing in rural America. Excerpts from twenty letters are:

> Somebody is getting millions from tobacco, but not the farmer. . . . We elected the association officials, now they can't be found. . . . The price of tobacco is 30 cents a pound, I got 15 cents from the pool. . . . Tobacco prices went down, yet officials in the cooperative make up to $22,000 a year. . . . The co-op officials turned traitor on us. . . . The whole thing is a tragic joke. . . . I received $317 for my tobacco, I could have got $1,100 outside the pool. . . . The pool paid me 7 cents a pound, then turned around and sold the tobacco for 25 cents. . . . I lost my farm because of Sapiro. . . . The Pool men lied to us. . . . The Sapiro didn't pay me, but it sued me. . . . Nothing you could publish would libel Sapiro. . . . That scoundrel should be sent up for life for sucking the life blood of farmers. . . . Smash him good for robbing us and making us loose our homes. . . . The sooner these leeches are given a dose of "go quick" the better. . . . My neighbor's wife went insane because they had to sell everything to get out of the clutches of Sapiro.[23]

As the trial got under way, scores of farmers tried to aid Henry Ford by offering to testify in his behalf. Some with insufficient funds to travel to Detroit, raised money in the local community and forwarded it by mail. Others sent in newspaper clippings or their own observations to be used as evidence. Hot tips were sent to attorney James A. Reed suggesting ways to trap the adversary.

As might be expected, considerable anti-Semitism appeared in this correspondence. Perhaps Accession 48 contains some of the most bigoted expressions of opinion in American letters. Since Ford had criticized the Jews in the *Dearborn Independent* over a period of several years, many believed Sapiro represented a Jewish conspiracy to dominate marketing of farm commodities, not only in the United States, but in the whole world. Much of this anti-Semitism came from the pens of those living in isolated rural areas where Jewish people were unknown. Since very few Jews engaged in agriculture, many accepted anti-Semitic dogma because they had no opportunity to get acquainted with them. As yet the racist terrors of the Nazi sadists were unknown, and the press and radio in the United States often repeated ethnic jokes as part of the matrix of American humor. Since Protestant churches often depicted the Jews as a despised people since the Crucifixion, the anti-Semitic clichés were accepted without deep reflection or personal experience.

To read the virulent quality of this rural bigotry is shocking. To quote lines from this correspondence is to expose the basic ignorance that lies beneath the surface of the so-called noble American living in the land of the free and the home of the brave. Such statements as the following are typical of this dementia:

> I think Ford is right about the Jews. . . . Sapiro is a shrewd little Jew. . . . The Bible says Jews will return to Palestine, but they want to get all the money out of America first. . . . The money-hungry California Jews used one-sided contracts and took the farmers for millions. . . . The dirty devils of Jews should be run out of the country. . . . Sapiro should be kicked out because he is trash. . . . That skunk of a Jew being allowed to do such things to this country . . . Who finances the wheat, the Jews; who buys 85 per cent of the wheat exported, the Jew . . . It is the speculator, the gambler, the parasite, the commission man, the Jew financiers that we are trying to get away from.[24]

Yet in this sewer of diatribes, a few rose above the gutter to decry anti-Semitism. After the *Dearborn Independent* had made the allegation that Aaron Sapiro, Bernard M. Baruch, David Levy, Otto H. Kahn, and Mortimer Fleischhacker formed a conspiracy to get a strangle hold on the American farmer, the Kansas *Farmer* stated, "We take no stock in the Ford theory of a gigantic conspiracy to get control of the worlds markets."[25] The Danville *News* in Virginia noted that Ford's phobia against the Jews was well known, but his charges of a conspiracy had little support. The paper added that in New York the Morgan banks were presided over by an Episcopalian, the Governor of the Bank of England belonged to the Church of England, and the Director of the Paris Bourse was a Catholic. The Henry Ford charges against Sapiro and his cooperatives were absurd and should not go unchallenged. "We are now seeing the harm that enormous wealth in the hands of one man can do when that man has neither the education nor information, and when he allows his prejudices on any subject to run rampant, regardless of the facts."[26] Many individuals wrote to Ford calling Robert Morgan's articles a pack of lies and the biggest swindle in the world. Others stated they were well treated by the Sapiro associations. Still others simply requested, "Stop my subscription to your Jew-hating paper."

The Sapiro-Ford trial attracted considerable attention, but after thirty-eight days of court proceedings the public began to lose interest in the contest. During the trial, James A. Reed, Ford's attorney, secured a ruling from the court which abrogated Sapiro's claim that Ford had libeled all Jewish people as well as himself. In addition, the suit placed the responsibility for anti-Semitism on Henry Ford rather than on the editors of the *Dearborn Independent*. This reduced the issues to one main question, had Ford defamed Sapiro's character?

The Sapiro attorneys presented Sapiro as a humanitarian devoted to the abolition of a farmer's economic woes through his cooperatives. For his noble efforts he had been maligned by Ford and his associates. These attacks had destroyed farmers faith in the marketing movement, thus causing hardship to both Sapiro and the rural Americans. For the defense, James Reed argued that Ford had never used the word "conspiracy" in his literature. Furthermore, the criticisms of the Sapiro organizations were justified because the evidence suggested that Sapiro had received excessive fees for his services, his cooperative officials were over-paid, and the farmers suffered the tyranny of salaried middle men who got their money first and let the farmers take what was left.

The day before Henry Ford was to appear in court as a witness, he was involved in an auto accident which required hospitalization and prevented him from testifying in court. Meanwhile, the defense presented the court with affidavits signed by fourteen people charging that Sapiro had tried to bribe certain jurors. At this point, Judge F. S. Raymond declared a mistrial and adjourned the case for six months.

On July 7, 1927, Ford published his apology to Sapiro, retracted his statements about Jewish people, and promised to "act honorably and to repair the damage as far as I can."[27] The parties to the suit then settled the dispute out of court.

This sordid affair tarnished the Ford image, gave solace to the members of the Ku Klux Klan, and encouraged the elements in American society which thrive on hate. Today it is difficult to meet a well-read Jewish person who is not familiar with Henry Ford's association with anti-Semitism in this country. Frank E. Hill and Allan Nevins, in their definitive work on Henry Ford, believe his blunders did not greatly diminish his standing with the masses. Their hero still exemplified the virtues most prized by rural Americans.

The evidence indicates that Ford's attacks on Sapiro's cooperatives did not cause their failure, but merely nudged them in this direction. These associations had serious difficulties and many of them had failed before the *Dearborn Independent* exposed the various malpractices. When Sapiro was asked why so many of his ventures collapsed, he replied that "death came after he had severed connection with the associations often because the rules he laid down were not followed."[28]

In reviewing these years, the central issue is not the motives or popularity of Henry Ford, but rather, was he right in rejecting the basic ideas inherent in the farm cooperative movement? The answer seems to be a resounding, "no." Joseph G. Knapp, who has studied the cooperative endeavor for fifty years, recently concluded that it is clear that farm cooperatives are successful. They have increased the dignity of individuals by giving them a sense of ownership, they have provided a choice of markets rather than dependence on a single dealer, they have provided yardsticks to measure competition in business, and they have trained farmers to participate more actively in business and community affairs.[29]

This success can be seen in the rapid growth of these cooperatives. In 1920, less than one million farmers used cooperatives to handle one billion dollars worth of business. In 1967, farm marketing cooperatives had a membership of 6.5 million, with a total business volume of over $16.5 billion. Farmers investments in these organizations in 1968 reached $3,900 million. Today, rural telephone cooperatives serve half a million farmers, while rural electrical cooperatives provide service for over five million farm families. Farm elevator cooperatives for handling grain and petroleum products are commonplace in all major agricultural areas.

Although Henry Ford maintained an interest in farmers, he failed to grasp the complexity of agricultural problems. He emphasized improving production of crops but did not grasp the importance of improved marketing and distribution of these commodities. As a result he contributed little to the farm cooperative movement in the United States.

VIII

Ford, Science, and Rural Ecology

Henry Ford's interest in farming runs like a thread throughout his life. Today one can sense this preoccupation as one strolls across the grounds of the Ford Motor Company at Dearborn, or pores over the bulky files in the Ford Archives. Carved in stone above the entry to the old administration building on Shaeffer Road are the words: "Industrious application of inventive genius to the natural resources of the earth is the groundwork of prosperous civilization." In his business correspondence, as early as 1907, one can find his secretary requesting information about the latest in animal husbandry, synthetic fertilizers, agronomy, horticulture, and agrobiology. In 1910 he asked to be put on the mailing list of all publications of the United States Department of Agriculture and the major agricultural experimental stations of the country. These requests usually added the cryptic note, "Bill me for the costs." When Julius H. Barnes, President of the United States Chamber of Commerce, visited Ford in 1922, he was amazed to learn of the manufacturer's genuine concern about the scientific aspects of American agriculture.

Apparently the quest for knowledge in this field remained insatiable. In 1940, seven years before his death, he tried to trace the rumor that a new wheat strain had been grown in Asia which produced large heads and heavy yields on plants only seven inches high. Officials in the Ford Motor Company branches in Shanghai and Yokohama were asked to assist in this search. When these leads failed, the hunt shifted to Korea. Finally a Baptist missionary in Honan province in China reported seeing a wheat variety which produced 17 percent greater yields. He lacked information, however, as to the length of the wheat stem. Further contacts were made with the Henry Lester Institute of Scientific Research in China, with officials of the South Manchurian Railroad Company, with faculty members of St. John's University in Shanghai, with the Fan Memorial Institute in Peking, with Dr. A. C. Sowerby, a leading scientist of the Royal Asiatic Society, and with offices of the United States Department of Agriculture in Shanghai. Although these investigations brought minimal results, the sixty pages of correspondence reflect the determination of Ford and his associates to secure scientific data on farm problems.

Much of Henry Ford's scientific thought reflected long-range vision. His love of nature, his concern for conservation, his hatred of waste, his disgust with filth, his desire to re-cycle used products, and his attempts to utilize unused farm plants and commodities for industrial purposes, all suggest modernity. He could well be called a precursor of the present day ecology movement. Perhaps Thomas Edison had been right when he once declared that "Ford's foresight was so long it sagged in the middle."

Ford's mind was restless, speculative, with a penchant for the unexpected. Some said his mind ran down twenty tracks at the same time. When asked on one occasion how he would improve the newspapers in the United States, he said he would discover a way to reclaim the ink in old newsprint so the ink and paper could be reused over and over again. When asked for his solution to a coal strike, he suggested the coal be burned in the ground in its native state with the heat piped out like electricity while the smoke and ashes remained under ground. "Science is all about us," he observed, and "an attitude of discriminating receptivity is the beginning on the higher road to knowing."[1]

As early as 1908, the British made attempts to secure a motor fuel for trucks in Africa by distilling alcohol from sugar cane and the prickly-pear cactus. In World War I research continued under the supervision of the British Alcohol Motor Fuel Committee. In the United States, the Hart-Parr Company of Charles City, Iowa, in 1908 equipped some of their tractors in Idaho, Colorado, and Cuba with alcohol-burning carburetors. The company claimed alcohol made a more satisfactory fuel than gasoline or kerosene and required only slight modifications on the carburetion system.[2]

With the outbreak of the World War I, Henry Ford became interested in the production of alcohol as a motor fuel. He set up a laboratory in the Engineering Building, he subscribed to *The West-*

ern Brewer to read about distillation techniques, he imported Danish potatoes for conversion into alcohol, and gave out interviews to the newspapers. He claimed the supply of gasoline diminished every year, but the alcohol resources were as unlimited as air and water because it existed in all vegetation. It could be distilled from such things as grain, sugar cane, potatoes, trees, cactus plants, the vegetation in swamps, and even from garbage. Since lumber mills left half the trees in the sawdust, this too could be salvaged. In addition, the breweries could now provide alcohol for internal combustion engines rather than the "stuff that destroys brawn and brain."

The brewery issue proved timely because the Anti-Saloon League and its followers had dried up several states, including Michigan. A San Francisco brewer, in 1917, fearing his state would also kill John Barleycorn, wrote the Ford Motor Company saying he had heard that Ford officials were advising Michigan brewers to convert their distilleries into industrial alcohol plants. He wanted full particulars and suggested, "When you get too thirsty in Michigan, come out to California and we will buy you a drink, but don't wait too long as nobody knows how soon we will go dry. . . ."[3]

These Ford pronouncements made potato farmers jubilant because if potatoes could be converted into motor fuel, the demand for farm crops would increase and prices would rise. Many farmers wrote Ford asking how many gallons of motor fuel could be extracted from a bushel of potatoes. Did the Danish potatoes have the most starch content, how many should be planted to the hill, should the eyes of planted potatoes face up or down, and should they be planted in the light of a full moon?

Helpful suggestions came from all sides. Some insisted sorghum produced the best alcohol, others mentioned straw, corn stalks, pig weed, and Russian thistles. One farmer believed mixing alcohol with carbolic acid would get the best results, while another thought barley should be used for making industrial alcohol, with the by-products sold as breakfast food. The editor of *The Wisconsin Agriculturist* claimed big distillers bought grain from farmers, extracted two gallons of alcohol per bushel, and then sold the bran back to the farmers for more than they had paid for it in the first place.[4] One perceptive fellow lauded the alcohol motor fuel saying that if his whiskey jug went dry, he would get a nip out of the tractor gasoline tank.

During the depression of 1920-23, farmers complained that farm crops went down in price while the cost of gasoline went up about ten cents in the last decade. They hated to sell livestock to pay fuel bills. A farmer near Hawley, Minnesota, wrote Ford in 1923 reporting potato growers going bankrupt in the Red River Valley because their crops brought less than the cost of production. Millions of bushels were left on the ground to freeze because they could not be sold at a profit. If Ford turned these waste crops into fuel, farmers could escape paying tribute to Standard Oil and Wall Street.

Although the Ford Motor Company experimented with alcohol distillation from 1915 to 1918, the efforts were feeble and inconsistent. When the United States entered the war in 1917, one of the Ford secretaries answered a correspondent by saying, "Ford has kind of lost interest in these recent gasoline substitutes." The British also had discovered that alcohol could not compete in price with petrol. One reason for this is that the fermentation of vegetation leaves only 16 percent alcohol, the rest being impurities and water. In order to distill the alcohol out of the mixture, high temperatures must be provided. To use heat to produce fuel, is a process which defeats its own end.

Yet the intriguing idea persisted in Ford's mind. He tried converting wood to sugar by treating it with hydrochloric acid and then converting the sugar into alcohol. As late as 1938, he was still saying cars could be powered from vegetables, and an acre of spuds should furnish enough engine fuel to plow 100 acres.[5] But Ford's secretary, W. J. Cameron, confirmed that all research indicated that alcohol blends could not compete with petroleum products.[6]

A second scientific problem intrigued Henry Ford when, in 1923, Harvey Firestone informed automotive manufacturers that the British monopoly of crude rubber was responsible for the doubling of its price in the American market. Since crude rubber prices had advanced from 15 to 37 cents a pound in three months in 1922, Firestone solicited the aid of Ford and Thomas Edison to help break this monopoly and lower the cost of automobile tires.[7]

Tire manufacturers had long been dependent on imports of crude rubber. After Charles Goodyear's discovery of vulcanization in 1844, Brazil remained the source of supply in the sap of the Hevea Brasiliensis trees in the Amazon jungles. Henry A. Wickham, in 1876, smuggled out 70,000 seeds from Brazil which were planted in the Royal Gardens at Kew, and later became the initial stock for rubber plantations in Malaya, Ceylon, India, and the East Indies. This cost Brazil the sole control of rubber and won Wickham a knighthood.

Faced with this problem, Ford and Edison decided to extract rubber from plants other than rubber trees and other tropical rubber-producing vegetation. William H. Smith directed the research work in Dearborn, where credence was placed in the earlier work of Harvey M. Hall, of the Carnegie Institution of Washington, D.C. During World War I, Hall had believed rubber could be derived from Rabbit Brush and milkweed plants which yielded from 3 to 6 percent rubber. The Bureau of Plant Industry of the United States Department of Agriculture encouraged these views.

When the press announced that Ford chemists would produce rubber from domestic plants, farmers congratulated the "Motor King" for converting weeds into cash. They said they had been fighting milkweeds, sunflowers, pigeon grass, and sow thistle for years. Now they could be sold on the market. All agreed the raw materials were plentiful.

In 1924, Ford and Edison decided to conduct further experiments in Florida. Over 7,000 acres were purchased near La Belle, Florida, and another 22,000-acre tract near Fort Myers, where Ford maintained a winter home. In 1929 Thomas Edison set up a laboratory near Way Station, Georgia, where various plants were tested for rubber bearing qualities.

Early in 1930, efforts were made to cultivate goldenrod to produce synthetic rubber. These flowers grew wild in Georgia, and from the 70 varieties, Edison chose the *solidago levenworthii* for his first experimental plots. H. G. Ukkleberg, a graduate of the University of Minnesota, directed the rubber projects from 1933 to 1936. He recalled that 10,000 different plants were tested, with the goldenrod the most promising. It had a fair amount of rubber and could be harvested like grain. The rubber remained entirely in the leaves. "We'd just strip the leaves off and test individual plants," stated Ukkleberg, "then we would cross the highest producing plants until we managed to increase the rubber yield from 3 to 6 percent."

Even though the goldenrod yielded some rubber, the meager results, together with the withdrawal of Firestone from the project in 1936, the advancing age of Edison, and the arrival of the Great

Depression, all combined to close the project. Still the experiment cheered rural Americans, giving them the hope of raising their own tires in the back yard.

Meanwhile, Ford established a rubber plantation in Brazil in 1927, where he secured concessions from the Brazilian government to use 2,500,000 acres on a tributary of the Amazon river. Here the workers discovered they could build hospitals, control disease, install sewers, operate railroads, airports, stores, schools, and dam the river, but they found it very difficult to grow rubber trees. It seemed that when rubber trees, accustomed to jungle growth, were cultivated on plantations they died from exposure to wind, sun, and rain. But by 1941 these plantations were growing disease resistant trees created by grafting techniques and producing over 750 tons of latex. After spending 20 million dollars on the venture, the company sold its holdings to the Brazilian government in 1945.[8] J. L. Mc Cloud, a Ford chemist, believed that one of the chief mistakes was a lack of expert botanists in the first years, which resulted in planting the wrong kind of trees in improper soil. By the time the technical problems were solved, Ford had lost interest in the enterprise.

Alert to the value of publicity, Ford exploded one of his journalistic bombshells in 1921 when he exclaimed, "The Cow Must Go." To replace her, he proposed artificial milk made synthetically. His dislike for dairy cattle stemmed from life on his father's farm where milking had been a disagreeable chore. Milking was hard work and it had to be repeated twice daily, a ritual which enslaved farmers and made the expression, "We must go home and milk the cows," the nation's number one killjoy. Anyone who has been kicked off a milk stool, or had a cow step in the milk bucket, or been hit across the eyes by a flailing cow's tail on a hot summer evening will understand why there are few romantic poems about milking on the farm.

Ford claimed these animals were unsanitary and inefficient. A scientific process would eliminate cows because there were no reasons why chemists could not discover the cow's secret of converting vegetation into dairy products. When interviewed by the editor of *Farm and Fireside* in 1925 he said, "Why should a farmer spend a lot of time taking care of a bunch of cows? It takes 20 days of actual work to grow and harvest the grain crops on a dairy farm. The rest of the time is spent taking care of animals. It is all wrong." When asked why he owned 150 head of excellent Durham and Ayrshire dairy cows and one of the best dairy barns in the state, he replied that these were kept just to prove they were all wrong.[9]

Mixed reactions followed. Members of the Near East Relief Committee rejoiced, thinking the new synthetic milk would save thousands of babies from starvation. Besides, tuberculosis, sometimes carried in cow's milk, could be avoided. City people hoped the innovation would reduce the cost of living.

On the other hand, a Minnesota farmer predicted that efforts to make cowless milk would fail because God made milk and Henry would have to go some to compete with the Almighty. He added laconically that the mechanical cow might merit consideration if it would eat stumps and rocks. Perhaps a new kind of gizzard would make Minnesota boulders as palatable as bran. The rocks and stumps removed, Ford could sell more cars.[10] Dr. E. V. Mc Cullum of Johns Hopkins University claimed Ford knew about as much about milk as he did about history. The Centralia *Hub*, referring to Ford's tin cows, explained how delightful it would be to go to the garage in the morning, crank Bessie, hear her four cylinders explode, turn the spigot, and return to the breakfast table with the family milk pail foaming on your arm.[11]

In similar vein, the Great Falls *Times*, announced that Ford had doomed the cud-chewing cow. Horses were not essential, cows were not essential, nothing was essential except tin cans. Maybe Henry Ford was not essential.[12] The Vancouver *Daily World*, noting the date was the twenty-third of March, claimed that this meant that "Henry has just nine months in which to get the cows out of the ranches by Christmas."[13] Farm journals ran cartoons depicting Ford's mechanical cow with captions to the effect that these were produced on an assembly line, sold F.O.B. Detroit, and shipped knocked down in crates, but equipped with interchangeable udders.

Yet it was the soybean which gave Ford his best opportunity to produce synthetic milk and to apply science and technology to farming practice. The "Ford and the Beanstalk Story" originated as another panacea for the depression following the crash in 1929. Rejecting the Townsend Plan, the Ham and Egg formula, the nostrums of Huey Long, Father Coughlin, and the Technocrats, Ford came up with his own self-help solution which called for closer cooperation between industry and agriculture. If industry could absorb more farm products, this new demand would raise prices of farm crops. Since by-products were going to waste, chemists would discover ways to convert wheat, corn, carrots, cabbage, sunflowers, straw, weeds, and corn cobs into products with commercial value. A Ford chemist recalled that after work stopped on the goldenrod, a laboratory was built in Dearborn in 1937 where research centered on waste products on the farm. Ford would suggest, "Now we've got all this useless waste, let's see if we can do something with it."[14]

After some experimentation, Ford experts chose the soybean as the most promising raw material. The beans could be grown in all parts of the nation, they were remarkably drougth-resistant, and they added valuable nitrogen to the soil. The Ford Motor Company did not discover the soybean, for it had been cultivated in Asia for centuries before written records were kept. Chinese peasants rotated it with other crops to bring new nitrogen to exhausted soils. In most Asian countries it ranked next to rice in importance for food because it contained proteins, fats, and vitamins needed for good health. An ancient proverb called it the poor man's meat and the poor man's milk. Introduced into the United States in 1904, it was used for cattle forage. During World War I, the Department of Agriculture, searching for a cheap source of protein, discovered the soybean as a soil fertilizer. Interest languished, however, until Ford officials began to advertise its virtues in the 1930s.

The company spent over a million dollars on soybean research in 1932 and 1933. Three hundred varieties of the beans were planted on 8,000 acres on the Ford farms. In the laboratory a processing machine weighing six and one-half tons extracted the oil from the beans, first crushing them into thin flakes, then exposing them to a gasoline solvent which absorbed the oil. The solvent was recovered again by distillation and reused. Thus the machine delivered in a continuous process both the soybean oil and meal. The oil made a superior enamel for painting automobiles and yielded a fluid for shock absorbers. The soybean meal, containing almost 50 percent protein, could be molded into horn buttons, gear shift balls, distributor cases, window trim strips, and electrical switch assemblies. Although the Ford company never claimed any original inventions in these processes, their efforts led to expanded use of farm commodities and demonstrated the advantages of cooperation between agriculture and industry.

The saga of the soybean reached rural America through the press as well as by exhibitions and demonstrations. At the Chicago World's Fair in 1933, the Ford Motor Company set up an Industrialized American Barn next to its Exhibition Building at the Century of Progress Exposition. This barn had been equipped with a soybean processing machine which converted a ton of beans into 400 pounds of oil and 1,600 pounds of protein meal. Here millions of visitors saw examples of how a farm crop could be converted into such products as plastic radio cabinets, table tops, buttons, ashtrays, steering wheels, glycerine, enamel, soap, paint, linoleum, oleomargarine, toilet powder, varnish, glue, and protein supplement for livestock.[15]

Farmers bombarded Henry Ford with questions. Some wanted to know where they could secure soybeans for seed, and which of the several hundred varieties was most desirable. If Manchu beans were 2,350 to the pound, how many should be planted per acre? Was it true that soybean milk had the same composition as dairy milk, namely 3.5 percent protein, 4.8 percent carbohydrates, 3.5 percent fats, and .70 percent minerals? Was it true that Ford's processing machine in the Edison Institute in Dearborn could extract oil from soybeans at a cost of 15 cents a bushel? A Texas boasted he had a soybean plant six feet tall with 650 pods and wanted to know if this was a dwarf? One farmer wanted to know to what extent the lecithin in soybeans strengthened the nerve tissue, heart, and the liver of human beings.

Since his factories used huge quantities of cotton and woolen cloth in the manufacture of automobiles, Ford sought improved methods of manufacturing textiles. Cotton had been used from force of habit, but had to be transported a thousand miles. Linen cloth had the longest fiber and made the strongest thread, but it required hand labor. The work was laborious, dirty, and enveloped in an unpleasant odor. Ford planted 600 acres of flax on his farms and mechanized all the operations. He anticipated saving 30 percent on his cost of woolen cloth, while the flax linseed oil could be used in paints.[16]

In 1937 his scientists developed a fiber from soybean protein and were credited as the first to spin a textile filament from protein derived from a vegetable source.[17] At the New York World's Fair of 1939, the Ford exhibit demonstrated the production of textiles from soybeans. The protein meal was mixed with various chemicals to form a thick tar-like solution. This liquid was forced through a screened spinneret with 24 apertures, each three one-thousands of an inch in diameter. The tiny strands passed through a chemical bath, were then wound on rolls for bleaching, and then spun into thread. The material could be woven into blankets, upholstery, or clothing.[18]

These innovations evoked considerable attention. *The Progress Guide* stated, "Go into the field and pick yourself a suit, all wool and acres wide."[19] Henry Ford appeared at a convention with his entire outfit made of soybeans, except his shoes. He envisioned a new fabric four times cheaper than wool. Since his laboratory produced 5,000 pounds of synthetic wool daily, he believed the importation of wool from abroad would be unnecessary. He also tried to induce the Federal Government to use the fiber to manufacture soldier's uniforms in World War II, but these efforts failed because the soybean process proved less economical than conventional means. In addition, the synthetic rayons, nylons, and dacrons proved to be too competitive.

Additional publicity accompanied Ford's venture into plastics. In 1909, Dr. Leo Baekeland, a Belgian scientist, made a synthetic resin plastic material which carried the trade name "Bakelite." Later, John Hyatt, of the Hyatt Roller Bearing Company, searched for a plastic to replace ivory billiard balls because of the scarcity of ivory. From a chemical reaction with gun cotton cellulose, he made a celluloid billiard ball which became the genesis of celluloid plastics seen today. In the automobile industry, distributors were made out of plastic material because it provided good insulation capable of resisting 15,000 volts of electricity. The coil cases of the 1915 Model T were constructed from a plastic formed out of wheat gluten with an asbestos binder. Horn buttons, instrument panels, and ornamentations were also plastic. In an interview with William L. Stidger in 1943, Ford suggested that his most significant contribution to society might be soybean plastics. Since they were molded rather than cast or stamped, production costs were greatly reduced. Traditionally, they were created from cotton cellulose and wood pulp, but later the raw materials included soybeans, corn, wheat, hemp, and China grass. Ramie was also used, a fiber which wrapped Egyptian mummies three thousand years ago, and which retained its strength over the centuries.

News photos in 1940 showed Ford hitting the rear deck of a plastic car body with an axe without inflicting damage. He insisted plastic car bodies weighed a thousand pounds less than steel ones, yet they could withstand ten times more shock than steel. Thus a car could roll over in the ditch without crushing, making the plastic models the safest cars on the road. After demonstrating some of the uses of the new material, however, the Ford Motor Company discontinued publicizing it.

In the meantime Henry Ford carried out considerable research on foods. The construction of the Ford Hospital in Detroit gave him an opportunity to try out his food faddist ideas. At one time he advocated eating only fruit for breakfast, proteins for lunch, and starches for dinner. He insisted Americans ate too much, that gluttony produced a sluggish brain, and that people should eat only when hungry. He believed people would live to be a hundred years old if they ate and exercised properly. Contemptuous of obese individuals, he admonished, "Cut down on the rations and you won't need doctors. Eat your dessert first and you won't eat so much."[20]

Dr. F. Smith, a staff doctor at the Ford Hospital, reported that Ford's views on diet and health often reached the absurd. When a friend of his returned from South Dakota, where the hot winds gave him sunburn and sore lips, Ford took a look at his friend and said he had been eating too many eggs. On another occasion, when one of his guests fainted at one of Ford's old-time dances, Dr. Smith suggested the man needed fresh air and a trip home. Mr. Ford asked his guest if he had drunk milk during the day. When the guest admitted this fact, Ford told him to go back and choose his partner for the next quadrille. Sometimes Ford visited heart patients in his hospital where he told them to disregard the instructions of the doctors, but to get out of bed and lie on the floor twice a day for half an hour, and eat celery, corn, and carrots until they were all right again. Once Dr. Smith treated Ford for a severe case of bronchitis, but the patient refused the medicines because the doctor could not describe the manufacturing process in their production. In making another call on Ford on his birthday, he ordered him to bed because he had a temperature of 103 degrees. Ford refused. A few days later Ford saw Dr. Smith who admitted he had been unable to diagnose the problem. Then Ford explained that he always ran a mile on his birthday and finished off with a hot shower. This was the cause of his fever.

To satisfy this curiosity about the relation of diet to health, Ford hired Dr. Edsel A. Ruddiman, a boyhood companion, to experiment with foods. Dr. Ruddiman received his M. D. from Vanderbilt University and served as professor of pharmacy at that institution for twenty years. He joined Ford in 1926 and remained with the company until 1942.

At one time, Ford instructed Ruddiman to prepare a biscuit possessing all the vitamins required for good health. Like a good soldier, the chemist created a biscuit out of soybeans and various chemicals. Ford ate these and offered them to friends who were in no position to refuse them. Harold M. Cordell, one of Ford's secretaries, described the all-purpose vitamin biscuit as, "an awful tasting thing."[21] On occasion, Ford invited guests to dinner where he served nothing but a soybean menu; soybean hors d' oeuvres; soybean soup, soybean bread, soybean beans, soybean croquettes, soybean pie, soybean coffee, and soybean ice cream. The Ford Motor Company published booklets with dozens of recipes explaining how to prepare these delicacies.

The good word spread. Dietitians and Home Economics teachers testified that soybeans were high in vitamins A and D, that they were 100 percent digestible, that one pound of soybeans contained as much protein as two pounds of beef steak, and that soybean milk proved easier for babies to digest than cow's milk, and with a diminished degree of burping.[22] Dr. Ruddiman made the soybean milk by rubbing the beans with water to produce a white liquid rich in protein, then adding elements to make it equivalent to dairy milk. Later he recalled:

> Most of my work was with soybeans and Ford wanted to know how good they were for food. I did a lot of chemical analysis on them, separating them into fats, proteins, and carbohydrates and feeding them to rats. . . . Ford came in frequently and made suggestions, or to see what the results were. I guess I was responsible as anyone for making soybean milk. . . .[23]

All this gave Ford another chance to repeat his earlier slogan, "The Cow Must Go." In April, 1944, he prophesied that cows would be obsolete in five years, because soybean milk could be produced for three cents a quart. When a Georgia dairyman told Ford he did not like the taste of milk from cows fed soybean meal, Ford replied, "Get rid of the cows."

But sentimental and vested interests defended the cow. The *Southern Dairy Products Journal*, in an editorial entitled, "Can the Soybean Say Moo?" wondered if Ford had estimated all his costs when claiming synthetic milk could be produced for less than five cents a quart? Paul V. Chapman, Dean of the College of Agriculture at the University of Georgia, defended the cow by saying Americans would not accept a vegetable drink as a substitute for a

glass of cold cow's milk; neither would a plate of sprouting soybeans replace a nice thick juicy steak.[24]

Yet synthetic gains were made. The Detroit *Free Press* in 1938
noted the whole world had once laughed about Henry's mechanical
cow, but now companies were making candy out of soybeans and
sweet potatoes. The paper pointed out that Washington Carver had
extracted three hundred products from the peanut, and that soybeans were now in everything from high class foods to door knobs.

Much of Ford's interest in agriculture during the 1930s centered
in chemurgy—a science putting chemistry to work in industry for
the direct benefit of farmers and indirectly for society in general. To
fight the depression, three hundred leaders of agriculture, industry,
and technology met in Dearborn in May, 1935, with Henry Ford
and Francis P. Garvin, president of the Chemical Foundation, as
joint hosts. Here was born the National Farm Chemurgic Council,
an organization designed to cope with the economic ills of farming.
These leaders decided that some destination other than the human
stomach must be found for the surplus products of the soil. Industrialists, farmers, and scientists would seek to advance the industrial use of farm crops through applied science and technological
innovation. Although Ford had attempted to move in this direction
fifteen years earlier, he had acted alone; now he prepared to cooperate in this endeavor with others. He opened the conference by
saying men's sustenance issued from the soil and not from merchant's shelves. When industrial centralization caused harmful congestion in the cities, men must return to the soil. Science as a new
frontier could conquer the agricultural depression. The conference
pledged cooperation and adopted a resolution calling for less re-
liance on man's vain intellect and placing more on nature's laws.

With the assistance of twenty-five state chemurgic councils,
almost a million dollars were raised to encourage research with
farm products. Efforts were made to convert pine trees into cellulose and paper pulp, to extract starch from sweet potatoes, to secure
rubber from native plants, and to produce industrial alcohol from
corn, barley, rye, wheat, potatoes, and grain sorghums. "Argol," an
alcohol blend with gasoline, might utilize the crops grown on fifty
million acres and bring farmers half a billion dollars annually. New
jobs for half a million workers would be created. The Argol plant
at Atchinson, Kansas, went into production and produced alcohol
which was mixed with gasoline and burned in automobiles and tractors. Although observers claimed the alcohol additive made motors

easier to start, produced less knock, and gave smoother performance than gasoline alone, the product could not compete with the petroleum corporations.

Naturally these efforts stirred interest. The United States Department of Agriculture established a soybean industrial research laboratory at Urbana, Illinois. Katherine Dos Passos, writing for the *Woman's Home Companion*, noted that state chemurgic councils were cooperating with federal government laboratories, state universities, and privately owned laboratories.[25] Since the Germans had manufactured antifatigue pills from soybean flour which could sustain soldiers on a 30-mile hike, it was urged that the United States should do likewise. In addition, soybeans could be used as filler in sausage, as a base for water paints, as a body for beer, and for making enamels, solvents, and for the hardening of steel. Experts at Iowa State College at Ames recommended soybeans for fattening beef cattle. Various business firms used the beans for producing printing ink, breakfast foods, and insecticides. The Ford Motor Company sold soybean meal to farmers for feeding livestock and poultry. The Ford processing plants at Saline and Milan, Michigan, exchanged the farmer's beans from the field for 44 percent soybean meal. These developments help explain why the soybean acreage in the United States jumped from one million acres in 1934 to twelve million acres in 1944.[26]

Something of the extent of Henry Ford's concern for rural Americans can be seen in his concern with the boll weevil, the enemy of cotton growers. This pest is thought to have originated in Latin America, spreading across Mexico and into Texas in 1892, then moving eastward through the cotton belt, reaching the Atlantic in 1916. Government officials estimated the annual loss from 1920 to 1924 as $300 million. Cotton yields in Georgia and South Carolina were cut in half in 1921. Losses since 1900 were equivalent to 500 shirts for every male in the United States.[27]

When this beetle emerges from the larva, a white curved grub, it grows into an insect one-third inch long, grayish-brown, and resembles a huge fly. Using its sharp beak as a sword, the weevil attacks the flower buds and green bolls of the plant, causing the leaves around the buds to discolor, flare out, and turn a sickly yellow. The buds drop off but the damaged bolls hang to the plant, becoming stunted, and, if late in the season, rotted. The female cuts a hole in the square (bud) and lays the eggs, which hatch in three days and the life cycle begins over again. A single pair can produce twelve million weevils in a season. They are not attracted to light, hibernate in winter, thrive in damp weather, feed entirely on cotton plants, and will feign death by playing possum. Natural enemies are direct rays of the sun, ants, birds, and forty-five other insects. Methods of control include spraying with calcium arsenate, and plowing under all vegetation to destroy the beetle's food supply.

Since the cotton crop produced an income that exceeded the gold mines of the world, the boll weevil challenged entomologists and state and federal agencies. All combined to fight the billion-dollar bug.

At the Ford Motor Company, William H. Smith headed the research on the boll weevil situation. He used the familiar technique of asking branch managers to secure the latest information in their region. The manager in Manchester, England, forwarded three articles on the subject which described the problem in Egypt; the French official in Bordeaux explained the use of chloropierine in Algeria to treat the cotton seed before planting, while the Danish representative stated that cotton was "inextinct in Denmark." Company officials in the United States forwarded information from the National Boll Weevil Control Association in New Orleans, and from the Bureau of Standards in Washington, D. C. The United States Geological Survey referred to the arsenic deposits in western states. The manager in Atlanta stated that an old gentleman had been selling a boll weevil poison called "Shuford's Killum Quick." He made the discovery of a nicotine mixture when a friend sent him some boll weevils in a snuff box. When the box was opened all were dead. His formula used snuff mixed with water, syrup, and banana, and letting the solution stand for four days. The solution sold for $15 a hundred pounds.

It appeared that one of the better ways to defeat the weevil was to add nitrate fertilizers to the soil which pushed the cotton plants to an earlier maturity, thus destroying the weevils time table. Since cotton placed a heavy drain on nitrogen in the soil, 65 percent of the commercial fertilizer sold in 1924 went to Southern states. If Henry Ford secured Muscle Shoals, he could provide cheap fertilizers which in turn would combat the weevil. R. R. Moton, of the Tuskegee Institute, addressing a conference in 1923 stated that 85 percent of the Blacks in the South lived on farms. They were in poverty because of an inability to buy fertilizers and produce good cotton crops. He added, "If Ford gets Muscle Shoals, he will make Calcium Arsenate to kill the boll weevil, whereas today we cannot get arsenate in sufficient quantities to prove effective at any price."[28]

Although Ford failed to get Muscle Shoals, he distributed thousands of pamphlets to cotton farmers explaining the habits of the weevil and the best methods to war against their ravages.

Meanwhile, Henry Ford continued his interest in ecology by waging a battle against waste. Because of his phobia, engineers in his company tried to salvage everything from floor sweepings to platinum. Wood shavings were converted into charcoal briquets, formaldehyde, creosote, and ethyl acetate. Coal derivatives yielded coke, benzol, and ammonium sulfate, while the slag from steel furnaces was used for surfacing roads. In 1925 the company sold coke commercially as well as ammonium sulfate as fertilizer. Eighty-eight gas stations in Detroit sold benzol to auto drivers at the same price as gasoline. Seven tons of Dearborn garbage were distilled daily in the River Rouge plant where it yielded alcohol, refined oil, and gas suitable for heating purposes. Residues were mixed with sand and sold as fertilizer to greenhouses. Tests were made to extract soap from the sewage in Detroit. Sale of the various Ford by-products in 1928 amounted to $20 million. The New York *Times* in 1930 claimed Ford threw nothing away, not even the smoke from his factories. Wilhelm Leopold, editor of the Munich *Neueste Nachrichten,* on February 10, 1924, facetiously suggested that, "We should not be too shocked to read one day that Ford makes use of the high temperature of his fevering patients in his hospital for the drying plants of his factory."

Ford's preoccupation with farming reflected humanitarian motives as well as his own financial interest. He admitted that if he wanted customers, he must be a customer as well. Perhaps this is why he talked about the cooperation of industry and agriculture. At the same time, he was serious about conservation of natural resources. He often said that automobiles should be grown, not mined from the earth. News releases from his offices reminded Americans that Ford used straw mixed with sulphur and a rubber base to form "Fordite" used to manufacture steering wheels for the Model T. To make a million cars in 1935, his factories consumed cotton from 433,000 acres, wool from 800,000 sheep, hair from 87,000 goats, leather from 30,000 cattle, lard from 20,000 hogs, linseed from 17,000 acres of flax, sugar cane from 13,000 acres, corn from 12,000 acres, and soybeans from 60,000 acres. W. J. Cameron, in one of his Sunday Evening radio hours, got down to such fine points as explaining that the beeswax used in electrical systems required the work of 93 million industrious bees.

In spite of Ford's scientific bent, he never spent much time fraternizing with professional scientists. He avoided scientific organizations, stayed away from meetings of learned scholars, and ignored status symbols. He respected sciential experts and often sought their advice, but his personal friends were practical, self-made fellows who worked with their hands and had the common touch. Thomas Edison, Luther Burbank, John Burroughs, Harvey Firestone, and Washington Carver fit his style—men who got things done without putting on airs. Ford and Edison shared their devotion to technology and had similar views on education, religion, money, and the Puritan ethic. Firestone and Ford had industrialization, mass production, and a competitive spirit in common. Luther Burbank and Ford appreciated the land and its ability to produce the abundant things of life. They had an affinity for nature, the mysteries of botany, and possessed the sensitivity of such naturalists as Henry Thoreau and John Muir. Henry Ford visited Burbank's home in Santa Rosa, California, in 1915, during the Pan American Exposition in San Francisco. Later he was impressed with the three thousand experiments that Burbank had conducted by 1923 to produce better potatoes, fruit, flowers, and trees. The botanist estimated that his thirteen acres would be worth a billion dollars an acre if all his new creations were put to use in the world. Today, in Greenfield Village in Dearborn stands a small building which was Burbank's original experimental shop in Santa Rosa—a fitting tribute to a man who had been a benefactor to millions.

Ford also developed a strong friendship with George Washington Carver. The two met at a meeting of the National Farm Chemurgic Council in Dearborn in 1937, where Carver spoke about new methods in farming. When interviewed, Ford deferred to Carver saying, "I agree with everything he thinks and he thinks the same way I do."[29] Carver had taught at Iowa State College and at Tuskegee Institute. When the boll weevil damaged cotton crops, he had urged planting peanuts. The humble Black scientist discovered 300 useful substances in the peanut, and 188 products in the sweet potato. Before his death in 1943, peanuts, once thought of as limited to the circus and baseball games, ranked next to cotton in value in several states.

Ford maintained this friendship, visiting Dr. Carver at Tuskegee and inviting him to stay at the Ford winter home at Ways,

Georgia, where the Ford school was named for the scientist. He also brought Carver to Dearborn as a guest where he could continue his scientific work. At times the two shared their eccentricities in food, such as eating dandelion and grass sandwiches. Carver believed Ford right in predicting the demise of the cow because, "with the abundance of food stuff that we have in nature's garden, there is absolutely no sense of anyone going hungry."[30]

Supporting his agricultural theories, Ford used his own farm to prove the blessings of science and technology. In 1922 he operated his farm near Dearborn without a horse on the place. Five years later, he insisted all farm work for small grain could be done in twenty days of the year. The land could be plowed in two days, cultivated in five days, harvested in two days, leaving ten days for fencing, ditching, and fertilizing. Labor-saving machinery, intensive specialization, and efficient organization would do the trick. By reducing the cost of production, lower prices for farm commodities would not be disastrous; all this had been proved by the auto industry. Ray Dahlinger, who supervised seven hundred men on the Ford farms in 1924, often sent forty plowing outfits into the field at one time, much like the bonanza farmers in the Red River Valley in the 1890s.

Ford took a personal interest in his farming operations. Fred Black, one of Ford's associates, emphasized that Ford's priorities were first the events at Dearborn, then his farms, and lastly the River Rouge plant. Ray Newman, a farm foreman, said Ford could be seen out early in the morning driving through the fields. He had various trails cut through the fields and woods where he hiked along at a rapid pace. Above all, Ford loved the land. As with Pearl Buck, the soil was the "Good Earth." As a result, he spent most of his adult life buying land in Michigan, in the Southern States, in New England, and in Great Britain. After his death, officials of the Ford Motor Company attempted to compile a history of his real estate deals. The records of L. J. Thompson reveal that as early as 1902, he purchased fifty-one acres in Dearborn and Springwells townships for $4,000. Each year he added to his holdings, until in 1915 he owned 2,843 acres with a cost of $3,754,045; in 1931 his acreage in Michigan reached 8,486 acres; by 1947 he had invested $14 million in land, most of which was used for agricultural purposes. Elmer See of Walled Lake, Michigan, commuted to his work in the automotive factories in Detroit for over thirty years. He recalls that as he drove along the highway he could see the Ford fields of wheat, corn, and alfalfa, the dairy barns, the farm machinery at work, and the hired hands in the field. These fields extended to within eight miles of downtown Detroit, the world's automotive industrial center. They remained intact up until the death of Henry Ford in 1947—a symbol of the manufacturer's abiding involvement in American agriculture. Today, the 10-story Central Ford Motor Company Office Building stands off Michigan Avenue, where a few years ago these acres waved with fields of corn. The parking lots, the black top, the Keep-off-the-Grass signs, and the tract houses of suburbia reflect changing times.

Admittedly, it is difficult to measure Henry Ford's scientific and technological contribution to rural life in America because techniques for measuring them are often unreliable. The voices of some need not represent the views of the multitudes. Although Ford's work impressed many, not everyone worshipped the "Great White Father of Fair Lane." Some critics claimed his words outran his deeds, that his press clippings overshadowed his performance, that he dabbled in science instead of initiating well-planned research programs. Those who hated men of wealth accused the Motor King of purchasing hobbies because he had more money than he could invest in his business. Still others accused him of being ignorant of the cultural arts and devoid of sympathy for philanthropy; hence he turned to things he knew best, science, farming, and the practical aspects of technology.

On the other hand, a careful examination of the record will prove that his scientific interest in agriculture was genuine. Over the span of years, he never apologized for his agrarian background and his love of agriculture. He believed science and technology led to Progress. Convinced of this fact, he became a propagandist for the cause. He talked science, saying its application to technology would lead to the promised land. To the skeptical, he preached faith in the machine, to the doubter, he suggested innovation, and to the conservative, he advocated change. Thus the automobile, truck, and tractor must replace horses, and machines eliminate cows. Farmers would become fully mechanized, while chemurgy would develop industrial uses for farm crops. Waste must be eliminated in farming and in industry. Solutions to farm problems lay in individual enterprise, not with paternal governmental agencies. By today's standards, Ford's attitudes toward national politics, labor organizations, and social responsibility seem a bit naïve. Yet his views on technology, conservation, ecology, and the mechanization of rural America were generally prophetic, enlightened, progressive, and often far ahead of his times. In appropriate fashion, the American Society of Mechanical Engineers in 1939 presented Henry Ford a medal for, "Distinguished service in science and for great and unique acts of an engineering nature that have accomplished a timely benefit to the public."[31]

IX

Ford's Politics and the Common Man

Henry Ford's political pull among rural Americans during the height of his popularity from 1914 to 1929 approached the incredible. The press called it the "Ford Craze" because nothing quite like it had entered the annals of our political history. Here was a man limited in formal education, devoid of cultural interests, one who gave few public speeches, and a shy personality who sought quietude. Usually he exhibited about as much interest in politics as a hermit. Nevertheless, he excited the little people, those who had failed to make the grade. Out in the great open spaces where the farm families rode in Model Ts and Ford trucks moved in a cloud of dust on summer days, voters accepted the notion that since Uncle Henry made a good car he could enter the White House and manage a good government. Thus a sort of mass hypnosis flowed from the Ford image. This, no doubt, is why they gave him strong support in the presidential primaries in Michigan and Nebraska in 1916, ran him for senator in Michigan in 1918, gave him support in the presidential nominating convention in Chicago in 1920, and urged him to lead a third party movement.

For one who insisted that he had virtually no interest in politics, this political veneration seems most unusual. Such support never gravitated to John D. Rockefeller, James J. Hill, the Vanderbilts, or the Mellons. Senator James Couzens, puzzled by events in 1923, complained, "Why Ford for President? It is ridiculous. How can a man over sixty years old, who has done nothing but make motors, who has no training, no experience, aspire to such an office. It is most ridiculous."[1]

But millions thought Ford qualified for public office and frequently told him so. He paid his factory workers five and six dollars a day; this pleased the laboring man. In financing his company he licked the tar out of Wall Street; this appealed to those in debt. He wanted Muscle Shoals to make cheap fertilizers; this delighted the farmers. He criticized the Jews; this catered to the bigots. He advocated soft money; this provided solace to the poor with an ingrained weakness for inflation. Above all, he was well known. Each Model T leaving his factories advertised his name. A Nebraska editor in 1916 believed it easy to account for his appeal to the rural electorate because, "When the list of his employees and those who use his cars is subtracted from the vote in any general election, not much of the polling strength of that commonwealth remains."[2]

Ford's political baptism occurred in Michigan where friends circulated petitions putting him on the presidential preference ballot of the Republican Party in the spring of 1916. According to Ernest G. Liebold, Ford's secretary, the first impetus came from correspondents who urged the auto maker to run for the office of President of the United States. As these letters increased, Liebold called the matter to Ford's attention. His initial response was negative. On one occasion he said he would not take political office if it were handed to him on a silver platter. He thought the filing of his name was a joke and he did not want anything to do with political campaigns. When he asked that his name be kept off the primary ballot, the request came twenty-four hours after the lists had been closed.

Subsequently, the Republican ballot presented the names of Senator William Alden Smith, William G. Simpson, and Henry Ford. Smith had served six terms in the House of Representatives in Washington, D.C., and one in the Senate. Woodrow Wilson carried the Democratic banner.

The election did little to electrify the citizens of the Wolverine state, although it provided a few comic overtones. Senator Smith gave some bland speeches, while Ford refused to engage in forensic battle and stayed home. Critics said that Ford had voted only six times in his life and then only because of the urging of his wife.

The April election returns showed Ford the winner with 83,058 votes, Smith, 77,872, Theodore Roosevelt, 1,074 and Charles E. Hughes, 303.[3] Ford had surprised those who believed he would fail to carry a rock-ribbed Republican state against a seasoned campaigner like Senator Smith. The *Independent* attributed the victory to Ford's powerful hold on the popular imagination of the common man.[4]

Two weeks later Ford pulled another surprise in the Nebraska presidential primary by almost defeating Senator Albert B. Cummins of Iowa, and running ahead of Charles E. Hughes and Henry D. Estabrook. Early returns gave Ford the lead, but final results put Cummins ahead of Ford by a scant 464 votes.[5]

These events raised the question as to why Henry Ford was being supported as a candidate for the office of President of the United States. His popularity had to rest on factors aside from the fact he manufactured Model T cars.

Some cynics claimed elections brought out the numbskull vote. A Michigan newspaper said people cast their ballots in a moment of absent mindedness, like doodling when making telephone calls— the hands being occupied while the mind relaxed.

The temper of the times suggests that the political support for Henry Ford in the midwest in 1916 stemmed from the candidate's devotion to pacifism. The outbreak of war in Europe in 1914 divided Americans on military preparedness, military conscription, and the manufacture of munitions. The debate over these issues was bitter. In 1914 Ford suggested the word murderer should be embroidered on the breast of every soldier and sailor. Every man in the army was either lazy or crazy. If the United States became involved in the conflict, and he were asked to make munitions, he would burn down his plants before accepting these orders. "I don't believe in preparedness," he added. "It's like a man carrying a gun. Men and nations who carry guns get into trouble. If I had my way, I'd throw every ounce of gun powder into the sea and strip the soldiers and sailors of their insignias."[6] When informed of the death of twenty thousand soldiers in one day's fighting without changing the battle line on the Western Front, he vowed he would gladly spend half his fortune if it would shorten the war by one day.

These pacifist doctrines had been reinforced by midwestern farm journals which attacked corporations for profiteering in munitions making. Steel companies were accused of gouging the government shamelessly in armor plate contracts. The *Nebraska Farmer* on March 29, 1916, claimed the war lords wanted to draft men into the army and compel them to work for low wages, while they connived to bring about a war so that millions would roll into their coffers. "A fine lot of patriots they are," added the journal. James Pearson, Nebraska's Lieutenant Governor, believed the primary election in his state proved that midwestern farmers disliked President Wilson's preparedness policies and turned to Ford as a peace candidate.

This may explain why Henry Ford ran much better in the primary races than Theodore Roosevelt. T. R. had alienated many Republicans when he bolted the party in 1912 to head the Bull Moose party. He had attacked Wilson's foreign policy as being too timid. Responding to Wilson's "Too proud to fight" speech, Roosevelt sneered, "Professor Wilson, that Byzantine logothete, supported by all the flubdubs, mollycoddles, and flapdoodle pacifists."[7]

The pro-Ford crowd, with more exuberance than tact, ridiculed the Rough Rider, calling him the egotist of Oyster Bay, an incorrigible politician, and the strenuous one who wanted to saddle European militarism on dear old Uncle Sam. A Massachusetts farmer promised Henry Ford he would round up fifty thousand voters in his state to defeat Roosevelt.

The role of Henry Ford in American politics in 1916 cannot be evaluated without reference to the "Peace Ship" episode. Although the basic facts in this venture are well known, the significance of these events needs further interpretation.

Henry Ford had grown up in a family that hated violence and war, and it was not surprising that he joined the American Peace Society in the fall of 1915. There he met Rosika Schwimmer, the Hungarian pacifist, in November of that year. Madam Schwimmer believed that any war which ended in a complete military victory for one side would eventually lead to further conflict. Therefore she wanted to stop the European war before the militarists were ready to quit fighting. She urged the establishment of an organization which would provide a forum for continuous mediation of international disputes. Neutral countries could provide this service by calling a conference. When Woodrow Wilson refused to call such a meeting, Madam Schwimmer and other pacifists toured the United States soliciting support for the idea. It was on one of these tours that Madam Schwimmer met Henry Ford, who was eager to help implement some program of direct action. Later in a meeting in New York, the Peace Ship venture was born. A group of delegates would go to Europe as negotiators to offer mediation to the warring parties.

Since the expedition needed passengers, telegrams were addressed to prominent people such as Thomas Edison, William Howard Taft, Luther Burbank, William Jennings Bryan, David

Starr Jordan, and Ben Lindsey. Many refused the invitation, but the *Oscar II* pushed away from a Hoboken dock on December 5, 1915, with 83 delegates, 54 reporters, 50 technical advisers, 18 college students, and three photographers—an array which Charles E. Sorensen called the "strangest assortment of living creatures since the voyage of Noah's Ark."

Losing sight of the pilgrims' real mission, journalists stressed the bizarre, such as the prankster who sent two caged squirrels to Ford; the newsmen who organized themselves into the Friendly Sons of St. Vitus, and the cable to Rome to get the blessing of Pope Pius VII, who happened to have died in 983 A.D. Editors tossed off such phrases as "Ford's Folly," the "jitney-peace excursion," and "more innocents abroad." The Boston *Traveler* commented: "It is not Mr. Ford's purpose to make peace. He will assemble it."[8]

During the fourteen-day voyage, morale plummeted. Here was a divided reaction to President's Wilson's message to Congress on December 7 which called for military preparedness; Henry Ford, the stabilizing influence among the leaders, came down with a cold and spent much of the time in his cabin; and Madam Schwimmer proved rather dictatorial and domineering. When the *Oscar II* reached Oslo, after surviving submarine-infested waters, Ford left the party on December 23 and returned to the United States on the *Bergensfjord*. This gave the impression that *he* was trying to get out of Europe by Christmas. The peace delegation visited Sweden and Denmark, however, and then received permission to cross Germany by train to Holland. A committee for continuous mediation scheduled other meetings in Stockholm and at the Hague. But by January 15 the peace party disbanded, with students and delegates returning to New York.

Obviously the Peace Ship adventure suffered from hasty planning, questionable actions, and a bad press on both sides of the Atlantic. The London *Times* referred to the members of the Ford Mission as faddists, propagandists-socialists, suffragists, and social reformers who tried to turn disgust into approbation.[9] One news item merely announced that the Ford Peace Party arrived in the Hague to hold its meetings in the Zoological Gardens.

Although this mission was vilified in many quarters, the venture is now beginning to be seen in better perspective. The endeavor contained genuine idealism, with a desire to save humanity from war and death. One of the college students who made the trip, Christian A. Sorenson, of Grand Island College in Nebraska, spoke for youth when he gave a speech aboard the *Oscar II*. He warned against making America an armed camp, he opposed military conscription, he decried the wasted bodies on battlefields. Speaking metaphorically, he suggested gathering all the skulls of Europe's dead and building a pyramid a mile square and reaching to the clouds. With a giant pen dipped in the blood of Verdun he would write militarism as a monument to greed and war. He pleaded:

> Let us hear from the wives who will be widows and the young maidens who die of broken hearts. Let us hear from young men in shops and farms who will fall in trenches, there to die like cattle and be burned like piles of rubbish. The English verse puts it aptly; "Damn the army; damn the war. Oh what bloody fools we are."[10]

More recently, Walter Millis saw the ridicule of the Ford Peace Ship as the "undying shame of American journalism."[11] The idea of continuous mediation relied on the concept that the building of a new world depended on how the war ended. If one could read history backward and envision a negotiated peace in 1916 with neither Allies or Central Powers defeated, perhaps the postwar collapse of Europe might have been avoided. Had this occurred, governments might have been spared the forces of Communism, Fascism, and Nazism. Today the concept of continuous mediation lives in the charter of the United Nations. In this sense, Ford and his associates were ahead of the times. Perhaps Ford's expenditure of nearly half a million dollars in behalf of his principles did not represent failure. He could take consolation in the words of Rabbi Joseph Krauskopf of Philadelphia who attacked the critics of Ford in 1915, saying, he would "rather a thousand times be branded a fool in the service of humanity than be hailed a hero for having shed rivers of blood."[12]

Against this background of dramatic events, Henry Ford's entry into politics evoked considerable enthusiasm among farmers and working people, many of whom wrote to Detroit to voice their support. An unsolicited tribute from North Carolina stated, "Now I want you to fight the munition manufacturers. I am just a humble farmer, but my three greatest desires are to vote for Ford, own a Ford, and see Ford elected president by the greatest majority given any man."[13] A preacher wanted more prayers, not ammunition, to support Ford.[14] A steel worker in Duluth, Minnesota, who could speak seven different languages, offered to hit the road to plug for

Ford votes.[15] Citizens of Parker, South Dakota, printed handbills announcing, "No names are greater in the whole universe than George Washington, Abraham Lincoln, and Henry Ford."[16]

Fearing that Ford might feel inferior because of his limited education, many proffered such consoling thoughts as: universities often extinguished the spark of genius in students; and after all, a shepherd boy, David, wrote the Psalms, Jesus missed a formal education, Joan of Arc was an untutored peasant, and Abraham Lincoln had little formal training. Besides, Ford had accomplished more for humanity than any first class grammarian in the nation. America would not reject him because he lacked training in orthography, etymology, syntax, and prosody.

During the summer of 1916, promoters of third party movements attempted to lure the auto magnate into their fold. Members of the American Party, now seventeen years old, begged Ford to lead them because he could cure the ills of society and act as a Moses to guide an unhappy nation out of Egypt.

The Prohibition Party made a serious effort to entice him to accept one of their posts of leadership. Daniel B. Poling, a prominent clergyman, on June 30, 1916, asked Ford to head the party in the coming election. A ticket based on Peace and Prohibition could poll three million votes and perhaps capture the government. During the Prohibition National Convention in St. Paul, Minnesota, in July, Poling called for unparalled sacrifices to promote peace, prosperity, and prohibition. Voters should elect prohibition, write woman into the Constitution, take the profit out of war, stop killing peace, save America and the world.[17]

But Ford refused to encourage these zealots. His secretary notified correspondents that Ford had no interest in politics and would not accept a nomination to a third party. In response to fan mail, G. S. Anderson, Ford's assistant secretary, drafted a form letter to answer those urging Ford's candidacy for nomination of president. This letter stated that Ford had repeatedly declined to run for office and "We do not believe any influence could be brought to bear to alter his decision. . . ."

At the Republican Nominating Convention in Chicago on June 7, the question arose whether Republicans and Progressives could cooperate. If they could unite, Wilson might be defeated; if they could not, and Roosevelt ran on the Progressive Party ticket, Wilson would win the fall election. The militarist faction criticized Wilson's foreign policy and urged Roosevelt's candidacy, while the doves feared Wilson's rearmament policies might lead to war. Since Charles Evan Hughes was the only candidate who could satisfy both factions, he received the nomination on the first ballot with two hundred fifty-three and one-half votes. Henry Ford received thirty-two votes, running behind Hughes, Weeks, Root, Cummins, Burton, Fairbanks, Sherman, and Knox, but ahead of La Follette, Borah, Harding, Willis, Mc Call, DuPont, Wood, Wanamaker, and Brumbaugh.[18] Meanwhile, the Progressives met in Chicago, where Theodore Roosevelt withdrew and threw his support to Hughes. Thus the Progressive Party came to an end as a significant factor in American politics.

After Woodrow Wilson accepted renomination at the Democratic National Convention in St. Louis on June 14, Henry Ford drifted toward his camp. Within thirty days, his secretary E. G. Liebold was sending out the word that Ford would not oppose the re-election of Wilson. In October, a Ford advertisement, costing $58,800 which favored Wilson, appeared in 500 newspapers. During the fall campaign, the Democrats made good use of Ford's statement that, "I spent four hours with him the other day and found him the most humane man, the most sensible man, the most businesslike man withal, I ever encountered."[19] There seems to be no doubt that Ford's endorsement helped swing California for Wilson in the election.

During World War I, political feelings had run high and by 1918 the Republicans were determined to gain control of Congress from the Democrats. To Wilson, bent on establishing a League of Nations, the composition of the Senate seemed crucial. Although Michigan was traditionally Republican, Henry Ford might save the day. With this in mind, President Wilson invited Ford to Washington for a conference on June 13, 1918. E. G. Liebold, who accompanied Ford on the trip, later recalled, "I remember Mr. Ford coming out of the White House accompanied by the President who came to the door step and finally bid him good-bye. Mr. Ford got in the car and said, "He wants me to run for Senator."[20]

Subsequently, Ford entered the primary election on both party tickets. He defeated James W. Helme on the Democratic slate 30,791 to 8,414, but Truman Newberry won the Republican primary with 114,963 votes to 47,100 for Chase Osborn, and 71,800 for Ford.

To win the senatorship would have been a difficult task for Ford because Michigan was heavily Republican with an able opponent heading the ticket. Truman Newberry, a Yale graduate and an attorney, served in the Spanish-American War, owned part of the Packard Motor Company, and later became Secretary of the Navy in Theodore Roosevelt's cabinet. He campaigned vigorously, and received $176,568 in support from the Republican organization in Michigan.[21]

Although fully committed to Wilson's idealism, Ford failed to take positive political action. He seemed to accept the honors but evade the responsibilities. One newspaper reporter complained, that instead of campaigning, Ford had gone fishing, more concerned about the size of the bass than his candidacy for the United States Senate. "He hasn't spent a cent, paid for a banner, bought the boys any drinks and cigars, hired a press agent, made any speeches, or kissed a baby since the Democrats endorsed him in June."[22]

Although Ford remained inactive, his friends put up a good fight. Ford-For-Senator Clubs were organized, campaign literature published, and news releases given to the press. A poor farm boy had risen to a leading manufacturer of automobiles, trucks, and tractors. He had converted his factories to war production, making Liberty motors, steel helmets, army trucks, Eagle Marine boats, and small tanks, and had turned his hospital over to the government to care for the wounded. He was the Kaiser's greatest enemy. Here was a man of action, not a speech maker.[23]

In opposition, the Newberry forces stressed personalities rather than issues. Ford had rapport with the common man, but lacked intellectual ability, foresight, and political acumen. He had produced great industrial works, but the Senate was not a factory. It made laws, not Lizzies. The editor of the Chicago *Tribune* commented bitterly, "If we had a Senate full of Henry Fords, the best thing the people of the United States could do would be to put out to sea in lifeboats."[24]

Ford's earlier pacifistic utterances were also exhumed and used to discredit him. His statements that he did not believe in boundaries, that nations and flags were silly, that nobody should respect a rotten country, and that after the war he would pull down the American flag from his factories and replace it with a flag of all nations—all these remarks were aired again in public. Rumors claimed he had shielded pro-German workers in his factories, and that he had threatened to withdraw all his money from banks which subscribed to the Liberty bond drives.

This mud slinging continued, with the Newberry faction insisting Henry Ford used his wealth and influence to procure a draft deferment for Edsel. The Detroit draft board first put Edsel in Class 2 under the original provisions of the law. He appealed to the district board for an industrial exemption. This board rejected his appeal and reclassified him Class 1. He appealed to the President in Washington and this appeal was pending when the new draft regulations took effect. His case, like others, was brought under new regulations and, in accordance with the information contained in the new questionnaire, Edsel was placed in Class 2-A as having dependents and in Class L as being indispensable in industry.

Although Henry needed his son to turn out war materials, and took a position which later experience proved reasonable, the short tempers of wartime prompted the opposition to shout "slacker" and "coward." Some claimed Edsel remained safe in a padded office chair while the less privileged died on the battlefields. Automobile stickers appeared with the words, "His Country Needs Edsel. Where is He?" and "I Helped Keep Ford Out Of The Senate." Comments circulated saying Ford was more successful in keeping his boy out of the trenches than he was in getting other boys out by Christmas.

The pro-Ford supporters claimed Newberry had spent $250,000 in the primary election, an amount equivalent to buying votes at $3.05 per ballot. He had contributed money to churches to purchase the minister's influence in his behalf. Ford campaign workers put campaign literature into farmer's cars parked on the small town streets on Saturday nights. Handbills admonished, "Notice the Lavish Use of Money for Newberry."

When Newberry defeated Ford by a vote of 217,088 to 212,751, the Republican camp rejoiced, while the defeated claimed campaign money had whipped Ford just as it sabotaged William Jennings Bryan in 1896. The downcast sent Ford condolences pointing to his good showing at the polls, called attention to the lies about him in the newspapers, and told him to stay in politics.

In retrospect, this election has been viewed as tragic in its implications. Had Ford put forth a little effort, had he carried the fight to the opposition, had he campaigned with vigor, he would have been senator. The importance of this race can be seen in the special session of Congress convened to consider the adoption of the League of Nations. In this session, the Republicans held forty-nine seats, the Democrats forty-seven. If Ford had been elected, the division would have been forty-eight to forty-eight. With Vice-President Marshall having the deciding vote, the Democrats could have organized the Senate committees and Henry Cabot Lodge would never have been chairman of the Foreign Relations Committee from where he effectively fought America's entry into the League of Nations. By being overly reticent and perhaps overly sensitive about his great wealth, Ford's soft approach helped defeat the crusades to which he was most deeply committed.

Again, had he shown some of the fight before the election that he manifested afterwards, the course of events would have been reversed. After the defeat he demanded a recount of the votes. When this failed he petitioned the Senate to investigate the cost of the Newberry primary campaign. The Senate vote for such an investigation was delayed until December, 1919. Meanwhile, the Federal Department of Justice impanelled a Grand Jury in Grand Rapids, Michigan, and Newberry and one hundred thirty-four of his associates were indicted. Revelations at the hearing were sensational. Each Newberry agent had been allotted $3,500 for twenty weeks of electioneering and money had changed hands like in a gambling casino. The Federal Corrupt Practices Law had been violated as well as the Federal statute against bribery. The defendants were also guilty of using campaign funds for their own purposes. Truman Newberry received a sentence of two years in prison and a fine of $10,000. He appealed his case to the United States Supreme Court which, on May 2, 1919, ruled five to four that Congress had exceeded its powers in trying to regulate a state primary election, thus Newberry's conviction was nullified. He resigned after four years in the Senate.

During the early 1920s, national politics hit the doldrums. Warren G. Harding, the darling of the ultraconservatives, occupied the White House. Harding had gone to Washington with misgivings about his ability and then demonstrated how justified his qualms had been.

This general discontent may have given birth to the Ford-For-President boom in 1920–23, although the specific motivating factors remain rather obscure. Some thought Henry Ford got the presidential bug during the Michigan primary in 1916, while others believed E. G. Liebold had been a moving force to elevate Ford to the White House.

At any rate, one hundred thirty-seven people met in Dearborn on May 24, 1922. After oratory lauding the manufacturer, a Dearborn Henry Ford-For-President club was formed. Later similar clubs sprang up all over the country. Part of the movement was spontaneous, with requests to enter the race coming from various organizations and from farmers individually.

As might be expected, Ford's initial reactions were indecisive. He seemed perplexed by the situation, kept his thoughts to himself, and remained distrustful of advice. One of the most resourceful of men in material things now stood at a loss in the presence of a problem which any Tammany leader would have undertaken with confidence. Even his own advisers were confused.

Speculation about Ford's availability for this office continued throughout 1923. Early in January, William J. Cameron, editor of the *Dearborn Independent*, let it be known that Ford did not discuss the presidency with anyone because his mind was on a thousand other things. By June the odds were changing, for E. G. Liebold released information indicating Ford would give consideration to an offer of the presidential nomination by any responsible party. At this point he would not object to activities supporting him. It is well to remember, however, that Ford never officially announced his candidacy for the office on any party ticket, nor did he ever say he coveted this honor.

Nevertheless, the absence of a formal commitment did not hinder him from acting like a politician hungry for votes. During the summer months when scores of newspapers ran banner lines, "Ford's Hat in the Ring," the motor magnate offered no denials. When Nebraskans wished to enter his name in the primary, he acknowledged the people's right to make a free choice of candidates. Arthur Brisbane wrote numerous laudatory editorials in the Hearst newspapers, while the press in general spoke of the seriousness with which professional politicians took Ford's candidacy.

Perhaps Mrs. Ford, with a woman's intuition, could see the bitterness that would accompany her husband's splash in national politics for she was incensed over the whole matter and accused Liebold of putting Henry up to it.

Regardless of family feelings, the Ford-For-President movement exploded, sending shock waves through the political camps of all parties. Convincing evidence exists to prove that had a popular referendum been held in July, 1923, to elect a president of the United States, the winner would have been Mr. Ford. Public opinion polls, newspaper analysis, and the views of astute politicians of the day substantiate this conclusion.

During June and July of 1923, *Collier's Weekly* conducted a poll over a four-week period in which 258,000 individuals were interviewed personally by a number of field agents. The results of the straw ballot showed Ford defeating President Warren G. Harding 88,865 to 51,000.[25] The editor of *Collier's* believed this vote represented a genuine cross section of public opinion. Unless he removed himself from contention, future political thought would revolve around him.[26] The *Kansas Farmer* commented on Ford's grip on the people's imagination. He operated an open shop, yet labor unions did not fight him; he piled up wealth faster than John D. Rockefeller, but was not denounced as a malefactor of wealth.[27] The Boston *Globe* said the poll revealed Harding unable to obtain a majority vote of his own party.[28]

In similar fashion, the Autocaster nation-wide survey during June tabulated almost 700,000 ballots, with Ford receiving 276,000 votes to Harding's 140,000. Ford with a two-to-one advantage over the President, held great strength in all sections of the country. These results were substantiated by Carl Richards of Baltimore who personally interviewed two thousand families in the Midwest. He found amazing sentiment favoring Ford in spite of the fact no one knew whether he was a Republican or Democrat.

Taken somewhat by surprise, professional politicians raised their eyebrows. In May, Senator Pat Harrison predicted Ford had more than an even chance of capturing the Democratic nomination for president in 1924. He had more popular backing than any other candidate; if he entered the fight it would be Ford against the field. He would carry the Democratic South, score heavily in the middle and far West, and gain the support of laboring men in the East. "I am not inflating a boom for him," stated the senator, "but the fact is he is tremendously strong among voters."[29] Similarly, Senator F. Ashurst, after returning in May from a nineteen-state tour, reported a spontaneous Ford boom, with old party leaders upset by his personal following among the rank and file in rural districts.[30] Rural people believed he would give them low freight rates and cheap fertilizers, while those in small towns thought he would reduce the prices of consumer goods.[31]

Meanwhile, Ford himself made pronouncements during the summer of 1923 which sounded like campaign rhetoric. In July he called prohibition a dead issue raised to hide vital economic questions. The Eighteenth Amendment would remain in the Constitution. Four weeks earlier he had suggested the Army and Navy enforce the Volstead Act because these men didn't have anything to do in peace time anyway. If they got busy they could stop the rum runners and dry up the source of booze.

Turning to the matter of war, he believed armed force was required to maintain peace, but thought war would be eliminated when the conditions which produced it were eliminated. His Peace Ship was still sailing on. He insisted he had never run for anything nor from anything. Newspapers interpreted Ford's slogan as being "Abolish Poverty," based on the Motor King's comments that government should coordinate industry, agriculture, and transportation. Tariffs were silly and immigration laws unnecessary. Workers must get accustomed to maximum production, but working hours must be reduced, wages raised, and the cause of strikes removed. He stated, "I want to abolish poverty in America. I want to make a good home possible for every child. Low wages are silly. You can't get rich by making people poor. They can't buy your goods and there you are. Manufacturers must become interested in higher wages. Wealth wouldn't be such a curse if everybody helped carry it."[32]

The farm depression of 1920–23 created rural discontent which now found expression in the "Ford for President" crusade. His offer to buy Muscle Shoals had seemed like an effort to aid the farmer. The *Rural New Yorker* in June, 1923, concluded that farmers were giving Ford strong support for the presidency. Various farm groups sent long lists of petitions to Detroit carrying such messages as, "Come and lead us out," "You are the Moses for 80 per cent of us," "No more politicians, lawyers or generals for us." "You have ginger, gumption and guts."[33]

Part of this inspiration lay in the notion that the United States needed a business man at the head of government. Since Henry had been so prosperous perhaps some of this luxury would rub off on the rest of the citizens. Clearly the need of the hour was a good business man, not a newspaper man or a college professor. Others used the Populist vernacular to attack the millionaires taking the bread and butter away from the mouths of the working class. The special interests had created a Muscle Shoals scandal, a tariff scandal, the Newberry scandal, the election of Harding in the La Salle Hotel in Chicago scandal, and were still demanding their pound of flesh.

These Ford fans deluged the Dearborn offices with advice on how to achieve victory at the polls. Designs for campaign buttons were submitted, as well as slogans such as "Ford Will Give Every

Man a Job." Many asked for election banners to affix to their Flivvers. One suggested a caravan of Ford cars crossing the nation flying
Ford pennants and distributing campaign literature.

Efforts should be made to de-emphasize the jokes about the
Model T because no joke could be elected President of the United
States. Others insisted his platform should include specific planks,
such as raising the wages of postal employees, abolition of usury,
keeping Britain in her place, and soaking the rich. A few suggested
he repeal all laws starting with the Constitution! Religionists, at
times, interpreted Ford in the light of what they understood to be
Biblical prophecy saying, it is written: "He will rise up a people
independent of all power save His spirit alone."[34]

Yet all were not eager to see Ford win the election. Several
advised him to abandon the race because his enemies would murder
him like they did Lincoln, Garfield, and McKinley. Others such as
Thomas Edison thought Ford more valuable in industry than in
politics. He asserted, "I would hate to see Henry Ford president
because it would spoil a good man."[35]

Many resented Ford's strong support for prohibition. James
Couzens disliked Ford's statement saying any reputable businessman knew the use of liquor was unwise. Many rural folks wrote
stating they were against the damnable prohibition laws and would
vote against anyone who favored them.

Some envisioned Ford as a miser giving little to organized
philanthropy, whereas the Rockefeller Foundation had served millions. Even the hobos, meeting in their International Brotherhood
Welfare Association convention in Baltimore on July 22, 1923, refused to endorse Ford for the presidency. James Eads, the so-called
Millionaire Hobo, announced that the organization would oppose
Ford because he stood for supervised charity, and this led to too
much surveillance from the police.[36]

Still others objected to Ford's candidacy because he was already too powerful. If president he might abolish railroads and substitute Ford trucks. Besides he would bring his own office staff to
Washington and make the cabinet an adjunct of the Ford Motor
Company.[37] His campaign funds could never be accounted for
under any corrupt practices law. He would advertise "Ford" and no
court would know whether he was advertising the car, tractor, or
presidential ambition. He could hire and fire thousands and no one
would be able to tell if he was conducting his business or managing
a political campaign. His patronage would be greater than a dozen
senators. He would have pork barrel projects under his own control

such as fertilizer plants, water-power plants, coal mines, railroads, factories, and newspapers. He would be able to do more for whole communities than Tammany Hall could do for individuals. While Tammany had to mix business with politics underhandedly, Ford could openly do business and conduct politics. He would have the best of both worlds. When he sold a car he sold himself; when he sold himself he would sell a car. Ford would not be Jack the Giant Killer, he would be the Giant himself.

Unquestionably Henry Ford's venture into journalism had political repercussions. Although it is impossible to measure the degree to which his paper the *Dearborn Independent* attracted or alienated voters, it is safe to say that in the long run it proved to be unfortunate. Had Ford run for the presidency in 1924, his associations with the views expressed in this organ would have been used against him with devastating effect.

Perhaps miffed by what he considered unfair attacks on him during the Michigan senatorial race in 1918, Ford had announced on November 3, 1918, that he would spend ten million dollars on a weekly to express his views on national and international affairs. There would be no advertising to give merchants a chance to influence the news. Acting fast, he bought the *Dearborn Independent*, a local paper, and hired Edward Pipp to manage it. When the editor failed to get the project moving, he turned the work over to E. G. Liebold, Fred Black, and William J. Cameron. Cameron, formerly of the Detroit *News*, had gained attention by writing an inspiring bit entitled, "Don't Die on First."

The first issue of the weekly appeared on January 11, 1919, a 16-page magazine selling for five cents a copy, and promising to be the "Chronicler of Neglected Truth." During the first year, the articles took stands against speculative capitalists, monopoly, and the gold standard. Comments favored government ownership of railroads, telephones, and federal works programs to guarantee jobs for everyone. The paper backed conservation, women's rights, pacifism, and compared Wilson's League of Nations to the Decalogue. Many of the writings expressed clichés about good citizenship, the challenge of the future, and the virtue in doing one's best. Liebold claimed the paper had been used in colleges as examples of fine writing, but Allan Nevins thought it had a muckraking flavor, ten years after muckraking went out of fashion.[38]

Other newspaper writers tended to poke fun at the *Dearborn Independent* calling it the best paper published by a tractor plant. It was the "dearly born *Independent*," "a rattling good newspaper," "the Ford Flivver Exhaust," and a "four-cylinder paper with the usual Ford bore." With an editor by the name of Pipp, people would think it a poultry publication. When rumor claimed that Ford would start a chain of newspapers, one reporter declared that one paper was enough to accommodate all of Ford's ideas.[39]

Although this paper had a rural bias and two-thirds of its readers lived on farms or in small towns, the subscription sales were disappointing. To boost sales, Ford dealers peddled the papers by distributing them in parked cars along the streets. Subscriptions finally reached 657,096 in 1926, but the Ford Motor Company lost over $4 million on the 12-year publishing venture.[40]

On May 22, 1920, the *Independent* became one of the most controversial subjects in the nation when it began the first of ninety-one articles under the general theme, "The International Jew: The World's Problem."[41] This series claimed the Jewish people had conspired to foment unrest among Gentiles, creating factions, thus permitting Jews to get control of the world's politics and finance. As a result, Jewish leaders controlled Wall Street, the liquor traffic, housing, the clothing industry, the theater, gambling, prostitution, and jazz. Everything from the spread of Darwinism to the Black Sox scandal was blamed on Jewish demoralizers. "The Jew is the world's enigma," intoned the *Dearborn Independent*, "poor in his masses, he yet controls the world's finances."[42]

The primary sources for these articles were twenty-four documents known as *The Protocols of the Learned Elders of Zion*, which outlined the steps planned to establish a Jewish world autocracy. Although copies of the *Protocols* did exist, the conspiracy did not. Jewish leaders stated there had never been an organization known as the Elders of Zion, and the *Protocols* had been proven to be forgeries.

Needless to say, Jewish people struck back, passing resolutions, publishing pamphlets, and filing law suits against Henry Ford. J. Aaron Lazar of Philadelphia published *Progress*, which featured such articles as "Stop Ford and the Ku Klux Klan," "The Menace of Fordism," and "Henry Ford Back of Universal Terrorism." When the Grand Lodge of B'rith Abraham met in Atlantic City on May 28, 1923, the convention adopted a resolution denouncing Ford as un-American and his candidacy for the presidency as an insult to the fundamentals upon which this country was based.[43] Rabbi Nathan Krass termed the *Dearborn Independent*'s attacks contemptible, bitter, poisonous, unholy, and constituting one of the scandalous episodes of our times.[44] Finally, during the Sapiro trial in Detroit, Henry Ford issued an apology on July 7, 1927. This apology was welcome, but most observers thought it arrived rather late.

In the midst of these hot issues, rapidly shifting political events in the late summer months of 1923 torpedoed the entire Ford-For-President boom. When President Harding returned from his trip to Alaska he became ill in Seattle and died six days later on August 2 in the Palace Hotel in San Francisco. Calvin Coolidge's move into the White House erased much of the scandal of the Harding regime and gave encouragement for better days ahead. In October, Ford hinted he would support Coolidge in 1924 if he promised to enforce prohibition. In return, Coolidge hinted he might not be adverse to Ford's bid for Muscle Shoals. Ford endorsed the candidacy of Coolidge on December 20, 1923, much to the relief of the "Sphinx of Northampton," who showed his gratitude by sending Ford a telegram expressing his thanks for this timely support.

Mixed reactions followed, with many congratulating Ford for bowing out of the race, while others feared America had lost its chance to elect its greatest president. A disappointed Minnesotan believed Ford "had chickened out, leaving us who thought we had a leader for the great Armageddon, the fight between right and wrong, between man and money, between freedom and slavery, between Christ and Satan. We now wonder if we haven't been worshipping a Tin God."[45]

In the following years Henry Ford withdrew from active politics, content to issue periodic statements on his presidential choices. In 1928 he suggested Will Rogers might make a good president because we needed someone with a sense of humor. Actually he supported Herbert Hoover in 1928 and 1932, and Alf Landon in 1936. As the "Sage of Fair Lane" grew older, he drifted further into the conservative camp. Horrified by the innovations of Franklin D. Roosevelt and his New Dealers, Ford stubbornly went his own way, unable to understand the trend of events which engulfed him. His motto might well have been that old-fashioned one implying all the virtues, "to so live that you can look any man in the face and tell him to go to hell."

X

The Great Depression and
the Ford Response

The stock market crash of October, 1929, followed by the Great Depression, produced a trauma which shocked the American people. The reverberations hit virtually everybody and few escaped its pernicious economic or psychological effects. Henry Ford survived the debacle, but his image lost its luster and he never again regained the esteem and loyalty of the common folks, who, for the most part, had bestowed so much admiration on him prior to this disaster.

During the pre-panic days, Ford belonged to the elite of the business world, whose leaders were credited with creating the impressive progress made in industry, technology, and the miracles of production. President Calvin Coolidge had sanctified the decade with his well-known comment that "the business of America is business." As a result, businessmen believed they had raised the standard of living and were entitled to sit on Mount Olympus and give forth words of wisdom on all vital issues of the day.

While Henry Ford's earlier views had been liberal in tone and his social reforms appeared meritorious, his economic and political ideas after 1929 became more controversial. It seemed incongruous that he could be so far ahead of his time in his economic thinking in 1914 and so far behind in 1929 and the early 1930s. Raymond L. Bruckberger, the French critic, in his widely read *Image of America* in 1959, claimed Ford introduced a more significant revolution in 1914 than the Russian revolution of 1917. The Ford thesis demanding prosperity for the workers shattered Ricardo's gospel of minimum subsistence wages and made every laboring man a potential customer.

Ford proved that corporations must place the welfare of the employees ahead of profits and dividends.[1] In many ways he acted as a precursor of John Maynard Keynes by insisting the most evil men in society were the rich who hoarded money or refused to use it in productive ways. These practices dried up the economy and dragged the business cycle into a depression. In addition, Ford's attitude toward medical care, capital punishment, the treatment of those in penal institutions, and his insistence that society owed everyone a right to a good job seemed enlightened and progressive in spirit.

Yet after this innovation in economic thought, Henry Ford saw the American dream of prosperity for all turned into a nightmare, with farmers, wage earners, and the weak taking a beating in the collapse of the economic system. In this toboggan slide the Ford reputation also slid to new lows. He had plenty of company, for the other entrepreneurs and politicians moved, as David Donald, the historian, described them, "like classic Greek tragedians caught in a web of fate as pitiable figures trying to patch their ship when the hull was smashed beyond all repair."[2] The economic system malfunctioned because people involved in drastic changes were led by men who seemingly were unable to understand these changes and act accordingly.

As a result, Western Europe and the United States entered a false paradise based on the assumption that wisdom implied isolation in foreign affairs and laissez-faire in domestic matters. Warren G. Harding platitudinously talked about the inherited institutions of our forefathers, and his speeches, according to William McAdoo, looked like an army of pompous phrases moving over the landscape in search of an idea.[3] Calvin Coolidge, a man of inaction for which he was admirably prepared, worshipped the golden calf of business and insisted that if any man were out of work it was his own fault; those incapable of supporting themselves were not fit for self-government. Will Rogers said even the atheists prayed for the salvation of the country when Coolidge became president, while Frank Kent in the *American Mercury* thought Coolidge less a fighting man than anyone outside the Old Ladies Home.[4] After Herbert Hoover entered the White House, according to Allan Nevins and Henry Commager, he made more serious errors of judgment than any president since U. S. Grant. Recently some historians rate Hoover below Grant and Harding in stature, because his policies hurt more people and ruined more American lives.

What were these errors? It is over-simplifying the issues to say that most economists and historians suggest the major crime was the failure to follow the Henry Ford thesis of 1914, which insisted the prosperity of wage earners and farmers must be insured in order to provide a healthy economy for all. The tragedy grew out of failure to protect the weak against the strong. Violations of these rules, both here and abroad, while substituting a faith in the businessmen to see that the goodies trickled down to the common herd, proved disasterous. Leadership failed, and people paid the price in the nation's worst depression.

Under the doctrine of divine theory of economic grace, big corporations put too much of the profits into dividends, reserves, executive salaries, and bonuses and not enough into wages. While new machinery had increased the efficiency of factory employees by 33 percent during the 1920s, their wages remained about the same. With only one worker in twelve unionized, employees were unable to secure their rightful share of the nation's income when court injunctions broke strikes and business organizations championed the open shop. Thus while Andrew Mellon's aluminum shares sold for $500, North Carolina cotton mill workers got 20 cents an hour and women received $9.00 for a 70-hour week.[5]

The American farmer, representing one-fourth of the population in 1927, received an average of $548 income per family. While the national wealth quadrupled from 1900 to 1929, too much of it gravitated into the hands of the wealthy. Kenneth Galbraith revealed that in 1929, the upper 5 percent of the American people owned one-third of the wealth of the country and received one-third of the income; 21 percent of the families received less than $1,000 a year and 71 percent of the families had incomes of less than $2,500 annually.[6]

Consequently, when farmers and wage earners, comprising three-fourths of the population, ran out of purchasing power, the huge industrial machine came to halt, surpluses piled up in warehouses, and Americans had so much of everything that they almost starved to death. Instead of two cars in every garage and a chicken in every pot, people were living in garages, the whole eating situation had gone to pot, and people were singing, "Tomatoes are Cheaper" and "Only One Meat Ball." We had solved the problem of production, but not distribution and consumption. Had the wealth been more equitably divided, the other factors behind the depression, such as the stock market crash, decline in foreign trade, installment buying, interest rates, high tariffs, corporate thimble-rigging, and international monetary imbalances would have been less serious.

Even Henry Ford's vision became obscured. He had seen the importance of consumer purchasing power when he announced the $5.00 day, but he overlooked the fact that little men needed to be protected against the greed of powerful industrial giants and established wealth. The only referee strong enough to give protection would be the arm of the Federal Government. He forgot that a liberal idea could not be successfully implemented by rock-ribbed conservative political leaders. As James Madison had noted in the *Federalist Papers*, people have vested interests which take priority over the interest of the general welfare. The powerful tend to take care of themselves before becoming concerned about the status of their neighbor. Aware of the goal of a humane society, Henry Ford misconstrued the means and made the fatal mistake of slipping into the reactionary camp, supporting presidents Coolidge and Hoover, and after a brief honeymoon, turning against that wild man Franklin D. Roosevelt and his New Deal.

Meanwhile, the plight of rural Americans became catastrophic. Farm income dropped from thirteen billion in 1929 to five and one-half billion in 1932. After three years of depression, farm income reached the lowest ebb since the days of George Washington, while wheat touched the lowest level since the days of William Shakespeare.[7] From 1929 to 1932, four thousand banks failed, with losses to depositors of $3 billion. Thousands of hard-working farmers who had saved a little money for their old age, suddenly discovered their life savings were gone, and they soon learned that these banks, when reorganized, would repay only a small fraction of the losses. Prior to the crash, small-town bankers were the respected leaders in the community, now they were accused of mishandling funds and attempting to save their own money while betraying the depositors.[8]

In the cities, conditions during the last three years of the Hoover administration were also tragic. Wages declined 60 percent and salaries went down 40 percent. By 1932 there were from twelve to fifteen million unemployed. Senator Robert F. Wagner of New York, in a speech to the Senate in January, 1933, quoted a witness before the Banking and Currency Committee as saying, "There are no less than forty-five million people living in poverty, of which fifteen million are existing only with the help of charity, without which they would perish."⁹ Caroline Bird in *The Invisible Scar* insists the depression packed a bigger wallop than anything in America between the Civil War and the Atomic Bomb. It had more impact than both World Wars because nobody escaped and all individuals were hit.¹⁰ Yet in the midst of the crisis, Herbert Hoover, who had administered $100 million in 1919 to aid the starving in Europe, still clung to his dogma saying, "I am opposed to any direct or indirect government dole. To give aid to an individual we strike at the roots of self-government."¹¹

Unfortunately, farmers who were heavily mortgaged learned that business practices intensified the panic. In normal times a farmer, who suffered reverses and was unable to pay his promissory note to the bank, could renew the note by paying the interest. In the depression, however, the banks, facing declining capital and reserves, attempted to secure liquid funds and thus foreclosed the mortgages, sold the farmer's property at whatever it would bring, and pushed the farmer off the land or forced him into tenancy. Even after the New Deal was launched, the Federal Land Banks adopted the same policies of harsh collection of farmers' debts. Thus the agency of government, ostensibly designed to assist the poor, took actions which accentuated the financial problems.

These unhappy conditions were described by Remley J. Glass, a Mason City, Iowa, lawyer who witnessed the tidal wave of farm foreclosures in 1931 by insurance companies, loan agencies, and banks. Writing for *Harpers* magazine, he stated that farmers were asked to pay their debts with oats selling at ten cents a bushel, corn, twelve cents a bushel and hogs at two cents a pound. In the fall of 1932 it took a wagon load of oats to buy a pair of shoes, and a truck load of hogs would not bring enough money to pay the interest on a $1,000 note. Disregarding the inability of farmers to pay, creditors forced them to meet their bills in full or forfeit their property. Men who had worked for twenty-five years and sunk every dollar they possessed into their homes were turned out with only a few items of personal belongings. In two years almost 25 percent of the mortgaged farm real estate in Iowa went under the hammer. "The conditions in my county have been substantially duplicated in every one of the 99 counties in Iowa and those of surrounding states. . . ."¹² One elderly farmer, facing ruin, told the lawyer with tears in his eyes, "The Lord gave and the Lord taketh away,"¹³ but it seems unfair to place the responsibility for the breakdown of a faulty human economic system on the shoulders of the Lord.

A family at Norbeck, South Dakota, had lived on their farm for half a century. Their parents had homesteaded, built large farm buildings, planted trees, broken 600 acres of prairie sod, and paid their taxes. When the crash came, loans were secured to buy seed, feed, and fuel for the tractors. One day the agent for the land bank drove into the yard, presented a court order demanding full payment or evacuation of the home within twenty-four hours. At the same time, Herbert Hoover had proclaimed a moritorium on foreign war debts, but no moritorium could be arranged for American farmers caught in the cruel depression brought on by forces over which they had no control.

Conditions seemed to get worse. In Washington, forest fires raged because unemployed lumber jacks and farmers had set them in order to get jobs as fire fighters. In Oregon, thousands of bushels of apples rotted because they were not worth picking, while women in Seattle searched garbage cans for food. In Southern states, cotton went unpicked because workers could make only 70 cents a day, not enough to keep them in pork and beans. Seventy percent of the farmers in Oklahoma were unable to pay interest on their mortgages. Roads in the West and Southwest teemed with hungry hitch-hikers, while camp fires of the homeless could be seen along every railroad track. Most of them were tenant farmers who had lost everything.

As if to add realism to a Dante's *Inferno*, even nature turned against the midwest farmers. In a region requiring 20 inches of rainfall annually to raise grain crops, only 10 inches fell in 1931, creating a drought which dried up water holes and ruined gardens, crops, and hay land. A shortage of pasture necessitated selling livestock or trucking in straw from as far as 200 miles away. Some cut green thistles for hay. Groves of trees died. Grasshoppers thrived on the heat and drouth, stripping corn fields and alfalfa, and in gale winds they rattled against the sidings of farm houses like hail. In 1933, soil began blowing into the air, eventually causing 50 million acres to be blighted by dust storms which reached from Canada to Mexico. In 1935 fifteen different storms raked the plains, some of them lasting fifty-five hours and reducing visibility to 500 feet. Strong winds drove dust across the fields like drifting snow. Automobiles on the roads ran with lights on at midday, while the storms created too much static to use car radios. Hogs and chickens died from choking on the dust. Dirt drifted over fences in huge mounds, while Russian thistles tumbled across the prairies, matting against fences and blocking gates. Members of the Texas legislature wore gas masks in the state house during the storm on April 10, 1935.

The depression years were painful and left scars. Pioneers who had been industrious now saw their life efforts slip away. Parents were unable to buy books for their children, or to send their young people to college for lack of money. Inadequate income meant working with obsolete machinery. Things were repaired with wire; old tires were patched with boots, and rope lines were used on harnesses because leather was too expensive. Old shoes were sewed and half-soled with old tire casings. Many burned corn in the kitchen and some used cow chips for fuel. Young people hunted jackrabbits hoping to sell the pelts for a few cents. When Mike Wagoner, the elevator man at Millard, South Dakota, put up a sign, "Today's market: SHELLED CORN TWO CENTS A BUSHEL: CORN ON THE COB, THREE CENTS LESS," farmers in the vicinity knew the reality of a major depression.

On the eve of the stock market crash in 1929, Henry Ford seemed as myopic as the other big businessmen who thought the booming industrial economy would remain on a high plateau. Unmindful of the seriousness of events in October of that year, Ford accepted President Hoover's suggestion that business leaders refrain from slashing wages and follow a policy of retrenchment. Consequently, late in 1929, he raised wages in his factories to $7.00 a day, saying well-paid men would buy goods and thus create more jobs. In addition, he reduced the price of automobiles and in 1930 announced a $25 million program of expansion.[14] Optimistically, he announced on June 7, 1930, that business recovery had been more rapid than the decline of the previous year. Besides, Hoover had done everything anyone could to bring about improvement in industry. "Everything Hoover has advised or tried has been sound," he concluded.[15]

This time, however, the magic failed. Ford sales dropped from 1,145 million in 1929 to 874 million in 1930; his sale of passenger cars to farmers fell from 650,000 in 1929 to 55,000 in 1932. From 1931 to 1934, the Ford Motor Company lost $125 million.[16] During this collapse, Ford, like others, reduced wages and fired workers. His payroll dropped from $145 million in 1929 to $32 million in 1933.[17]

When it became apparent that prosperity had not lurked around the corner, Ford claimed he had been right all along in insisting the stock market rested on unsound foundations. Prior to the crash Ford had held that the stock market exchange encouraged speculators to seek profits from other speculators, all of which had nothing to do with production of more goods, lowering prices, and raising the standard of living. Betting on a horse race added neither strength nor speed to the race. The price of stocks reflected the hopes and fears of speculators not the true conditions of the industry. In fact, it had nothing whatever to do with industry. In addition, stockholders were nonproductive, absentee investors whose primary goal was profits. They were money makers not commodity makers. When the chief function of any industry is to produce dividends rather than goods for use, the emphasis is fundamentally wrong. If stock were sold in the Ford Motor Company, it would increase the cost of the car to pay dividends. Stockholders were a great curse, they knew nothing about the business, they interfered with those who did know, and were drags on the system. He often repeated, "You can't live off a printed bond and a pair of scissors."[18]

The bank failures of the Hoover regime reaffirmed Ford's hostility toward professional bankers, especially those in New York. He believed the depression had shattered their shabby careers and exposed their sinister motives. They had brought on the panic by taking all the money and sitting on it. Like stock brokers, they, too, were looking for profits, not service to mankind. They speculated with other people's money and tried to control all business enterprise. To invest in counterfeit stocks was as criminal as counterfeiting money. Most bankers were racketeers who should be compelled to take an oath to obey the Ten Commandments. The *Wall Street Journal* on March 16, 1934, quoted Ford as saying, "Bankers cannot put anything over."

These comments may seem strange coming from one who served as president of a Dearborn Bank and who used the services of banks constantly. Ford exonerated the local bankers in small towns, but he detested the financial tycoons on Wall Street, whom he accused of waiting for a company to get into financial trouble, then pouncing on it by making a loan with the provision that their bankers sit on the board of directors to control policy. The difference between honest and dishonest bankers was that honest men kept money circulating; unscrupulous bankers collected money and let it pile up until it clogged business activity and thus wrecked the nation's economic welfare. Congress should investigate them because bankers were the scavengers, the parasites, and the ogres.

Frustrated by the impact of the depression, Ford lashed out in all directions. Initially a false optimism prevailed. Alexander Legge, Chairman of the Federal Farm Board on November 28, 1929, said it looked as though industry would have to search for employees instead of laying off workers. Two months later, Andrew Mellon predicted a revival in the spring. In June of 1931, Ford made the naïve comment that one of the healthy signs of the times could be seen in people's strong desire to find work. He thought there was plenty to be done if people would only do it. By December, 1931, he foresaw immediate recovery because men had quit looking for Santa Claus and waiting for miracles and were now ready to go to work. People should begin looking for work at home. They could clean yards, paint fences, and be more self-reliant. Being unemployed did not mean being out of work, because one could do things even though not hired to do them. People should secure loans to be paid back later; they might plant gardens and produce their own vegetables. Charity hurt folks instead of helped them; the only thing worth giving was an opportunity. Charity was barbarous, the worst action in society with the exception of our prisons.

By 1934, some of Ford's views reflected the flowering of asininity. He thought the depression reflected only a state of mind which would pass when people became more flexible. The panic had been beneficial because it taught everyone to appreciate their neighbors and the simple things of life. He added, "If you lost your money, don't let it bother you. Charge it up to experience."

Furthermore, surpluses did not exist because all of man's wants had not been met. Curtailing production indicated despair, not hope. Government regulations were evil because they stabilized the wrongs in society, and to restrict farm acreages would rob men of useful labor and destroy food. He advocated the use of more efficient machinery in agriculture and increased electrical power. Above all, people should get back to nature in the country rather than crowd into cities to join the soup lines.

Most farmers thought the Ford talk either irrelevant or ridiculous. When a father could not feed his family, he was in no mood to listen to such platitudinous bilge as rolling up the sleeves and going to work. A family near Novi, Michigan, indignantly inquired why Ford could say the depression was a helpful thing when his income in 1930 was $30 million, enough to feed all the unemployed in Detroit. If Ford had to stand in a breadline for a cup of coffee and a ticket to a flop house or if he saw his babies become ill because of malnutrition, he might know something about the subject. . . . "He makes light of ills he never felt."[19] Another malcontent criticized Ford for saying the average man did not really want to do a day's work unless he was caught and could not get out of it, and then he himself proceeded to lay off 75,000 men in his factories.[20]

Protestations from a teacher stated Ford's workers were denizens of soup kitchens, while Ford failed to perform deeds but responded with an outpouring of words, "a turgid flood abounding in moral exhortations and noble ideas," while his profits in 1930 were equivalent to $257.52 per share on the 172,645 shares of stock owned by the Ford family.[21] An irate California fruit grower sent Ford a clipping from the *Wall Street Journal* for November 2, 1928, which featured a story entitled, "Ford Hails New Era with Hoover," and elaborated on the Motor King's notion that the job of a statesman was to clear the way for what Almighty God was going to do. The correspondent sardonically offered this advice; "Stick with your pistons and gear grease. As a prophet of the Lord you never would have got out of old Egypt land. . . ."[22] Another protestor demanded that Ford run a retraction in the papers denying his statement that farm prices for crops could never get too low. "I will not take any lip from you after we have been buying your cars and tractors. How do you suppose we can buy anything if we are working for nothing? Don't you know we are losing our farms."[23] Replying to Ford's remark that no one should be out of work because there was so much idle land in the country, an Indiana farmer asked, "Are you so ignorant that you can't see that we can't buy land held by real estate companies because we are broke, dead broke."[24]

The depression gave Henry Ford an opportunity to stress one of his pet ideas, however, namely the decentralization of industry and the back-to-the-farm movement. Undoubtedly his interest in water power suggested that this resource might be utilized more constructively in rural regions. As early as 1916, he had talked about these benefits. If waterwheels ground wheat and powered saw mills, why couldn't they drive rural factories? These would give farmers added security because they could work the land in the summer and the village factories in the winter months. "When it comes to sustaining life we go to the fields," Ford declared. "If the world were one vast machine shop it would die. We cannot eat and wear our machines." The *Dearborn Independent* on November 1, 1919, noted that soldiers returning from Europe had congregated in cities. The farm lads were fascinated by the bright lights and refused to return to the farm. In urban centers the inadequate housing forced them to live in tents, churches, and armories provided by the municipalities. As a result the cities became too large for their own good, while the country towns were too small. This dislocation of labor meant the nation barely produced enough food to feed the population. If the streams which rippled their way idly through the country were harnessed to produce electricity, thousands of bustling communities would spring up among deserted hamlets. As postwar jobs grew scarce, Ford saw city fellows taking off their silk shirts and drifting back to the farm where they belonged.

Conceivably, Ford may have been influenced by Edgar Chambless of New York, who in 1918 drafted a proposal called "Roadtown." W. L. Spillman, of the Office of Farm Management of the Department of Agriculture, revealed the plan, wisely to important leaders such as President Woodrow Wilson and Henry Ford. Chambless suggested decentralizing big cities by creating linear communities in which business, industrial, and home life would be housed on one long street and in one continuous structure. All transportation, heating, and public utilities would be underground. Since there would be no traffic above ground, there would be ample room for parks and gardens. The plan would merge urban and rural living, providing the advantages of both but none of the evils. Luther Burbank thought "Roadtown," practical as well as a necessity for the existence of civilization. John Dewey called it a remarkable integration, making for efficiency, because it combined work with recreative leisure—a balance fundamental to mental health. W. L. Spillman believed the ideas unique because this would eliminate congestion in urban centers.[25]

With some of these objectives in mind, Ford in 1918 acquired an old grist mill known as Nankin Mills on the Rouge river. Other plants were built to demonstrate that small streams could be used profitably for industrial purposes. As a result, small factories at Plymouth, Newburg, Waterford, and Northville manufactured drills, taps, and valves. Milan produced ignition coils, Milford turned out carburetors, and Willow Run built generators and starters. All these village industries were on water sites within 20 miles of Dearborn. In the early 1920s there were seven of these plants in operation, with the number increasing to twenty in 1934, employing 2,400 part-time farmers. In the late 1930s, the village industries employed less than 4,000 in the small plants and not over 6,000 workers in the larger factories at Ypsilanti, Green Island, New York, and St. Paul, Minnesota.[26]

Ford liked to retreat from the city and visit his village industries which were placed in romantic surroundings, flowing streams, flowering shrubs, and shade trees. He often spoke of the industrial cities as unnatural, artificial monstrosities where factories belched out smoke which begrimed the workers and forced them to live in crowded slums. In this sense, he anticipated the present ecology crusade to secure a better environment.

When Drew Pearson visited these village industries in 1924, he reported the farmer-workmen received $6.00 a day for four days in the plants with two days devoted to farming small plots. This decentralization had increased the speed of manufacture in making valves by 100 percent. It had cost 9.5 cents to manufacture a valve in the Highland Park factory in 1920; it cost 4 cents in the Northville village plant in 1923. Henry Ford claimed the workers took more pride in their work, while the family men on the farm created less turnover in the labor force than single men and transients who made up much of the labor force in the big cities. Certain heavy industries would remain in cities, but small parts manufacture should be decentralized in rural areas.[27]

As the Hoover depression rocked the nation, Ford re-emphasized his back-to-the-land proposal. He affirmed that man's roots were in the soil and the further he got away from the land, the greater his insecurity. No unemployment insurance could compare with an alliance between man and a plot of ground. Young men had left farming because of the absence of mechanical power and efficient methods to remove the drudgery of farm work. If industry cooperated with agriculture, both would benefit. In a conference with President Hoover in the spring of 1932, Ford pointed out that if factory workers could reside in the country, they could raise $500 worth of garden produce annually, enough to keep them off relief rolls in the city when factories shut down. Decentralization according to Ford did not mean moving factories into the South to secure cheaper labor, neither did it mean building branch factories across the country. The marriage should be a natural one in which advantages were mutual. The farm and factory were natural allies; they never should have been separated in the first place. "With one foot in agriculture and one foot in industry, America is safe."[28] He joined others in a drive to encourage chemurgy by which farm crops could be utilized in industry and talked about growing automobiles from soybeans and various farm commodities. In an interview with a reporter for *The Christian Science Monitor*, in April, 1933, he said, "We must harness the surplus of the farm to the surplus of industry. Isn't the soya bean a sign it can be done? Our automobiles are all to be painted with the oil from this humble bean. The farmer grows the legume and I pay him for it. Moreover, he will do the initial processing that fits it for industrial use, and I shall pay him for it. I shall use the oil to make paint and enamel and the other substances in the bean to make parts for the car, and he will buy my car, which uses the bean that grows on his land." Pointing toward the massive River Rouge complex, Ford added, "That plant will gradually be scrapped." The city offered little that could not be obtained on the farm. While opera houses and museums did not grow in rural areas, the advent of the radio, motorcar, telephone, and electric power had made rural living a modern existence.

As might be expected, the press gave Ford's view good coverage, partly because the industrialist made good copy, and in part because the depressive atmosphere during the panic made any word of optimism sound like a chorus of hallelujahs. The Detroit *Free Press* in February, 1931 said, "Ford Visions Dawn of New Epoch," The New York *Times* stated "Ford Seeks a New Balance for Industry," with Ford saying "Don't fear surplus—use it."[29] The Washington *Evening Star* on May 28, 1930, quoted Ford as saying too many people believed that Santa Claus lived in the city, but now that half of the people in Detroit were out of work they could go back to their farms because everything that grew could be used for some purpose. The Cincinnati *Post*, in 1933, claimed Ford's decentralization programs would stop people going around demanding that someone give them a job, because with their new skills they could now make their own jobs which would free them from the payroll habit.

Responses to the back-to-the-land crusade were usually favorable. People in distress longed for the security of a home of their own. When city people faced starvation and one thousand girls rioted to get twenty-five jobs advertised in New York city in 1931, with a million transients drifting across the country, with some Bethlehem miners carrying nothing but potato peelings in their lunch buckets, and with a score of Columbia University students selling their blood at hospitals to stay in school, there was something appealing about a little farm with green fields, a few cows, a garden, and a chicken coop full of poultry. At least the plan sounded more exciting than Hoover's grim comments about balancing the budget and economy in government.

Frequently farmers wrote Ford asking how they might link their farm with the Ford industrial system. One near Willis, Michigan, hired fifteen men each year, but since work was seasonal, he had to let them go in the fall. If he had a contract to produce auto parts, he could keep his men the year around. Another near Hastings, Florida, sent a picture of his 647 acres asking Ford to buy it and establish a colony for refugees in this back-to-the-farm movement. From Hoosick Falls, New York, came the request to join with Ford in manufacturing farm machinery in the winter months while reverting to farm work in the summer. One optimist went ahead and organized 560 farmers in North Carolina and requested a loan of $10,000 from Ford to get them started in manufacturing. The Agricultural Experiment Station in Vermont wanted to know what crop would be ideal for the farm and industry combination. A farmer near Waterbury, Connecticut, told Ford he was on the right track because France had sustained millions on tiny farms for centuries. Our government, instead of wasting money on relief, should buy huge tracts of land in the midwest, build small houses, provide electricity and get hungry people out on the land.

On November 8, 1934, Franklin D. Roosevelt, writing from the White House, informed Henry Ford that he had been thinking about the idea of getting people out of the dead cities and into the country. He believed it high time more attention be given to the location of smaller industries in small towns. He invited Mr. and Mrs. Ford to visit him in Warm Springs in November when they could have a good talk about these matters. Apparently nothing came of this invitation, however. Meantime, an official of the Russell Sage Foundation liked the notion of uniting farm and factory. If truck farms were laid out along a narrow-gauge railroad, the farmers could load their produce as the train moved along, like the assembly line in a factory.

Yet the average farmer found little hope in the Ford plan because the benefits seemed too vague and theoretical. There was no specific program he could support or agency he could join. Those who did write to Henry Ford usually received a form letter in reply from a secretary advising the correspondent to see his county agent because the Ford Motor Company did not do business with individual farmers scattered across the nation. In addition, in the 1930s, Henry Ford headed one of the most concentrated industrial giants, which hired 75,000 workers at the River Rouge plant but with only about 3,500 men in all the village industries. There seemed to be no evidence that other manufacturers would decentralize. Understandably, Henry Ford had urged these proposals because he was at heart a farmer with a sincere interest in agriculture. However, his dispersal of work looked more like a hobby than a policy backed by the National Association of Manufacturers. Then too, Ford's relief for the poor seemed provincial in its scope. He donated 17 tractors to welfare workers in Birmingham, Michigan, so they could plow their gardens. He placed 1,000 acres in Dearborn at the disposal of Community Cooperatives for growing vegetables, thus saving the city about $50,000 in welfare costs. In Inkster, a suburb of Detroit, where 1,500 Black people were destitute he sent trucks to pick up 86 loads of tin cans and ashes. He distributed food and plowed 500 acres for family gardens. Roads were improved and people were paid a dollar a day to help clean up the town. While these efforts were laudable, it looked as though Ford's efforts to save America were limited to people living within 50 miles of Detroit. W. J. Cameron, in 1937, stated that he could not cite any examples outside the Ford Motor Company where the experiment of decentralization of industry had been tried.

Many resented Ford's rhetoric because it seemed irrelevant in the face of immediate needs. A farmer at Red Wing, Minnesota, said his people wanted to remain agricultural rather than be invaded by industry, while a disappointed cattleman at Faith, South Dakota, complained, "You talk about industry helping us farmers. Out in this range country, where the wind and heat can curl your hair, what are you going to do with industry, manufacture jackrabbit overshoes, or Listerine for the coyote's halitosis. . . ."[30] An unhappy farmer at Harvey, Illinois, said he had read all about the back to the farm accounts but saw no relief. He had a family of eight, had been unemployed three-fifths of the time, and had no money to make such a move. He could purchase a farm for $5,000 which was worth twice that amount, but he could not make a deal. "I would be on the farm now if I were able to raise even $2,000. Hell no. . . . It is a nice thought 'Back to the Farm'—but I have no money in my pocket, so how am I going to get there. I will await your reply."[31]

It became clear that the years of the Hoover depression had shattered people's faith in the businessman's ability to protect the economic welfare of all Americans. Industrial leadership with its notions of a free market, the laws of supply and demand, and laissez faire economics had failed largely because the doctrine assumed men in power would make the judicious moves on a voluntary basis. Since the voluntary approach led to disaster, the voters went to the polls in November, 1932, and removed Herbert Hoover and his philosophy from office and ushered in Franklin D. Roosevelt and the New Deal. A majority of the electorate decided economic issues were too important to be left in the hands of a few individuals; henceforth the state would be empowered to regulate and initiate economic programs.

As the new era dawned, it left Henry Ford bewildered, frustrated, and discredited. When he fought the N.R.A., and various New Deal programs, his following melted away. To be sure, many followed his career as a manufacturer of automobiles, but they no longer accepted his political and economic views as gospel. The world had changed too fast even for a man who had done more to effect change in this country than any other industrialist.

The subsequent shift of interest of rural Americans from Dearborn to Washington, D.C., can be seen in the correspondence of those in distress. Instead of writing to Ford, farmers in increasing numbers addressed their remarks to officials in the nation's capitol where the power to effect reform resided. The letters filed in the library at Hyde Park, New York, and in the National Archives in Washington, D.C., suggest that farmers believed relief could be found in federal legislation rather than in the good intentions of business leaders.

In the meantime, recovery seemed painfully slow. Federal relief programs saved most farmers from complete ruin, and prices of farm commodities gradually improved. Henry Ford, however, attacked the legislation to reduce farmer's productive capacity as immoral and wasteful. As Will Rogers insisted, "farmers relief can't last much longer for the farmers ain't got much more to be relieved of."[32] He also thought Ford had more influence on American lives than any other man in the country. "He put wheels on our homes. A man's castle is his sedan. Life's greatest catastrophe is a puncture. . . . It will take a hundred years to tell whether he helped us or hurt us, but he certainly didn't leave us where he found us."[33]

XI

Ford and the Little Red Schoolhouse

Henry Ford maintained a vital interest in education throughout his lifetime. Although limited in his own formal training, he developed a philosophy of education and spent large sums of money supporting various enterprises, most of which provided educational opportunities for disadvantaged young people. Many of his projects were designed to help rural youth, giving credence to the notion that he never entirely got away from his own farm background.

He frequently said he was more interested in education than manufacturing. His observations led him to conclude that people did little reflective thinking; they let others arrange their indignations for them. Thought was not a series of illuminating flashes, it was the deep, dark mining amid the accumulated rubbish of the world's illusions and the world's laziness. He believed "Thinking is the hardest work there is, which is the probable reason why so few engage in it."[1]

Ford had faith in young people. He believed the older generation had failed to provide the kind of education designed to prepare graduates to cope with the modern world. As a result, they were frustrated, insecure, and rebellious. Ivory-tower teachers, losing touch with reality, were incapable of teaching youth how to accept responsibility or to get a job.

Since Ford's industrial career had been a pragmatic adventure, he naturally thought education should be pragmatic, functional, and utilitarian. He ascribed to the John Dewey principles of learning by experience, vocational training, and educating the whole person. He believed an educated person could do a lot of things, in-

196

cluding living a life which was useful and happy. On one occasion he said he was for any educational system which would turn out young people who were competent, happy, and who could earn a living without being victimized by a swindler of any stock market get-rich scheme.[2]

The Fords first became involved in a school in 1908, when they bought the 80-acre Valley Farm in Wayne County. When the Protestant Orphan Home in Detroit sought a site for a camp for boys, the Fords agreed to keep fifteen boys on the farm, using the house as a dormitory. It was their belief that farm life, together with training in farm work, would prove beneficial to these underprivileged boys.

Here the Ford philosophy of education first appeared. The boys, ages twelve to eighteen, attended school during the day, but after school they took care of the hogs, milked the cows, cleaned the kitchen, and did their own laundry. In the summer vacation they worked in the fields—haying, cultivating corn, planting apple orchards, harvesting grain crops, and doing the farm chores. They were up at 5:30 in the morning and ready for work at 7:00. All were in bed at 9:00. Tidiness was essential, while on Saturday night all took hot showers, fortified with plenty of soap, with no boy escaping until he had passed inspection of the director.

Throughout the year, Mr. and Mrs. Ford visited the farm on numerous occasions where they ate with the students, brought additional supplies, and made arrrangements to take the group to the State Fair, or on a boat trip to Bob Lo Island in the Detroit River, or to visit the Highland factory to see the assembly of Ford cars. Ford believed schools should teach good manners, discipline, and the dignity of productive labor. True education turned a person's mind toward work, not away from it.

Realizing that his farm boys were limited in training, Ford tried to prepare them for industrial jobs in the city. In 1916 he opened the Henry Ford Trade School in his Highland Park plant. The first class consisted of one instructor, six machines, and six Valley Farm boys. From these modest beginnings grew one of the most widely-known schools in the country. By 1948 ten thousand students had felt its influence, while educators hailed it as a radical departure from the generally accepted vocational schools.

The innovative feature which attracted most attention was Ford's idea that students should be paid for the work they did in training classes. In the early years, boys spent fourteen weeks in class, thirty-four weeks in shop work, and received four weeks vacation. They received $400 to $600 a year in wages, with an additional $2.00 a month in a savings account. Dental work was free of charge. The system provided a chance for young people to earn while they learned. Later in one of the Apprentice schools, students could attend classes for three years while receiving wages of $6.00 to $7.60 per day.[3]

Henry Ford held no brief for the notion that cash incentives for studying would ruin character; in fact he believed the opposite. Long class periods were provided to avoid frequent interruption. All shop work had commercial value. Students did departmentalized work rather than engage in projects. Accuracy and attention to detail were stressed, with the use of the most modern machinery available. Lucrative employment awaited students at graduation.

Ford criticized most schools for wasting years of a child's life, then turning him loose in a world he did not understand, to hunt for work he must learn how to perform. The so-called manual training classes in the public schools were inadequate because the training consisted of mostly useless odds and ends. What real value was there in working a month to make a door stop or lamp shade for mother at Christmas time? Such schools never permitted a boy to get into the heart of his work because everyone knew the end product of his hands had no market value. Ford argued that anyone with a trade would never have to start on a job as an unskilled worker. In most schools there was little kinship between what a person knew and what he could do. The aim should be to restore the vital connection between knowing things and doing things.

Some professional educators disliked the Ford emphasis on vocational training and insisted students under this type of tutelage were too much concerned with their work. They were too serious, too silent, too intense about their tasks. Some thought these schools were more of a factory than the factory itself. All this was disturbing because such an education developed too much specialization at too early an age.

As the Ford schools became better known, rural people suggested something be done to improve the education of farm families. Why didn't Ford establish schools to train city people for work in agriculture? Why didn't he sponsor radio programs to educate Southern farmers away from the one-crop cotton system. Ford should encourage rural schools to get back to the fundamentals of learning. Revitalized education would help eliminate conditions which produced worn out farms, worn out machinery and worn out men.

The educational interests of Mr. and Mrs. Ford were directed toward farm youngsters somewhat by accident. On a return from a Florida vacation in the spring of 1923, the Fords decided to visit the Berry School near Rome, Georgia. They had heard about this institution which combined training in agriculture with academic work to aid the poverty-stricken mountain children of the back country. On Saturday, April 7, the Fords arrived at the school where they met Martha Berry, the founder, and the entire student body. Since the struggling institution depended on charity to keep it alive, every effort had been made to impress the wealthy Detroit couple. A devotional program in the Chapel featured student participation. During the assembly period, a student gave a speech of welcome expressing the good fortune in having such famous guests on the campus and adding the timely note that the student body hoped Henry Ford would get Muscle Shoals because those in the South favored the project. At lunch, the visitors noted that the girls prepared all the meals without the aid of a cook.

The boys also were taught to work. They had built log cottages, fired kilns to make bricks for classroom buildings, maintained a large dairy, a laundry, and wood-working shops. Ford's eyes lit up when he observed a sawmill converting logs into lumber, and as the party drove by a field in which a Fordson tractor was working, Mr. Ford asked the driver to stop. Not waiting to open the door he vaulted over the side and started running toward the tractor calling to the boy driver to turn it toward him. When the tractor stopped, the father of all Fords cranked it. Indeed, the Fords and Berry Schools would meet again. Here was a school designed to equip young people to be more productive than they could possibly be if left to the environment in which they were born. Henry Ford could understand this type of education. He left the campus with the promise to send a disc harrow, some repair parts for the two Fordson tractors, and a new kitchen stove. They did not know they had embarked on an adventure which would cost them three million dollars over the next twenty years.

The Berry Schools were steeped in tradition, much of it sentimental, unorthodox, and humanitarian. The life of its founder, Miss

Martha Berry reads like a novel. She was born in a Georgian mansion near Rome. Her father made a fortune before the Civil War and recouped it during Reconstruction. When he died he left his daughter financially independent. Behind the Berry home, illiterate and semiliterate whites lived in the Southern Appalachian mountains. Their poverty ranked with the lowest in the United States. Large families lived back in the woods in log cabins where privation afflicted the mind and spirit. Yet their pride was immense; their waste in human resources tragic.

Martha Berry decided a day school would be desirable, so she deeded her inheritance to build a small whitewashed school across the road from the plantation. The first day of school saw twelve boys sitting on the rough benches. They attended school, but were often detained at home to do farm work. Miss Berry decided on a boarding school where the students could work for their keep. Thus she opened the Berry School in January, 1902, and began an industrial institution to serve the needs of the "Cracker" boys in the hills. Tuition was set at $25 but could be paid in farm commodities.

When financial difficulties grew serious, Miss Berry went to New York, seeking funds from friends, Wall Street brokers, clergymen, and she even managed to reach President Theodore Roosevelt in the White House.

When Mr. and Mrs. Ford visited the school in 1923, the institution had already gained some stature. The elementary and high schools enrolled 600 students, while over 3,000 graduates had known what it was to go through school working two days and attending classes four days out of the week. The annual budget was $75,000, while the real estate and buildings were valued at nearly a million dollars.

Henry Ford's interest in the Berry Schools increased because his views of education and taste in living matched those of Martha Berry. The school appealed to him because of its efficiency of operation, its opposition to waste, and its high degree of cooperation among the campus personnel. In the fields stood wheat and tender cotton stalks, while cattle and sheep grazed on the slopes. Boys in overalls worked in the fields, the barns, and the shops. Girls dressed in blue gingham operated old-fashioned looms to spin and card wool for making rugs, towels, table runners, counterpanes, and clothes of artistic finish. Everybody worked, and as much as possible the students earned all or most of their way through school.

Inspired by the vision of Martha Berry's dream, Henry and Clara Ford took delight in playing Santa Claus. After their first visit, Henry left word with the company branch office in Atlanta to send a new Ford touring car, two Fordson tractors, a rock crusher, and a carload of farm machinery to the Berry School. After the first trickle of monetary blessing, came the gushing flood of abundant cash. The financial records in the Ford Motor Company Archives reveal the building program for the Berry Schools during the 1920s as costing almost four million dollars. The Ford contributions were:[4]

1922	$ 1,639.10
1923	12,854.85
1924	42,406.88
1925	130,393.67
1926	300,000.26
1927	420,392.25
1928	210,871.62

These donations made possible the construction of the Ford quadrangle of three-story stone buildings in Gothic style. Today, as visitors enter the grounds, they drive through cornfields until suddenly looming up before them stands the magnificent cathedral-like structures, complete with ivy, lily ponds, and marble statuary—a university set among poetry and plowing.

With improved finances, the Berry Schools thrived, with a college division added in 1928 and enrollment reaching 1,000 in the 1930s. By 1938 the farm produce and livestock sales amounted to $100,000. The campus in 1941 had 125 buildings, 20,000 acres of forest, 4,000 acres of farm land, 80 miles of paved road, 1,200 head of pure bred Jersey cattle, and 25 active industries.

The Fords often spent part of their vacations on the Berry campus. Henry Ford enjoyed visiting the farm. He would drive tractors, stroll past the dam and water wheel, and watch the sunset from Mt. Lavender. He liked the home-grown, home-cooked meals in a homespun school.

Because the Fords admired the Georgia countryside, they began buying parcels of land twenty miles south of Savannah. Acquisition of old plantations continued until 70,000 acres were owned by them at the time of Henry's death in 1947.[5] The Ford residence at Vallambrosia, now over a hundred years old, had been one of the finest plantation homes in Georgia's coastal region. With the mild climate and abundant rainfall, two and three crops could be raised each year. Thomas Edison carried out his rubber producing experiments here and the Fords made it a winter home.

Characteristic of the restless energy of the man, Ford could not rest because at heart he was a builder. As he looked about him he saw tumbled-down ruins of a once thriving antebellum rural economy. Some of the prewar mansions with marble stairs had never been rebuilt. The thin, sandy soil, long since depleted by excessive cropping now supported struggling pine trees, weeds, and tangled brush. Any semblance of prosperity had "Gone with the Wind."

Poor soil, naturally, produced poor folks. Some families eked out a living on a few acres of vegetable gardens or picked up odd jobs in lumber mills. Tom Phillips, who worked for Ford in Georgia, said, "Before Ford came, there wasn't anything here. People was awful poor. When they got work they had to go off and get it, white and colored alike. Indeed, this was a poor place before Ford came here."[6]

As a result, people were, for the most part, undernourished, sickly, and ignorant. The predominant ailments were malaria and hookworm disease. Few knew the meaning of a balanced diet or the rules of sanitation. In addition, malaria ravaged the population with its recurring attacks of chills and fevers. The presence of malaria parasites in the blood deprived the patients of normal energy and destroyed their will to work.

Against these conditions, Ford moved with vigor on several fronts. Two medical clinics were built in 1931 at Ways Station and Richmond Hill to serve the 2,000 people in Bryan County. Dr. C. F. Holten and a staff of eighteen nurses worked to eliminate the malaria, or black water fever as it was commonly called. All those working for Ford were required to take a five-day treatment of atabrine followed by plasmochin, if tests proved positive. Those refusing to undergo these tests were dropped from the Ford payroll. Drainage of swamps reduced the mosquito germ carriers and sanitary privies were provided to curb the spread of hookworm. People came to these clinics from twenty-five miles around, often walking or riding in carts over muddy roads.[7]

To revive the sick economy, Ford pumped $4,267,020 into buildings, equipment, and other improvements on the Georgia plantations. He built a community house with twenty guest rooms, constructed a saw mill, and reconditioned homes. Scientific farming methods were employed to increase crop production and to raise the standard of living in the region.

When the people of Bryan County built a new school for white children, Ford provided transportation in school busses, free noon lunches, and medical and dental care. He offered to pay all costs except teacher's salaries. Then he constructed George Washington Carver School at Richmond Hill for black students attending grade and high school. All expenses connected with the school were paid by Ford. He contributed half a million dollars to finance these educational programs from 1936 to 1947.

Consistent with his educational theories, the Carver school provided classes in home economics, industrial shop work, and agriculture. Two hundred black children now had an opportunity to attend school and learn a trade. Evening classes for illiterate adults were also held.

Of all the Henry Ford educational enterprises, the best known are his Greenfield Village Schools in Dearborn. Here a million tourists a year visit the 200-acre site to view the magnificent collection of Americana. The complex includes the Henry Ford Museum, Greenfield Village, and five grade and high schools. This monument stands as a reflection of the donor's hope to "preserve in actual working form at least part of our history and tradition."[8]

The origins of this multimillion-dollar project are obscure, some saying Ford's sentimental nature drew him back to the simple life of his childhood. Others claim his abhorrence of waste encouraged him to preserve remnants of the past. Allan Nevins and Frank Hill believe he disliked the publicity rising from the Chicago *Tribune* trial where he allegedly made the statement that history is bunk. Returning from the trial at Mt. Clemens, Michigan, he told E. G. Liebold that he would create a museum to show people what had actually happened in the past years.[9] At any rate, he restored his family home in 1919 and began collecting antiques of all sorts.

When the Greenfield Village restoration took place in the 1920s, Ford reconstructed the little red brick Scotch Settlement house where he first went to school in 1871. Harold M. Cordell, an assistant secretary from 1921 to 1929, recalled helping restore the school by finding old desks, blackboards, and other paraphernalia. He said Mr. Ford could visualize perfectly the original features and was a perfectionist in supervising the refurnishing of the school.[10] The school opened in September, 1929, with thirty-two students in the elementary grades. A teen-age girl assisted the teacher because

Ford thought children learned faster when they taught each other. He said, "We adults would find life much pleasanter if we went about it as a child does—always wanting to learn, always sharing what we've learned, never satisfied with what we know, always wondering what we don't know."[11]

A bit later the McGuffey School for primary grades opened in Greenfield Village. The class met in a log cabin, a replica of the one-room school which William Holmes McGuffey attended in Ohio. Since Ford found the McGuffey readers to be the greatest intellectual influence in his life, he used them in his schools, reprinted thousands of them for general distribution, and urged educators to re-adopt them in the elementary school. These texts incorporated lively narrative; the stories stressed love of nature, events in rural life, and lauded the blessings of industry, thrift, temperance, kindness, and patriotism. Phonetics received strong emphasis, with the abolition of mysticism and dull sermonizing. Above all, stories were written in cheerful style, such as "The lark is up to meet the sun, the bee is on the wing."

In the McGuffey School the youngsters participated in varied experiences. In a playhouse they served their own meals and practiced good manners to develop poise. A small barn stocked with Shetland ponies and miniature farm implements added to the children's fun. Ford himself would sometimes fire up a small steam engine and thresh a few bundles of grain. An authentic old sternwheeler "Swannee," moored in a nearby lagoon, provided excursions as an orchestra played Stephen Foster music. Ford believed students were more likely to learn if their studies were accompanied by pleasant activities. Field trips and nature studies were designed to make education a part of life, not a preparation for life.

When critics accused Ford of putting students in a straitjacket, tying boys down to shop benches and girls to typing classes, he pointed to the flexibility in his system. When an artist set up his easel in the school yard, a painting class organized spontaneously. When George Washington Carver came to Dearborn and walked in the woods to listen to God's orders, a nature study group followed. Girls wove articles for their own hope chests. Radio students broadcast the chapel services and were paid for their work. Opportunities were enhanced, not limited. In 1938, there were six thousand students in all the Ford schools, a testimony to his dictum, "Don't try to do too much for your child. Your job is to help him help himself, not to help him shun responsibility."[12]

In 1930 Ford announced he would invest 100 million dollars in American education and hinted he might devote full time to academic matters. He invaded New England, rich in scholastic tradition, to establish three schools in Massachusetts. He opened Redstone School in South Sudbury, Southwest School near Wayside Inn, and Wayside Inn Boys Vocational High School. He stressed quality rather than quantity and limited enrollment to a total of a hundred students in the three institutions.

Of these, the boys vocational school revealed the most daring innovations. The thirty-one boys were not taught in formal classes, but learned by solving daily problems. If a tractor needed to be overhauled, the students learned how to grind valves and install new piston rings; if the kitchen ceiling fell down, they studied plastering by patching it; if they needed flour for baking, they learned how to run a grist mill; if they needed water, they dug a well, and if the lights went out, they repaired electrical circuits. During the four years, every boy became familiar with the basic processes and machines of modern farm and industry.[13] Moreover, they were paid $2.00 a day, part of which went for board and the rest for clothes, amusement, and savings.

The spawning of Ford schools included a number of McGuffey-type institutions in the Upper Peninsula in Michigan where the Ford Motor Company held mining and timber property. These were certified by the State Department of Public Instruction and administered by the local township Board of Education. Ford, however, financed the teacher's salaries, transportation of school children, and dental care.[14] This type of funding of public schools was probably unique in America. At least six schools were maintained in full or in part by Ford in towns which manufactured parts for the Ford Motor Company. Records in Dearborn show an expenditure of over $200,000 for these schools from 1939 to 1945.[15]

As one looks at Henry Ford's educational endeavors, they seem to reflect his compulsion to prove that certain types of training and practice could enhance human potential, especially those in rural environments. For example, traveling in England in 1930, he observed that British agriculture seemed to be a rich man's recreation and a poor man's penury. When he heard that farm hands received $3.10 in wages a week, he concluded the economic theory had to be wrong. He thought the virtues of capital had been exaggerated at the expense of labor. Why should large land owners hide behind laws of supply and demand, controversies about rent, interest, and the rewards of speculators. Why should capitalists dominate the rural scene when labor gave land its value?

Intrigued by the maldistribution of wealth in rural England, Ford launched an agricultural experiment which combined the principles of a corporation farm with a profit-sharing wage system. He established Fordson Estates, bought land, improved machinery, and utilized the latest scientific methods in farming. The hired men drew a weekly salary of $10 a week and divided the excess income from the sale of farm commodities at the end of the year. At the end of ten years, the results were impressive on virtually all counts. Wages increased 25 percent, and the profit-sharing added another 60 percent to the incomes of the 181 farm hands working the 5,000 acres. Their combined savings totaled $240,000. Thus Ford claimed that putting 50 percent of the farm income into wages was profitable, just as paying high wages in the Ford automobile factories had been profitable. The trick was to put money into wages instead of paying stockholders or excessive interest to banks and loan companies. In a sense, Ford opposed the economic views of vitually all farmers and large land owners, who believed that a hired man should never be paid more than the minimum wage. His own experience had taught the reverse to be more healthy for all concerned.

Henry Ford saw education in broad terms as encompassing a person's total experience. This meant more than reading books, it implied observation, sensory perception, personal reactions, and individual involvement. He evidently had this in mind when he made his famous statement in 1919 that history was more or less bunk. Much later, in an interview in 1940, he admitted he used to get the devil for making this statement but refused to retreat from his earlier comment. "Now," he added "I say history is bunk—bunk—double bunk. Why, it isn't even true. They wrote what they wanted us to believe, glorifying some conqueror or leader or something like that."[16]

What Ford really resented was the deliberate reduction of history to dates, wars, textbooks, and rationalizations. With this in mind, he took action by establishing one of the largest educational exhibits in the nation, namely the founding of the Henry Ford Museum-Greenfield Village-Edison Institute complex in Dearborn. Roger Butterfield claims these one hundred buildings house the most popular historical preserve in the United States under nongovernmental operation. "Its entertainment features are conspicuous, but its basic purpose is mass education."[17] In 1938 half a million people visited the complex, while during the 1960s approximately one million visitors each year saw this fabulous collection.

Ford began with the restoration of his birthplace, and he searched diligently to restore it to the smallest detail. The quest whetted his appetite for collecting all kinds of Americana. He visited a Pennsylvania farm in 1922 to examine an old threshing machine built in 1820, and he stopped in antique shops, sometimes buying nothing and sometimes buying the entire store, saying "Pack it up and ship it to Dearborn." His thousands of Ford dealers were told to be alert for antiques, and at one time he had eight secretaries doing research in locating specific museum pieces. The files show as many as one hundred letters written in the quest of a single item. This mountain of miscellany filled the old tractor building and overflowed into warehouses and yards.

Since permanent housing facilities were needed, Ford pursued his twin dreams, Greenfield Village and the Museum. He often talked about his objectives saying the farther people could look back, the farther they could look ahead. He wanted to assemble every kind of article used in America since 1607 because this would reproduce life as it was lived. Looking at things would give a truer impression than months of reading.

The Greenfield Village featured the New England commons with houses and shops representing colonial America. The originals and replicas included Edgar Allen Poe's cottage from Fordham, New York, Walt Whitman's house from Melville, New York, Barbara Frietchie's home at Frederick, Maryland, and Patrick Henry's house from Red Hill, Virginia. Inside were scores of spinning wheels, quilting frames, cooking utensils, trundle beds, candle molders, and various devices showing the progression in lighting from sperm oil to kerosene. A Michigan sawmill of 1817 and a general store from Waterford, Michigan, were moved to the village. Later acquisitions included Luther Burbank's office in Santa Rosa, California, and a courthouse where Lincoln practiced law. Adjacent to the colonial village is a cluster known as Menlo Park which stands as a memorial to Thomas Edison. Because of their long friendship, Ford recreated the Edison laboratories with meticulous care.

Although Menlo Park, New Jersey, had little industry, its fame rested on Edison's research and adaptations which helped bring the phonograph, the incandescent lamp, and a complete system of public lighting. The original Edison laboratory, a two-story clapboard building, served as experimental rooms, machine shop, and general office. Additional laboratories were in Fort Meyers, Florida, where Edison did research in winter. All these buildings were brought to Greenfield Village and placed in their relative positions. The trees, shrubbery, and names of streets were duplicated. Six inches of red New Jersey soil was shipped by the carload to complete the restoration. When, on October 21, 1929, the celebration to honor the 50th anniversary of the incandescent light was held in Dearborn, Henry Ford, with his arm around Edison, shouted into his ear, "This museum and all connected with it, is for the inspiration of youth."[18]

Mr. Ford disliked dead museums filled with Indian relics and stuffed owls. He wanted a living educational exhibit demonstrating the skills of the past. A pageant would greet visitors. Obviously, this would require a large stage. The result was a building covering eight acres. Shiploads of teakwood were brought from the East Indies to provide a beautiful inlaid floor covering 350,000 square feet. It is the largest teakwood floor in the world and is designed to last for centuries. The façade of the building is 700-feet long and 450-feet deep. The interior is supported by 180 columns encased in special steel radiation, creating a modern clean-cut design.

The exhibits are arranged to tell the story of agriculture, manufacturing, and transportation from Colonial days to the present. All inventions which have ameliorated the manual labor of mankind are shown, as well as the new scientific principles on which other inventors have based their research. Not included are instruments of death—swords, cannon, military equipment, uniforms, daggers, armour, and dirks. Even mousetraps are eliminated, because the constructive instead of the destructive elements should prevail.

The agricultural section presents the evolution of farm implements from crude colonial plows to modern farm machinery. Since Ford had an affinity for steam engines, the Museum features the most complete line of stationary, portable, and self-propelled farm steam engines that provided the first mechanical power for American agriculture. The transportation section includes stage coaches, mail coaches, one-horse chaises, gigs, calèches, buckboards, phaetons, buggies, rockaways, racing sulkies, victorias, carryalls, coupes, and two-horse sociables. The first Ford quadracycle of 1896 is a historical treasure, while early automobiles of various makes are on the floor. Emphasis is upon mechanical progress rather than the esthetic. Bruce Bliven, writing in 1937, described the collection as more modest than the Deutsches Museum in Munich, Germany, but he added, "the Ford collection is more complete than in Munich or anywhere else in the world."[19]

As the Museum became better known, people in all ranks offered to assist in the project. Farmers wrote saying they wanted to donate spinning wheels which had been in the family since colonial days. They asked Ford to accept their old beds, silverware, kettles, lamps, grandfather clocks, stoves, crockery, plows, flails, tools, and various farm implements. Some hoped to unload items at fancy prices. Since the value of antiques is difficult to establish, they set prices and hoped for the best. An Illinois farmer asked $5,000 for a threshing-machine patent signed by Andrew Jackson. A watch, supposedly carried by George Washington across the Delaware on his famous Christmas Eve boat excursion, could be purchased for $1,000. A shotgun, with the name C. Hanks inscribed on the stock, was described as belonging to "Lincoln's mother's relatives." Priceless violins popped up in every section of the country, with owners swearing the inscriptions were Antonius Stradivarius Cremonensis Faciebat, anno 1721, or anno 1725, or anno 1770.

Apparently Ford followed his hunches in buying antiques. He could pay $45,000 for a highboy and then complain when asked $10 for an oxen yoke. Secretaries usually told correspondents that most farm articles were worthless and thus were fit only as donations. If an item were strongly desired, however, a nominal price was offered. Many sent gifts to the Museum, satisfied with the honor involved. The Wohlbruck family in California donated their entire museum, which consisted of fifty-six freight cars of exhibits.[20] "Steam Engine Joe" Ryanda of New Ulm, Minnesota, gave Ford an early wooden-wheeled farm steam engine worth several thousand dollars. When asked why he gave this prize away, he replied simply, "Henry Ford asked for it."[21]

At times, Ford used farm machinery in the Museum to demonstrate how they worked to people living in rural communities. For several years he sponsored an old-time threshing bee to relive memories of the past. He instructed his curator, Fred Smith, to put sweep-horsepower machines and threshers in working condition for these demonstrations in the wheat fields of the Ford farms. At times an old Westinghouse steam engine provided the power. Mr. Ford enjoyed operating the engine and visiting with farm folks. In 1944 twenty-five hundred people attended one of these threshing reunions near Tecumseh, Michigan.

This intense curiosity about early America led Henry Ford into research projects in which he tried to probe historical events. Many of these studies pertained to life in rural communities. For example, after purchasing Wayside Inn, he became interested in the origin of the poem, "Mary Had a Little Lamb," found in the McGuffey readers. By persistent investigation and numerous field trips, he learned that the Wayside School had been built in 1789 and used until 1856, when it was sold. It was a red wooden building named Redstone because of the color of the rock at the site. Ford wished to preserve the school house because it was here that Mary took her lamb to school.

Mary was Mary Elizabeth Sawyer, born on a farm near Sterling, Massachusetts, in 1806. One cold March morning, Mary accompanied her father to feed the livestock. When they reached the sheep enclosure, they found two lambs had been born during the night. One was dead, the other almost dead. Against her father's wishes she took the lamb to the house, nursed it back to health, and kept it as a pet. One day her brother Nathaniel suggested they take the lamb to school. Fearing the teacher's disapproval, they hid the lamb under Mary's desk and covered it with a scarf. When Mary went forward to recite, the lamb tagged after her. The uproar that followed mortified Mary almost to tears as she led the lamb outside. Another student, John Roulstone, Jr., on the next day handed Mary the three original stanzas of the poem, "Mary Had a Little Lamb."

But in 1830, Mrs. Sarah J. Hale published a book of poems which included the Mary and her lamb in six verses. This led to a controversy. Did Mrs. Hale or John Roulstone write the original lines? Descendants of Mrs. Hale claimed the poem was entirely imaginary; there never had been a real Mary or a real lamb in the Redstone School. After a careful study of internal and external evidence and an evaluation of literary criticism, the Ford experts concluded that a "seam" did appear between the first three verses and the last three. But the American public need not worry. There was a Mary, she did have a lamb, its fleece was white as snow, and it did follow her to school one day. Having solved the riddle to his own satisfaction, Ford published a 40-page book under the title, *The Story of Mary and Her Little Lamb as Told By Mary and her Neighbors and Friends*.[22] On February 15, 1927, Thomas Edison wrote Henry Ford saying the first words which ever came out of his first phonograph were "Mary had a Little Lamb."

The significance of Ford's educational ventures is difficult to measure. In some ways he seemed naïve, possessing a virgin mind uncluttered with formal training and untrammeled by any scholasticism. Not circumscribed by traditions, he was free to explore, always cocksure he could improve anything that came under his observation. Denied advanced education himself, he could say university degrees meant nothing to him until he could see what a person could do with it. A college education did not always fit a man for success because many were too proud to work; they regarded education as an escape from it, and had thus educated themselves beyond their intelligence. They acquired academic equipment for professions for which they had no natural aptitude. He always returned to the principles of learning, living, and earning. Will Rogers quipped, "If Henry Ford can educate a college boy to make a living right after he gets out of college, Ford is really the greatest living American."[23]

He believed if we could afford wars, we could afford education. If we could spend billions on war, we could give American children their birthright. Youth should not be condemned but encouraged, given counsel, and understanding.

Ford agreed that the nation's strength rested upon our democratic institutions and technological know-how. He thought technology had been slighted in schools because few institutions taught courses in the history of technology. Most books revealed the outside of machines rather than the inside. Writers leaned toward verbalization rather than visualization. Therefore he encouraged the use of motion pictures in class rooms. The present increased interest in technology suggests that Ford was in many ways ahead of his times.

Significantly enough, his family will provided for the endowment of the Ford Foundation, with assets of 2.3 billion dollars, dedicated to the purpose of "advancing human welfare." Thus he left the greatest private legacy primarily to the advancement of education, in the broad scope of that term. In this sense, his efforts are still reflected as a powerful force in education today.

XII

"Dear Mr. Ford..."

The avalanche of correspondence addressed to Henry Ford over the years reflects something of the nature of the man himself, as well as something about his correspondents. This mail illuminates much of the social history of the period because it contains the candid views of Americans who commented on life as they saw it. Since Ford appealed strongly to the common man, he heard most often from farmers and middle-class folks who were living in the typical small towns of mid-America. Much of the evidence is subliterary in form, most of it is anti-intellectual, some of it is trivial in nature, but it all adds up to a perspective of the average man's estimate of the Detroit Flivver King. The analysis here focuses on Henry Ford as seen by those who felt impelled to write to him. After reading parts of Henry Ford's mail, what are the conclusions?

In the first place, the amount of this mail bulked large. After the announcement of the $5.00-day on January 1, 1914, an observer exclaimed, "Letters! Letters! Letters! It rains letters. It pours letters. Letters come by dozens, by grosses, by hundreds, yes, literally by thousands."[1] "Ford's mail is enough for a small town," noted the Detroit *Free Press*, "it is piled in boxes, crates, baskets and barrels. . . ."[2] The correspondence appeared in letters of one sentence, one paragraph, one page, and a score of pages. The flow included post cards, telegrams, blue prints, pamphlets, brochures, and yards of newspaper clippings. Although the exact number of letters cannot be determined, various men in Dearborn attempted to measure the volume. The *Ford Times* in March, 1914, stated that letters were arriving at the rate of 500 to 1,000 a day. Charles Zahnov, one of Ford's secretaries, said his office received 1,000 to 1,500 letters daily during the early 1920s. Edgar A. Guest, after visiting Dearborn in 1924, wrote an article for *American Magazine* in which he claimed, "Every day, 1,500 persons decide that the way out of their troubles is to write a letter to Henry Ford."[3] He probably exaggerated in saying 10,000 people wrote to Ford each week begging for help of some kind. William Greenleaf, however, in his *From These Beginnings*, accepts the Guest figures at face value, claiming that in 1924, Ford was receiving 500,000 letters annually.[4] In 1930 E. G. Liebold, writing to a correspondent in Massachusetts, reported that Ford's mail averaged several thousand letters daily. In these estimates it is not clear which letters were personal and which ones pertained to business affairs of the Ford Motor Company. It seems reasonable, however, to assume that over a twenty-year span, Henry Ford received from three hundred to one thousand letters a day dealing with personal matters and another thousand letters daily concerning business affairs of the company. This adds up to millions of letters during Ford's forty-four years in business.

Ford spent little time with this correspondence, however. At times a secretary would show him a letter which seemed to have special significance, but Henry was not a desk man. He thrived on movement; movement to inspect factory work or to consult with engineers in the experimental division. Committee work bored him. When sessions dragged, he frequently excused himself for a breath of fresh air and then never returned. He did much of his office work in his automobile, cruising around the Michigan countryside amid beautiful scenery and quiet vistas.

Meanwhile, back in the offices in the Engineering Building in Dearborn, a small secretarial staff handled the correspondence. Although all letters were not answered as was commonly believed, most of them received replies. In 1923 Harold M. Cordell, a secretary, devised fifty form letters to expedite replies. One form stated, "Mr. Ford, on behalf of himself and the company, wishes to express appreciation of the sentiment in your recent letter. . . ." Since Ford's signature appeared, many believed they received a personal note. William Wadell, another secretary, recalled reading and answering letters at a rate of three per minute. Due to this speed in handling, errors sometimes occurred. On one occasion, the wrong form letter went off to an English Countess implying that she had written requesting money. The woman became indignant and "wrote a sizzling reply giving us hell."

As might be expected, Ford received messages from a host of prominent people, such as Kaiser Wilhelm, Count Tolstoy, King Edward VII, and other European dignitaries. Seven presidents of the United States corresponded with him, some exchanging felicitations, others seeking advice and cultivating good will. Franklin D. Roosevelt, as vice-president of the Fidelity and Deposit Company of Maryland with offices in New York, wrote Ford on January 17, 1924, inviting him to spend a vacation at Hyde Park. Mr. Roosevelt mentioned that in November of 1923, four prominent citizens of New York came to him claiming Ford to be the greatest menace in the country. After Ford withdrew from the presidential race, the same four men returned to Roosevelt's office the next January to say they believed Ford to be a wise man, a great industrial leader with sound judgments and great vision. He added, "I take it you know the type of New York mind which performs gymnastics of this kind. . . ."[5] Twenty-one years later the two exchanged communications. President Roosevelt, returning from the Yalta Conference aboard the *Quincy*, wrote on February 22, 1945, "Dear Mr. Ford: I was happy to receive your nice telegram on the way to the Crimea. Now I am coming back and I think the international results have been excellent. I hope that you will come to see me this spring if you are in Washington or the neighborhood. . . ."

The preponderance of Ford's correspondence, however, came from humble folks, who regarded him as the neighbor next door or a relative of the family. Most common people had read so much about the billionaire that they thought they knew him personally. A Louisiana Farmer explained why he wrote in familiar terms because, "I have seen so much of your life recorded in the papers that it just seems I have known you all my life. . . ." This affinity became so powerful that even today some letters arrive in the Dearborn office addressed to Henry Ford, written by people who are unaware of his death in 1947.

The folksy quality of much of the Ford fan mail is noticeable. The letters reflect candor, a sense of rapport, a down-to-earth egalitarianism, and childlike simplicity. In this sense, the collection is unusual. The files of the Franklin D. Roosevelt Library in Hyde Park are full of laudatory sentiments, but they do not exude the folksy sentimentality found in the Ford Archives. Apparently correspondents saw Roosevelt as President of the United States, while Ford seemed to be the farm family on the adjoining half section.

As the warmth of spring put beauty in the New England hills, a farmer's wife near Ashby, Massachusetts, invited Henry Ford to visit them because the laurel would be in bloom in the middle of the next week. An Oregon family wanted the Fords to come out and have dinner with them and asked whether they liked their chicken boiled or fried. Approaching ninety years of age, a lively Virginian said she was getting her third set of teeth and second eye sight. She had invited her 36 grandchildren and 100 great grandchildren to her birthday party and hoped Ford would likewise show up for the event.

The chatty flow of family news included such minutia as the location of the farm house, the name of the township, number of cattle on the farm, and the status of the weather. Comments included such items as, "We planted our potatoes today, but the rest of the garden isn't up yet," "We have cabbage, tomatoes and peppers started in a box," "We have 85 chicks three weeks old," "Could you stop in and help us churn butter," and a Texan who explained, "We had a good rain here last night and I hope you had rain over your way."

Naturally, doting mothers told Ford how cute their cherubs were with curly hair and two front teeth. Some named their sons Henry Ford for good luck. "I just had a baby girl," purred a Maryland wife, "and since your wife's name is Mary and yours being Henry, I am going to name it Mary Henryetta Ford, if you don't mind. She is real pretty and weighed 10½ pounds at birth." A wife, seven months pregnant, said her 14-month old girl failed to cut teeth until 13 months old. "Mr. Ford do you think the next child will have the same trouble. Please write."

Although the wealthiest man in the land scarcely needed alms, surprisingly enough gifts of all descriptions poured into the Ford coffers.

Special holidays brought a torrent of remembrances in letters and cards. Many kept the Fords on their regular Christmas card list. Valentine's Day encouraged gushing sentiment some of which found expression in doggerel which had heart but not poetic form. Birthdays provided incentive for writing. Those with birthdays on July 30 often shared this coincidence with Ford, while those the same age sensed a fraternal kinship. Ford's seventy-fifth and eightieth birthdays brought messages from all parts of the country.

The newspaper references to Ford's humility appealed to ordinary people caught in the hum-drum of life. News emanating from the Dearborn offices was designed to enhance this folksy aura. For instance, the vacation trips of Ford, Thomas Edison, John Burroughs, and Harvey Firestone into the Great Smokies in the summer of 1918 and into the Adirondacks in 1919, were played up as the greatest adventure since Teddy Roosevelt and his armed battalions went game hunting in Africa. Here were he-men roughing it amid the wilds of nature. Candid camera shots revealed such exciting events as Edison sleeping under a tree, or the elderly John Burroughs beating Ford in a tree chopping contest. Rumors had Ford taking dips in the creek stark naked, and that Burroughs added to scientific knowledge by demonstrating that a skunk could be carried by his tail without dangerous repercussions.

Less well-known facts about these simple camping trips were that the party in 1918 had six automobiles, two Packards, two Model Ts and two Ford trucks. Tents, cots, stoves, ovens, electric lights, a refrigerator, and a large table capable of seating twenty people were provided and managed by a crew of seven men.

A mountain of mail reached Ford from rural people who wished to tell their experiences with the Model T. These memories remained in hallowed reveries. Over the years the Tin Lizzie had become personified and graced with the attributes of a good companion. Those who had spent years repairing the car and giving it artificial respiration viewed the passing of the era with regret, not unlike the departure of a life-long friend. In fact, when it was announced that the Model T would be replaced by the Model A, some purchased several Lizzies as a reserve to carry them well into the future.

Ford received many requests to make some kind of a trade, preferably the exchanging of some item for a brand new Model T. A farmer near Denver wanted to trade six mounted moose heads for a new car. One offered as bait an antique grandfathers clock, two hundred years old, with an eight day repeating strike, a calendar, a brass movement, and a carved cherry case seven feet tall. Other offers included Navajo Indian rugs, a six-horse team of horses, a McCormick-Deering grain binder, ten acres of cut over timber land, a stack of good prairie hay, four Shetland ponies, a steam calliope, a bundle of second mortgages, and a variety of second-hand cars.

Real estate deals were offered by many because they had heard of Ford's tendency to increase his acreage of farm land. Usually farmers and small town property owners described their holdings in honest terms, but city professional promoters often resorted to high-pressure tactics to complete a deal.

Many rural people assumed that a company which could buy railroads, mines, and forests would be in the market for small items

as well. They believed Henry Ford's credit was good. Those hoping
to get a better price from Ford than on the open market offered to
sell such commodities as wheat, corn, hay, cattle, hogs, sheep, and
poultry. One farmer offered to sell thirty-two registered Shorthorn
cattle for $10,000, but was told Ford had all the livestock he
needed. Others believed they could sell various attachments to
farm machines which they had built, such as anti-quack grass implements, or tractor mounted corn cultivators. One thought Ford
might like to buy his Russian wolf hound with a long intelligent
head, while a farm lad wanted to sell his three-legged pony.

Considerable correspondence involved rumors that Ford
planned to give away a certain number of Model Ts in whimsical
fashion. The gossip was usually vague, but the results wide-spread.
One rumor had Ford giving cars to women who refused to bob their
hair. The comment reflected the controversy in the twenties when
conservatives equated old-fashioned morality with Holy Writ and
St. Paul's reference to women's hair as their crowning glory.

Other misconceptions, equally fantastic, included Ford giving
new cars to all families in the United States whose name was
spelled Ford, or to those with birthdays were the same as his, on
July 30. Some believed they could get a free Model T by sending in
a certain postage stamp, or dimes with the Mint letters, F.O.R.D.
Other rumors included Ford selling his cars for $100 on his birth-
day, or on his son's wedding day, or on the day Virginia voted dry.

Henry Ford indeed did give away some automobiles to such
prominent people as Crown Prince Gustav of Sweden, King Alfonse
of Spain, Baron Krupp von Bohlen und Halbach, Thomas Edison,
John D. Rockefeller, Randolph A. Hearst, Fritz Kreisler, and John
Burroughs. From 1921 to 1942, he gave away approximately 200
cars, 23 trucks and 15 tractors.

Many tried to wrangle a new car from Ford while offering little
in return. A Colorado farmer who had driven his 1911 Model T
86,000 miles, thought this performance merited a new one. A gar-
dener in Wisconsin claimed his twenty-year old wine would cure
cancer and therefore he would exchange two quarts for a new car.
A young fellow in Oklahoma wanted a 1925 Ford to make an endurance run to Oregon, which would give him a chance to see his relatives and advertise the auto enroute. Some suggested Ford sell
cars at cut-rate prices without telling local dealers. Others simply
asked that he donate one for old times sake, to facilitate sales work,
to visit sick relatives, and as one writer put it, "If I had a Ford, I'd

think I had the world and all that's in it." A Hoosier farmer with a family of eight explained, "I hate to hafta ask this, but I am in bad health and need an old Ford so I can make a tractor out of it and thus farm my 32 acres. . . ."

While the proposals of farmers often seemed impractical, they were usually more realistic than the bizarre notions of city business-men, who wanted large sums of money to promote their ventures. An Indiana adventurer planned to scientifically propagate reindeer from Alaska to Labrador to produce enough food to last as long as the continent endured. Another prospectus outlined plans to salvage a galleon of the ill-fated Spanish Armada of 1588. A New York broker in 1924 offered to sell Broadway from 55th to 56th streets for $1,800,000!

Urgent appeals were made requesting his attendance at public meetings where his presence would highlight the program and guar-antee success. Promoters hoped he would make an appearance and perhaps give a few appropriate remarks. E. G. Liebold, in 1923, said these invitations arrived at the rate of approximately 30 a day. Ford detested these promotional schemes and refused to be made a freak in a sideshow to attract trade. Although he spurned the Chamber of Commerce organizations and the Civic Clubs, he did accept invitations to various events where farm machinery was demonstrated. He frequently showed up at State Fairs and the trac-tor demonstrations held in various agricultural communities. In July, 1918, he joined 80,000 people at the tractor show near Salina, Kansas, in what the New York *Herald* called "the monster demon-stration of the progress of motorized agriculture."[6] Reporters pic-tured the Detroit maestro as a better show than the tractors. He arrived sans golf clubs, sans valet, and sans a bulging pocket book. He trudged behind machines through plowed fields and rubbed el-bows with farmers. He refused to sit in Morris chairs, rejected 25-cent cigars, and chatted with the sons of the soil. On his fifty-fifth birthday, instead of celebrating with a champagne dinner, he spent the noon hour atop a hay stack talking to a small boy and viewing the countryside.

A considerable part of Ford's fan mail came from people who thought the industrialist was a social reformer who had, as the Munich *Neueste Nachrichten* puts it, "the rare gift of surrounding his whole work with a halo which portrays him as a champion of mankind."[7] In the early 1920s, Edwin Markham concluded, "I put the social gospel into words; Mr. Ford puts it into works."[8] If this gospel meant inculcating social and economic reforms into capitalism and laying hold on life with both hands, as Washington Gladden expressed it, then the policies of Ford in 1914 exemplified the new doctrine. The Ford Motor Company raised wages of most employees to $5.00 a day in January, 1914, and to $6.00 a year later, and changed to a five-day work week on April 5, 1922. A shared-profit bonus of $48,299,815.45 went to workers from 1914 to 1918.[9] Ford explained that it was better to make many comfortable than to make a few rich. He refuted Andrew Carnegie's notion that giving money to laboring men would pauperize them. "Aid the man who sweats," added Ford. "We believe social justice begins at home."[10]

This profit-sharing plan became the subject of ministers' sermons and high school debates. Wiseacres said Ford made Carnegie look like two cents because he put his money into workers instead of horses and yachts. A southern newspaper complained that men left their wives and went to Detroit to work for $5.00 a day, while the courts had to haul them home again. Farmers wanted to know why a man in Ford's factories should receive more for his labor than those working in agriculture. Ford's workers were indoors in comfortable shops out of the wind and rain and after eight hours they could go home. When they were broke they could strike for higher wages. Meanwhile the farmer worked sixteen hours a day, invested $10,000 in his farm, paid taxes, and at the end of the week he could not go to the bank and draw out $30. A cartoon depicting the traditional rural hostility toward the factory worker shows an enraged hired man waving his pitchfork in the farmer's face and threatening, "I want a share of the profits of this farm and $5.00 a day for eight hours work, or I'll quit and go to Detroit."[11]

Ford introduced various innovations such as a Sociological department under the direction of Dean Samuel S. Marquis. This agency, with a corps of some two hundred social workers, was established in 1916 to aid factory workers in such matters as health, housing, investments, and social life. Those refusing to follow instructions in financial and social affairs were put on probation or dismissed. Although the results were beneficial, some believed the supervision threatened the privacy of the individual. The company stores, operating from 1919 to 1927, introduced labor-saving techniques similar to the supermarkets of today. Customers moved along a counter and were served by clerks who transferred the goods directly from railroad cars to the counter. Prices were reduced because of the efficiency in handling large quantities. These commissary stores were too successful, however, creating opposition from the Detroit retailers, who threatened to boycott the Ford Motor Company. As a result, the eleven stores in several states were closed in 1927, even though studies by economists proved them highly desirable.

Another project with humane overtones came in 1914 when Ford agreed to finish building the Detroit General Hospital. He turned the management over to his secretary E. G. Liebold, who incorporated many of Ford's ideas of medical practice. The institution put doctors on a fixed salary, and hospital rates and doctor's fees were to be standardized for all, regardless of wealth. Patients were to be informed of costs in advance. In 1915 the charges were set at $3.00 to $8.00 a day for room and $3.00 a day for medical care, with the highest cost of a single operation being $250. Patients would receive the advice of several doctors rather than the guesswork of a single physician.

Although the hospital was recognized as one of the outstanding hospitals in the country, the mass production methods seemed too much like the Highland Park factory. One patient said he got undressed and sat down on a moving belt, "just like you was a flivver. The doctors line up along the belt, and as you go through each guy does his bit. It ain't like the old way when the doctor did everything. At the end of the belt, you're through, and they slide you right onto a bed that's got a little flivver engine and it takes you right to your room."[12] Liebold had the nerve to suggest that doctors punch a time clock, and he enforced a rule that no patient should be asked to wait over thirty minutes. In Accession 65 of the Ford Archives are some of Liebold's notes, as well as the observations of Dr. J. Janney Smith, one of the doctors on the staff. Liebold had written: Monday, hernia operations, Tuesday, appendixes removed, Wednesday, gall bladders, Thursday, hysterectomies, Friday, prostate glands, Saturday, Clean out the Place.[13]

Ford also established a mission house to treat alcoholics and drug addicts. He sympathized with the Anti-Cigarette League and published a 56-page booklet entitled *The Little White Slaver*, which attacked the habit as detrimental to health and morals. The evidence claimed that tobacco led to sallow skin, sunken eyes, loss of memory, heart disease, insomnia, giddiness, impaired vision, impaired digestion, and led to masturbation. Over six hundred requests for this type of literature reached Ford's office in 1914. On the question of alcohol, Ford gave limited support to the Prohibition movement prior to the adoption of the 18th amendment in 1920. He discouraged drinking among his employees and claimed overeating created an appetite for booze. During the 1920s he opposed liquor in all forms, barred its use in his plants, and announced he could not afford to risk expensive machinery and human lives to workers who poisoned themselves with drink. As a result, the temperance people praised Ford for his stand. A rural Methodist minister in New Jersey wrote, "Would that there were 10,000 Mr. Fords in the nation. Were it so, verily, verily, I believe the millennium gates would open wide."

Henry Ford also believed convicts could be rehabilitated. He thought prisons wasted human resources and laws prevented convicts from doing productive work. A prison should be an industrial enterprise, turning out goods for the benefit of all. Prisoners should be paid regular wages so as to support families at home. A jail should not be a tomb for the living, doing ill-directed, degrading labor. "We still believe things are more important than men. A criminal is a nonproducer, but society demands that he remain a nonproducer. This is flagrant waste." In 1915 Ford had five hundred convicts, many of them from Sing Sing prison, working in his factories. Eugene V. Debs, who knew something about prison life stated, "Henry Ford has taken thieves, pickpockets, prostitutes, burglars, dope-fiends, murderers, both male and female, who were supposed to be hopeless degenerates and has made men and women of them. There is nothing strange or miraculous about this. . . ."[14] Clarence Darrow suggested in 1930 that most Americans would be in jail if everyone who had violated a criminal statute had been apprehended. In writing to Ford he said our prisons were filled with derelicts as a product of our unscientific way of living. The schools and colleges had not reached this class. "No one knows as well as you do how most men can be adapted to useful and remunerative work. . . ."[15]

Consistent with his liberal views on social issues, Ford strongly opposed capital punishment because he believed it fundamentally wrong. He insisted the electric chair did not cure crime or act as a deterrent. He thought no person should favor capital punishment unless he himself were willing to perform the execution. Since few would take this responsibility, it was unfair to ask the state to do the killing. "It is wrong to kill a man" he asserted, "It does no good for the man and it does no good for society. But we want to kill because it is the easiest way of disposing of the problem."[16] As a liberal, at least prior to 1925, Ford denied the doctrine of total depravity and the assumption that men were conceived in iniquity and born in sin. In the Jeffersonian sense, he believed there was good in every person, that men could be appealed to on a basis of reason, and that justice should be a fundamental law of the universe.

Because of these humane philosophies, Ford drew appeals from do-gooders in all walks of life. The Anti-Profanity League showered him with posters admonishing people not to swear nor use obscene language. A California Sierra Health colony asked him to establish a sanitarium in the mountains for those with tuberculosis and other pulmonary diseases. One correspondent wanted milk stations which sold at reduced prices. Another hoped Ford would buy small farms for retired citizens in old age. If the widows of presidents Cleveland, Roosevelt, and Harding could draw $5,000 a year, why shouldn't a poor farm widow with four children receive a mother's pension?

Many Americans seemed to think of Ford as a department of justice, an attorney general, or policeman to enforce laws of morality. A woman in Georgia wanted him to curb vice, associated with Elks conventions. She claimed these annual sessions revealed greater laxity in morals than exhibited in ancient Rome. Fights occurred in back alleys, drunken hoodlums dressed in purple and elk heads performed familiarities in public, and all restraints were gone. A nude woman had been put in a store window as a display in full view of the public while the police failed to interfere. "Boozy girls are hauled about by drunken men screaming with laughter over pinches by promiscuous hands on any part of their bodies. Now Henry, I want you to do something about all this, because you are the richest man in America and maybe your voice will be heard. . . ."

A farmer near Fairbault, Minnesota, stated the breweries had controlled the state legislature for thirty years. Would Ford donate two new Model Ts so people could be brought to Anti-Saloon meetings and then home again in time to milk the cows?

After the holdup and murder of a paymaster and guard of a shoe factory in South Braintree, Massachusetts, on April 15, 1920, Nicola Sacco and Bartolomeo Vanzetti were arrested and brought to trial. During the trial the counsel for the defense claimed the two were indicted, not because they committed the crime but because they were foreigners who held radical political views. The jury declared Sacco and Vanzetti guilty and Judge Webster Thayer sentenced them to death. Governor Fuller permitted the executions to take place on August 23, 1927.

Two days before the executions, Vanzetti wrote to Henry Ford, declaring his innocence and stating that a review of the evidence would bring exoneration. This letter, undoubtedly his last, written to Henry Ford on August 21 from the Death House of the Massachusetts State Prison, is remarkably objective and rational:

> Dear Sir:
>
> Just this morning, I accidentally learned that you had asked or suggested the commutation of our death-sentence to life imprisonment to as to give us an opportunity of presenting eventual new discovered evidence . . . I have always claimed my innocence and I will die affirming it . . . . I am sure a new trial would vindicate my innocence; this is the only reason why I would prefer commutation to my execution. . . . consider me as very grateful to you for your request or suggestion in our case —also for my family. Yours, BARTOLOMEO VANZETTI.

The interest here is not so much the miscarriage of justice for a fish peddler which shocked the world, but rather the revelation of Ford's insight into human nature and his faith in the underprivileged.

Although Ford's interest in social reform never completely vanished, it diminished with advancing age. By 1928 he had mellowed, losing his zeal for humanitarian causes and lapsing into reactionary modes of thought. Occasionally he made remarks to the press, but the zip was gone and his ideas, like his Model T cars, were fast becoming obsolete. Advancing years brought on a nostalgia for the old days, and he turned to collecting antiques for his museum and reviving square dancing. This was his revolt against the tempo of the jazz age, the hip flask, and the Charleston.

Henry had learned to dance in the 1870s when dance orchestras produced rhythm and harmony. The Fords had held old fashioned dances intermittently over the years, but the pressures of business curbed their social life. In 1923 they secured Benjamin Lovett of Boston to teach square dancing to various groups in Dearborn. Henry Ford bought instruction books, drew diagrams on the floors of offices showing the position of the feet for certain dance steps, and ran his secretarial staff through the routines. He provided dance classes for school children in Dearborn because he believed this taught youngsters poise and polite manners. For a time dances were held weekly in Fair Lane to which company personnel and guests from Grosse Pointe were invited. Henry was an indefatigable dancer who, according to one writer, gave as much attention to a dance step as to marketing Lizzies in Manchuria.

With great enthusiasm he organized "Ford's Fiddlin Five," a group averaging 70 years in age, to tour the country reviving old tunes and demonstrating that the old steps of the hoop-skirted belles of grandma's days could be more graceful than the bobbed-haired flappers clogging the Charleston. As a result, the fad caught on, with old-time fiddlers emerging to scratch out the Virginia Reel to the call of the do-si-do. The Ford Motor Company sponsored fiddling contests in which local and state winners went on to a national contest. Excitement ran high in rural communities and small towns on Saturday nights when these contests enlivened the scene.

For a time, this revival prospered, with thousands participating in the new craze. At one dance in Detroit in 1925, some six thousand people filled the hall with over two thousand turned away. These dances continued until the Second World War, but in the 20-year span, thousands followed Ford's dance manual *Good Morning* which was designed to revive the old music and to counteract the forces of jazz.

The advent of radio in the early twenties provided a sensational medium of communication. By 1922, a hundred broadcasting stations were reaching a million homes in the United States. For the first time, the home had been opened to the sounds of the world. Farmers on the plains used barbed wire for aerials to tune in their crude sets. The Crosley, Atwater Kent, and Montgomery Ward Airline came with separate speakers and were powered by a six-volt storage battery.

With the introduction of chain broadcasting, the Ford Motor Company began offering a program of folkdance music in 1926. These came on Friday nights with an orchestra beating out such tunes as "The Arkansas Traveler" and "The Girl I Left Behind Me." This folksy program, like the Saturday Night Barn Dance program from Chicago, appealed to the musically uneducated, who enjoyed the lively tempo and rhythm of the folk music and the nasal twang of the caller.

Generous fan mail reached Detroit, especially from the rural areas and small towns. Since this was the only orchestra music many rural people heard, they wrote Ford to express their gratitude. "Three cheers for Ford. We danced the whole hour even though we are 80 years old. . . ." "Your program is the best on the air. . . ."

Because Henry Ford had great wealth and a humanitarian image, the requests for financial aid were voluminous. Dr. Samuel S. Marquis, who headed the sociological work at the Ford Motor Company, in 1916 estimated the requests for money averaged $6 million a month, while Edgar Guest in 1924 claimed it would cost $400 million a year to meet these demands. These files in the Ford Archives make grim reading. The pages might well be edged in black for they contain the frustrated cries of the poor. Here the souls of the weak, discouraged, and afraid are laid bare; people whose dread of poverty outweigh their shame in begging for money. These letters suggest the prevalence of poverty and substandard living conditions even in the day of the so-called prosperous 1920s.

A Canadian farmer wrote to Ford saying his wife cried every night because he could not pay the dealer for his farm machinery. Another farmer near Lexington, Nebraska, had been crippled when hit by lightning so his 73-year old mother had to do the work. His life insurance policy had lapsed, and he hoped Ford would reinstate the policy. A doleful account from a rancher near Glendive, Montana, in 1923 stated he had been hailed out one year, burned out the next and left without feed for his livestock. The family wondered if Ford would purchase their beautiful agate, keep the commission and forward the rest.

The deepest concerns were for the children, first their necessities, then opportunities which might make life easier for them than it had been for the parents. A mother near Fowlerville, Michigan, explained that her children needed stockings and shoes to keep out the cold. She had mended their clothes until they were nothing but patches. She added that she had never asked for aid before in her life and hoped to God she would never need to do so again. A rural widow in Indiana, unable to pay a $700 loan on her house, faced foreclosure and the loss of her personal belongings. An unemployed teacher near Marion, Pennsylvania, lived on a forty-acre farm without horses or a tractor. She was unable to send her son to school because of poverty. She did not want charity but wanted to exchange her books for some money. "I will try anything honest and honorable that will keep my children in school. Please don't put me down as a beggar. I am just a frightened mother, insecure, worried, and desperate."

The requests for jobs were legion. A Swede in North Dakota said he had raised nothing but failures in wheat farming and one more would ruin him completely. He wanted work for himself and two sons in Detroit. A farm family, after losing their property near Chambers, New York, traveled around picking up odd jobs but found no steady employment because it was the same old story, times were hard, business was dull, companies were not hiring people and now a baby had come to add to the difficulties. They had heard that Ford had bought a railroad and perhaps they needed help on the section gang putting in ties. Convicts who have served time frequently applied for jobs because they had heard Ford's well-known statement that he had never met a really bad man. A former prisoner who received a position in the Ford branch factory in Atlanta, Georgia, said he now had hope and sunshine flowing into his life.

Perhaps the most pathetic letters were written by the aged and those in bad health. A rural free delivery father in Ohio had a wife crippled with rheumatism and a family of eight children stricken with scarlet fever. If no assistance could be found he would have to break up the family. A woman in Minden, Nebraska, wrote to Mrs. Ford saying her husband had been sick for twenty years and bed-ridden for five years. "But I have no money. When I read that you had so much money that you didn't know what you were worth, and that you sometimes stay up all night thinking about how to spend your money, I thought I would write you. . . ." A retired school teacher in Oregon owed a $500 mortgage, had $1,075 in other debts, and with no teacher's pension plan, she could get only $7.50 to $15.00 a month from the state and then only if she signed away her home to the state and took a pauper's oath.

Yet many poor people were more cheerful. An Arkansas farm wife wanted a $150 loan to move to town and start a grocery store because after forty years of fighting nature they were now prepared to become capitalists. A perceptive woman said she had saved up a little egg money amounting to $100 and wanted Ford to invest it in any way he saw fit.

Some wrote Ford asking advice in investing money, buying stocks, and how to bet on various presidential races. Others wanted remedies for hay fever, varicose veins, fallen arches, the hives, and gas on the stomach.

Religious leaders looked to Ford as a potential donor. Churches needed money to fund building projects, to send missionaries to the foreign field, and to carry the gospel to the unwashed sinners. During the 1920s most people had read that Mr. and Mrs. Ford belonged to the Episcopal Church and gave it financial support. *The Lookout*, published by the Methodist Church on August 20, 1922, stated Ford prayed daily for wisdom, his creed was the Sermon on the Mount, and his highest purpose in life was service. The *Christian Herald* claimed Henry read a chapter in the Bible every day and had the Scriptures handy in all rooms of his home. Most people, however, had not heard that in earlier days Ford had said he was born an Episcopalian but had not worked at it since, that he could get along without kneeling to pray, and that anyone going to heaven or hell would take their knees along with them. On one occasion when asked what he thought of the church he said he favored them because they were good places for young people to meet and mate up. At another time when asked if he attended church he said, "No, the last time I went somebody stole my car."

Individuals often used religious rhetoric to clothe their requests for charity. One correspondent asked for money "for God says in the Good Book to help the poor, and I am one of the poor." A Wisconsin farmer needed a new car to get to town so he argued that the Bible teaches if one had two coats one should be given the poor. "So if you want to do good, give us a car and the Lord will richly bless you." An ingenious man in Illinois in 1923 asked Ford for a loan of $2 million for eighteen months. Although he never explained the need for the money, he wrote 435 letters to Ford in less than two years. He usually included the note, all filled in with the exception of Henry Ford's signature. In these letters he mentioned the beauty of brotherhood and that God loved a cheerful giver.

For the most part, Henry Ford's notions of philanthropy reflected the Puritan ethic of hard work, frugality, sobriety, and self-reliance. Charity had no place in the civilized world except to take care of the infirm, the aged, and the sick. Able-bodied men should be given work, not cash; only weaklings accepted charity. Giving away money might seem desirable to the donor, but it usually ruined the character of the recipient. Ford continued to argue that doles, free meals and free lodging, and Community Chest agencies should be condemned. There should never be any unemployment in the first place. Cities should provide work for those who could not find it themselves. Funds should come from taxation not from voluntary contributions. Hard realities rather than soft sentimentalism, and utilitarianism rather than alms became the Ford credo. "I am against charity because it lowers self-respect," said Ford," "Society does not owe any man a living, but society does owe him a chance to work."[17]

Above all, Ford liked to see where his money went; where results might be seen with his own eyes and measured by his own standards of value. As a result, his philanthropy went primarily to trade and vocational schools, museums, technological research, hospitals, and occasional outright gifts in cash.

According to the records in Accession 384 of the Ford Archives, Henry Ford's net income from 1913 to 1947 amounted to $139,200,761.83, his total tax deductions were $34,055,046.20, which included contributions of $15,259,997.58.[18] Although it is impossible to secure figures which are absolute because of the difficulty in defining what constitutes gifts and what were normal business expenses, it seems fair to assume Ford gave away a sum of money ranging from $15 million to $25 million during his lifetime. Of this amount, it is estimated that he gave almost two million dollars to individuals. While he never achieved the more sophisticated and systemized programs of John D. Rockefeller and Andrew Carnegie, his contributions were respectable when compared with others of great wealth. Much of Ford's wealth was tied up in factories and machinery and did not represent money in the bank. While he could veto the request of a widow forced to pawn her wedding ring to buy food, he none-the-less possessed enough sympathy for the unfortunate masses to justify their faith in him to the extent that large numbers felt impelled to write to him as "Dear Mr. Ford. . . ."

XIII

Ford in Retrospect

Henry Ford profoundly influenced life in America during the first half of the twentieth century. His greatest contribution lay in his demonstration that mechanical power should supersede animal power in transportation and in agriculture. He realized that the nation was moving toward the era of the internal-combustion engine, and, sensing this change, he joined others in meeting the demand for automobiles, trucks and tractors. As a manufacturer of these power units he shared with approximately two thousand other companies in bringing about the demise of the horse in the United States. Never fond of farm animals, he scorned those who bragged about the value of "the old gray mare," who devoured much of the oats and grass on the farm. His thesis was "you couldn't fix a dead horse with a monkey wrench." As a result, fifteen million Flivvers proved the feasibility of motor transport in agricultural regions. These tough vehicles plowed through mud roads and rattled into farm yards with such persistent fortitude that they were regarded as an integral part of rural life. When the number of horses and mules in the nation fell from twenty-eight million in 1917 to two million in 1965, the transfer of labor from farm muscles to motors was virtually completed.[1] In fact, the Statistical Reporting Service of the United States Department of Agriculture in 1962 discontinued listing the number of horses on farms because they were no longer significant to farm production.

This application of science and technology to American agriculture produced impressive results. At Henry Ford's birth in 1863, each farmer in the country had access to 1.4 horsepower; eighty-four years later at his death, each farmer commanded 10 horse-power. In 1863 one farmer could produce enough food to support five townspeople, while today one farm worker can support thirty city people. From 1937 to 1957 the agricultural output per man-hour increased 60 percent compared with 28 percent in industry.

As the new technology provided the machines which made obsolete the "Man with the Hoe," power farming removed much of the drudgery in farm labor and brought the luxuries of city life to rural America. Henry Ford participated in this transformation. His success was phenomenal. The Ford Motor Company, founded in 1903, grew into an industrial giant which by 1922 had manufactured five million cars and two hundred thousand farm tractors—all val-ued at approximately $3 million.[2] When Henry resigned the presi-dency of the company in 1945, his cash bank balance was $685,034,892. Twenty-three years later the company had $9 billion in assets and $14 billion in annual sales.[3]

Not only had Ford helped to provide a technology for rural America, but his economic philosophy cheered the farmer and aver-age wage earner in the country. He practiced the doctrine which held that mass production and efficiency in management could re-duce the prices of manufactured products, which, in turn, would increase sales, thus bringing an abundance of the good things of life to virtually all members of society. There was nothing new in this doctrine which for years had been advanced by the proponents of free private enterprise. Most capitalists, however, rejected their own gospel by avoiding competition and by creating monopolies which put emphasis on profits, not on price cuts. The remarkable feature of Ford's program was that he actually did reduce prices and, for this determined stand, the common man rose up to call him blessed. Although it took Ford some time to reach these goals, his record in price reduction is remarkable. In 1908 his Model T tour-ing car sold for $850. It went to $950 in 1909, then dropped to $690 in 1911, $550 in 1913, $490 in 1914, $360 in 1916, and to an all-time low of $290 on December 2, 1924. At this time the roadster sold for $260.[4]

These were economic facts which rural Americans could under-stand. They knew of no other industrial performance to compare with it. When a farmer could go to town and buy a Model T at a price below that asked for a good team of horses, he knew he had a bargain, and when he drove to the local garage where he could buy half of the five thousand Model T parts for less than fifty cents, he also knew he had a good deal.

For the most part rural folks liked Ford because they saw him as a business maverick who made a fortune without ruthlessly exploiting others. He never appeared as the finance-controlled, absentee-owned, and impersonally-managed industrial order which characterized big business in the United States. On the contrary, he placed industrial production at the service of the common man and built his company without benefit of special privilege. He fought the Seldon patent which limited manufacturing, he opposed monopolies, trusts, and combinations. His defiance of Wall Street appealed to farmers who had long hated the money power in the East. Looking at the Ford image in the 1950s, Peter F. Drucker concluded, "He won the following of the farmer, the urban middle class, and the workingman."[5]

People with little money believed Ford used his wealth judiciously. When he introduced the $5.00 working day in 1914, it seemed like Santa Claus rather than the exploitation of the laboring man. When the publisher of the New York *Times* heard the news, he asked, "He's crazy, isn't he. Don't you think he's gone crazy?"[6] Rural people did not think Ford had gone insane, neither did they agree with the *Wall Street Journal* which deplored this action as unscientific and unethical; a move which would destroy incentive. The *Journal* claimed Ford had committed economic crimes which would return to plague him and the industry he represented. To double wages and distribute ten million dollars in profits was to apply Biblical principles in a field where they did not belong. These old arguments implied that good incomes would corrupt the poor but make virtuous the rich. It suggested that the underprivileged would squander their money on luxuries while the overprivileged were entitled to them. Ford shattered this snobbery, claiming no man could raise a family and own a home on the old wage rates.

The average man did not think Ford misused his money. He had financed the Peace Ship venture in an effort to stop the bloodshed in World War I; he offered to buy Muscle Shoals to produce electricity and fertilizers for farmers; he said education was the greatest force in civilization and spent millions on schools which provided vocational training for young people; he tried to rehabilitate convicts, favored abolition of capital punishment, and initiated special programs for minority workers; he financed research on soybeans and other farm crops in an attempt to find industrial uses for agricultural commodities; he experimented to find ways to salvage products out of garbage, sewage, weeds, wood shavings, ashes, and rubbish; he melted down old cars to recycle metals and save natural resources; he stressed sanitation and cleanliness, and took pride in the neat appearance of things.

Personally a man of simple tastes, he disliked the ostentatiousness of high society, avoided scandal in his home life, retained an affinity for old machinery, old songs, old school books, old dances, and old fashioned morality. In a sense, he represented the values of middle-class Americans.

Above all, rural people never forgot that Henry Ford had been raised on a farm, that he milked cows, sawed wood, dug fence post holes, and operated a steam threshing engine for several years. This part of him was genuine and not to be confused with dilettantes who dabbled with farming as a hobby. Farmers knew no men of great wealth who had Ford's agrarian bent and who farmed thousands of acres up to the day of his death. In addition, Ford used the farmer's vernacular when he talked about the use of power machinery in agriculture, the improvement in marketing, the building of better roads, the scientific principles in chemurgy, and the maintenance of individual freedom which gave dignity to those living on the land.

Part of the Ford charisma came from his bias against the traditional enemies of the little man: the metropolitan bankers, the financial speculators in real estate, the stock market and grain pits, the professional experts in law, economics, and theology, the blue bloods in society, those living off capital, and the general run of city slickers. By attacking the top dogs in an affluent society, his rhetoric gave comfort to the weak and the disinherited. His pronouncements, even though fallacious or only partly true, were music to the ears of debtors who thrived on panaceas.

All rural Americans, obviously, did not revere Ford and his empire. The number of the disenchanted increased when the Great Depression discredited businessmen and alienated a large segment of the population. The progressive ideas of Ford's earlier career now seemed obsolete, and his opposition to the New Deal and his fight against organized labor in the 1930s seemed to indicate that time had passed him by. For the sake of his own reputation he had lived too long.

Much that has been written about the Henry Ford legend tends to merge the real with the myth. One cannot work in this vast literature without noting the magnitude of a mythology which makes it almost impossible to discern the facts. And the passage of time has only embellished these myths.

For example, every school boy knows that Henry Ford was the first to dream of the feasibility of manufacturing a low-cost automobile for the masses. Knowing that America was moving from the age of steam power to gasoline power, he founded his company in 1903, and in October 1908, produced his first Model T. Hence, he has been envisioned as a modern Moses who, standing on Mt. Sinai, looked into the future and saw the transportation revolution—an era where even the common man would be mobile, propelled in vehicles over ordinary country roads.

But in the constant re-telling of this fabulous story, people have assumed that, since Ford was fantastically successful in using mass-production techniques to produce a low-priced car which the average man could afford to buy, he was the first to think of the idea and the first to implement this dream. To give Ford credit for the origin of a cheap car for the masses is to distort the facts. The idea is simply not true.

Before trying to dispel this myth let us first look at the legend. Henry Ford gave it credence by collaborating with Samuel Crowthers in writing the autobiographical *My Life and Work*, in 1925. Here Mr. Ford, in 1909, is quoted as saying:

> I will build a motor car for the great multitude. It will be large enough for the family but small enough for the individual to run and care for. . . . But it will be so low in price that no man making a good salary will be unable to own one—and enjoy with his family the blessings of hours of pleasure in God's great open spaces.[7]

Crowthers went on to say this announcement was greeted with derision and people said if he attempted this he would be out of business in six months. Besides it would be futile to make a low-priced car because only the wealthy were in the market for automobiles.

Since Ford had said he would make an economical car, his words were repeated without seriously questioning his originality. Hence writers repeated the story. In typical fashion *Holiday* magazine in July, 1957, stated:

> Ford was the first motor maker to see the cheap auto as something that would change America's way of life. . . . When other automobile manufacturers were designing expensive playthings for rich men who could afford chauffeurs and mechanics, Ford

was thinking of a vehicle that would carry a farmer to market, enable the factory worker to live away from the smoke of the factory and make it possible for middle-class families to take vacation trips. . . . The car had to be light in weight and easily assembled so that its cost would fit the average man's pocketbook.

The public relations people of the Ford Motor Company in 1963 mailed out thousands of copies of advertising which included the statement, "Henry Ford had a dream that if a rugged, simple car could be made in sufficient quantity, it would be cheap enough for the average family to buy."

In the first place, there seems to be some confusion as to when Ford received his initial vision concerning the building of a low-priced car for the masses. In the 1920s he maintained this intellectual breakthrough occurred in 1909, when the Model T first began to find a ready market. Allan Nevins and Frank Hill, however, in their definitive biography of Ford, point out that he had told John W. Anderson in 1903 that he favored manufacturing automobiles by quantity production of a simple standardized design, like turning out pins or matches. From 1904 to 1909, Ford often opposed Alexander T. Malcomson, one of the partners in the company, who favored the building of more expensive cars. The best evidence suggests that Ford favored mass production techniques in 1903; that he favored building a lower priced car from 1904 to 1908, and that he grasped the idea of an economy car for the masses in 1909.

If this is an accurate estimate of the chronology, then there is nothing unique, startling, or innovative in the Ford pronouncements. Since the basic inventions of the automobile occurred in Germany, France, and Great Britain from 1885 to 1900, there had been plenty of speculation about automobiles before Ford began talking about them in 1903. Over five thousand automobiles were manufactured in France by 1900. Seeing they were successful, thousands of people naturally hoped to see the price reduced enough to fit the budget of the average income.

Scores of inventors and manufacturers had attempted to produce low-priced cars for the masses many years before Ford voiced his opinions. In England, the Adams-Hewitt automobile was advertised in 1900 as "A small car, cheap, with standardized parts for the common man."[8] Therefore all the elements in the Ford vision had been enunciated several years before the Detroit Motor King got into the act. When he did speak, he merely repeated an aspiration which had been on the lips of multitudes and which had been carried in the advertising of manufacturing companies.

Unquestionably the most devastating evidence available to shatter the myth that Ford first dreamed of a cheap car for the masses is found in a letter of Charles E. Duryea written on January 31, 1896, and addressed to the editor of the *Horseless Age*. After referring to the prize to be offered at an auto race in New York during the year, Duryea stated:

> . . . .It seems to the writer that this is offering a premium for speed, whereas the crying need today is not speed but better construction and better operation, and possibly to suit the desires of the masses, less cost. . . . We require in the horseless carriage a mechanism so simple as not to get out of order easily or give trouble to the unskilled operator, and a carriage so arranged as to be comfortable to use, viz. it should be clean, free from objectionable odor, vibration or possible danger. If it is simple in construction it will, in all probability, become cheap in cost, when the supply approximates the demand, so the item of cost is not a large one and if the construction is given proper prominence.[9]

Here the whole Ford theory is wrapped up in one letter, seven years before the organization of the Ford Motor Company. Charles Duryea speaks of a simple, reliable car, produced in quantity for unskilled drivers, cheap in price and designed for the multitudes. What did Ford ever say which goes beyond this in originality?

Meanwhile, in the United States, Ransom E. Olds insisted that a simple, inexpensive, utilitarian auto should be produced. Consequently he built 425 cars in 1902 and sold them for less than $400. In 1903 he sold 2,500 of them, and announced at the Detroit Auto Show that the era of the fad had terminated and the era of utility begun. He predicted that within ten years the car in general use, "will be one of 750 pounds in weight, small, compact, and simple in construction."[10] The Oldsmobile, marketed through twenty-six agencies, featured leather tops, curved dashboards, a two-passenger seat, a rear engine, and a steering rod. They looked like horseless buggies but they met a ready demand. By 1905, Olds had sold 6,500 cars at $500 each and Gus Edwards had written, "In My Merry Oldsmobile." Mitchell Wilson in *American Science and Invention* insists that, "The father of the automotive mass production was Ransom E. Olds. . . . He was the first to preach and practice the idea of a cheap car for the masses."[11]

Ford was late in getting into the business of manufacturing economy cars for the common man. When his first Model T appeared in 1908, there were at least twenty-four companies which were already building low-priced, simply-constructed automobiles. The *American Agriculturist* on October 1, 1908, stated that these twenty-four different makes sold from $250 to $900. The journal pointed out that these autos were popular with farmers because they could traverse plowed fields, snow banks, and mud holes, and could clear tree stumps, boulders, and ridges of turf on old wagon trails. The *Horseless Age*, in November, 1909, explained that the Pope-Tribune appeared in 1904 and sold for $650. The Brush car came out in 1907 with a price tag of $500. In 1908 the International Harvester Company, with assets of $100 million, manufactured high-wheel auto buggies, selling for $750. By 1910, one could purchase a Sears Roebuck Model L car complete for $370, or a Reo runabout for $500, or a Maxwell for $600, or a Hupmobile for $750. The advertisements in *Collier's* in April, 1907, featured a Walthem runabout at $400, a Cadillac Model K for $800, while the Ford Model K sold for $2,800.[12] All these cars were lower priced than Ford's first Model T which sold for $850 in 1918. In fact, the Cadillac sold for less than a Ford in these years.

From 1903 to 1908, the average price for all Ford cars sold was $1,600. Therefore, if Ford had long believed in low-priced cars as the wave of the future, he was slow in moving in this direction. Not until 1910 did the Ford Motor Company begin its spectacular reduction in prices, a trend which reached its low in 1924.

Again it is well to remember that when Ford began building automobiles in 1903, most of the cars on the market were in the low-priced field. Allan Nevins points out that in this year, two-thirds of the automobiles sold in the United States cost less than $1,375.[13] Hence the initial effort of manufacturers had been to reach the consumer of average means, rather than to produce cars for the wealthy men of leisure. What happened was that the early automobiles were too cheap and simple in construction. Since most of them were too small, light, and unreliable, more expensive ones were designed to eliminate these earlier mechanical weaknesses. When the Model T arrived, this represented the second cycle of low-priced cars, not the first cycle.

A more accurate appraisal of the whole episode would be to say that automobiles reached the public in the late 1890's. Meanwhile, the public demanded modest priced cars for popular use and scores of companies attempted, with varying degrees of success, to achieve this goal. After a decade of experience, Ford finally introduced his Model T in 1908 and the assembly line in 1913. This coupled with new marketing techniques and technological innovations made the low-priced car a reality. Henry Ford deserves credit for being eminently more successful than his competitors. For this achievement, his place in the history of technology is immortal. Yet, in praising him, we should not give him credit for something he did not accomplish—namely, to become the first man in the world to think of the desirability of making low-priced automobiles for the masses of common people.

In spite of the fact that Henry Ford's role in American technology is better known than other industrialists, many questions remain unanswered. For instance, in the absence of a careful study of Ford as an inventor, one may ask, what specific inventions did he make? What machines did he invent? Was his creative mind more adept in finding practical ways to use the knowledge of others than in making original technological discoveries? If we associate Thomas Edison with the phonograph, Eli Whitney with the cotton gin, Alexander Bell with the telephone, Emile Berliner with the microphone, Otto Mergenthaler with the linotype, Cyrus Mc Cormick with the reaper, and the Wright brothers with the airplane, what specific accomplishments can be associated with Henry Ford?

Since Ford popularized the automobile, many suppose that he invented it. Myths die hard. The credit for inventing the automobile goes to Europeans. Robert Street's patent of May 7, 1794, in England is commonly accepted as the first effort to describe an internal combustion engine.[14] He suggested that a vapor, secured from heating tar or turpentine and drawn into a cylinder by a piston, could be exploded with a flame to create motive power. The first motor to achieve commercial success was built by Jean Etienne Lenoir, a Belgian residing in Paris.[15] On January 4, 1860, he patented a model equipped with a carburetor which mixed liquid hydrocarbons to form a vapor which exploded in a cylinder ignited by an electric spark. These engines burned illuminating gas and since they did not use compression they were almost noiseless. By 1865, at least five hundred of these motors were in use in France, England, and the United States.

Meantime, Nikolaus August Otto, a shop clerk in Cologne, Germany, read about the Lenoir engines and speculated about the new power which some day might replace the steam engine. Working with his brother William and Eugen Langen, who had capital and business experience, they patented an engine on April 21, 1866, which received the Gold Medal at the Paris Exposition of 1867. These engines were improved at Cologne in 1872. Here Langen hired Gottlieb Daimler as chief engineer and William Maybach as head of production. By 1875, the company had sold 2,000 Otto engines in Germany and about the same number in England. These were the engines exhibited at the Centennial Exposition in Philadelphia in 1876 which aroused the interest of American engineers. The genius behind the Otto motor lay in the incorporation of the four-cycle principle as basic to the success of the gasoline engine and has remained as standard design to the present day. Because of these achievements, historians usually refer to Otto as the father of the automobile, tractor, and airplane. Once the gasoline engine had been perfected, its power was soon harnessed for transportation. Gottlieb Daimler and Karl Benz attached motors to tricycles and automobiles in 1885–86, and Emil Lavassor and René Panhard ran their first automobiles in Paris in 1891. Charles and Frank Duryea of Springfield, Massachusetts, built an auto buggy, which, according to their testimony, ran on April 19, 1892.

If Henry Ford did not invent the automobile, but did manufacture the Model T automobile, then it might be asked, what in the Model T represented a new invention? Here again, mechanical novelty is difficult to discern. Most of the basic automotive inventions had already been made by 1908. The motor, differential, electrical systems, steering wheels, universal joints, magnetos, windshields, pneumatic tires, and even planetary transmissions had been discovered before this time. To be sure the Model T was a dependable and simply-designed automobile which was easy to handle and repair.

Its creation, however, represented the efforts of a team of engineers, rather than the inspiration of one man, Henry Ford. The records at Dearborn show that much of the design and experimental work was done by Joseph Galamb, C. Harold Wills, Harry Love, C. J. Smith, Gus Degener, and P. E. Martin. The chief tool designers were Oscar Bornholdt and William Pioch. Fred Diehl and Carl Emde were the experts in materials and specifications. William C. Klann worked out the tractor assembly, while Clarence W. Avery helped develop the assembly line technique. William Knudsen was largely responsible for establishing branch factories across the nation, and James Couzens provided the brains for the business details. Charles E. Sorensen for forty years supervised production methods in the factories in Dearborn. Thus innumerable inventive-minded men were involved in the creation of the Model T and its system of mass production, which focused power, accuracy, speed, and continuity and other principles to manufacture a standardized product in great quantities. Perhaps Ford best represented the team approach rather than the achievements of a genius working alone.

There is some mystery concerning Ford's interest in science. Some writers denigrate his scientific achievements, saying he was ignorant of mathematics, that he hated books, that he shied away from literature, that he couldn't read a blue print, and that he had to see three-dimensional models before he could visualize mechanical apparatus. Charles E. Sorenson, in his memoirs, states that, as pro-duction manager of the Ford factories for forty years, he never saw Ford with a book in his hands. Others said he was a mechanic for whom tools and machines were his books.

These generalizations need modification, however. Although his formal education had been limited, he maintained an interest in engineering and scientific developments which far transcended that of the average mechanic. His personal library in his home in 1947 included 2,249 books, 90 transfer cases of periodicals, 20 cases of printed materials, 10 cases of blueprints and maps, and 67 scrap books containing 22,080 pages of newspaper clippings covering the years from 1911 to 1947. All this filled 652 linear feet of library shelving space.[16] An inventory of his books reveal a strong scien-tific bent. These titles include such general works as Richard Hakluyt, *The Principal Navigations, Voyages, Traffiques and Dis-coveries of the English Nation*, 10 volumes; Hornaday's *American Natural History; The Works of Darwin*, 15 volumes; the collected works of Jules Verne in 15 volumes; and the writings of Dickens, Emerson, Poe, Holmes, Whittier, Prescott, and a 50-volume set of McGuffey's Readers.

More specialized books carried such titles as *Principles of Pharmacy, Organic Chemistry, Drugs and Medicines, Soldering and Brazing, Electric Cranes, Submarine Engineering, Refractive Fur-naces, Farmer's Cyclopedia of Agriculture, Diesel Engines, Boiler Explosions, Water Bacteriology, Sewage Disposal, Glass Blowing, Mathematics for Engineers*, and *Internal Combustion Engines*. Al-though it is impossible to know how much Ford actually read, the scattered notes in some of the margins indicate he consulted many of these works, especially in his earlier years. Some notion of his scientific interests can be seen in his personal collection of scientific instruments, valued at $3,000, which he kept in his office. These included telescopes, rheostats, condensers, induction coils, voltmeters, ammeters, pyschrometers, tachometers, galvanometers, compensators, potentiometers, millivoltmeters, and pyrometers.[17] One would conclude that the man who had wheels in his head did not acquire his mechanical knowledge through a process of intuition. Undoubtedly he made use of all types of experience to enhance his understanding of technology. A Detroit newspaperman thought that when it came to engines, cams, differentials, ball bearings, pulleys, lathes, electrical equipment, steam engines or anything to do with machinery, he was about the best educated man on earth.

Regardless of the divergent views about Henry Ford—his inconsistencies, his mercurial patterns of thought, his need to assemble his own mind, his idiosyncrasies, his flashes of genius, his iron-willed stubbornness, his visionary impulses, his proclivity for the unconventional, his egocentricity, his idealism, and his emergence to the status of an mythological enigma—his place as the king of American industrialists will remain enshrined. As a builder he accentuated the mechanization of America by manufacturing the Model T which helped put the nation on wheels and put himself among the billionaires. The farm lad, who learned to use his hands, and went to the city to put together his first auto buggy in a tiny brick building on Bagley Avenue in Detroit, went on to gain world fame.

This fame was the result of his ability to mass produce a practical automobile which had a universal appeal. Dr. Samuel S. Marquis, dean of St. Paul's Episcopal Cathedral in Detroit, thought the Ford car was Henry Ford done in steel. It was not a thing of beauty or art, but of utility, strength, power, and endurance in engine and chassis, but somewhat ephemeral in its upper works. "With top torn, body dented, upholstery gone, fenders rattling, and curtains flapping in the wind, you admire the old thing and speak softly and affectionately of it, because under the hood the engine occasionally on four, sometimes on three, often on two, and now and then on one—keeps rhythmically chugging along and keeps going when by all the laws of internal combustible things it ought to stop and with one weary expiring gasp fall to pieces and mingle with the mire its remaining grains of dust. But it keeps going. . . ."[18]

The people who were born too late will never understand the pride and affection folks had for the Tin Flivver. It is an experience of special significance to people in all ranks of society. Charles A. Lindbergh knocked around in a Model T when he was earthbound, prior to his flight to Paris. William F. (Buffalo Bill) Cody bounced into Oakland, California, in 1918, riding around Lake Merritt in a Ford touring car to advertise his famous show. When Babe Ruth visited the same city at the height of his career with the New York Yankees, he was met at the railroad station by the mayor in a big limousine. A newsman showed up in a 20-year-old Ford, however, picked up the Bambino, and rode at the head of the parade in the worst looking Model T in the city of Oakland. Pancho Villa, the Mexican outlaw, used a Model T on his retreats into the mountains of northern Mexico. Marie Nelson, a missionary to Angola, Africa, used a loud speaker on her Ford to announce the time of devotions, while a Chinese newspaper editor in 1922 observed that the word automobile and Model T were synonymous in China.

Today, the historians still find it impossible to delineate the life, work, and character of Henry Ford in terms of absolutes. This study of his impact on rural America is only one perspective, with an attempt to look at the "Sage of Dearborn" through the eyes of those who held him in highest esteem—the grass-roots Americans.

Notes

The basic research for this book was done in the Ford Archives of the Ford Motor Company in Dearborn, Michigan. During the past twenty years this huge collection of material has been housed in several different places. In 1949 much of the material lay in the Engineering Building. During the early 1950s they were in Ford's home at Fair Lane. Since 1960, the collection has resided in the Central Office Building of the company in Dearborn, in the Ford Rotunda, and at the Henry Ford Museum.

Documentation of this material is indicated under the source, *Ford Fair Lane Papers*. This citation refers to the business records of the Ford Motor Company, business correspondence, Henry Ford's personal files, and reminiscences recorded by people who had knowledge of Henry Ford and his business associates.

Since many of the letters written to Henry Ford were sent by people who would prefer to remain anonymous, their initials rather than their full names will be cited in the footnotes. This rule applies to individuals who wrote personal letters to Mr. Ford, not to those engaged in official business.

The Ford–Ferguson File refers to the 40,000 letters and documents used by the Ford lawyers in preparation for the suit brought by Henry Ferguson in the early 1950s. Each letter was numbered.

1. *Ford Fair Lane Papers*, Mrs. John P_____, Rome, Georgia, to Henry Ford, Dearborn, Michigan, June 3, 1918. Accession 62, Box 4.

2. Grace Hegger Lewis, *With Love From Gracie: Sinclair Lewis, 1912–1925* (New York, 1955), p. 108.
3. John B. Rae, *Henry Ford* (Englewood Cliffs, New Jersey, 1969), p. 171.
4. Sidney Olson, *Young Henry Ford* (Detroit, 1963), p. 4.
5. Brooklyn *Eagle*, New York, March 14, 1932.
6. *Ford Fair Lane Papers*, President of the United States Chamber of Commerce, Washington, D.C., to Joseph Stalin, Moscow, U.S.S.R., July 20, 1944: "I wish to extend to you the greetings of one of America's greatest businessmen, Henry Ford." Joseph Stalin to Mr. Lambe, Washington, D.C., September 21, 1944: "Thank you. I am surprised at this, but pleased because I consider Mr. Ford one of the world's greatest industrialists. Will you please give him my best regards and may God preserve him." Accession 23, Box 38.
7. *Breeder's Gazette*, *op. cit.*, p. 290.
8. Barcelona *Diario del Comercio*, September 17, 1924.
9. Will Rogers, *Wit and Philosophy from Radio Talks of Will Rogers* (New York, 1930), p. 33.
10. Marshall W. Fishwick, *American Heroes* (Public Affairs Press, Washington, D.C., 1954), p. 136.
11. Peter F. Drucker, "Henry Ford, Success and Failure," *Harper's*, July, 1947, p. 2.
12. Rae, *op. cit.*, pp. 151–52.
13. *Ford Fair Lane Papers*, Harold M. Cordell, "Reminiscences," p. 8. Oral History Series, Accession 65.
14. *Pipp's Weekly*, vol. II, February 25, 1922, quoting the Grand Rapids *Herald*.
15. *Ibid.*, vol. I, May 15, 1920, p. 12.
16. *Ford Fair Lane Papers*, Fred Smith, "Reminiscences," p. 10. Oral History Series, Accession 65, Box 15.
17. Rae, *op. cit.*, pp. 172–73.
18. Allan Nevins, *Study in Power* (New York, 1953), vol. II, p. 343.
19. *Christian Advocate*, August 24, 1906, p. 1060.
20. New York *Times*, March 2, 1924.
21. Fishwick, *op. cit.*, p. vii.
22. Frank Bonville, *What Henry Ford Is Doing* (Seattle, 1920), p. 13, quoting the Chicago *Herald*.
23. San Francisco *Chronicle*, March 16, 1927.
24. *Ibid.*, January 27, 1928.
25. Leo Gurko, *Heroes, Highbrows and the Popular Mind* (New York, 1954), p. 49.
26. Frazier Hunt, "Henry Ford's 1940 World," *Hearst's International*, January, 1922, p. 72.
27. Arthur Pound, "The Ford Myth," *Atlantic Monthly*, January, 1924, p. 44.
28. *The New Yorker*, November, 1951, pp. 41–42.
29. *The American Thresherman and Farm Power*, April, 1922, p. 12.
30. *Southern Cultivator* (Atlanta, Georgia), June 1, 1900, p. 2.

31. Philip Kinsley, *An Interview with Henry Ford*, reprinted from the Chicago *Tribune*, July 12, 1935, p. 11.
32. Bascom B. Clarke, *The Musings of Uncle Silas* (Madison, Wisconsin, 1904), p. 208.

CHAPTER II

1. *Horseless Age*, December, 1895, p. 7, quoting the New York *World*, November 17, 1895.
2. Philip Van Doren Stern, *Tin Lizzie* (New York, 1955), p. 13.
3. *Ford Times*, vol. 4, 1911, p. 97.
4. Minneapolis *Journal*, October 6, 1899.
5. *Breeder's Gazette*, August 24, 1904, p. 292.
6. The Macon *Daily Telegraph*, July 10, 1906, quoting the Philadelphia *Public Ledger*.
7. *Breeder's Gazette*, *op. cit.*, p. 290.
8. *North American Review*, June, 1906, p. 807.
9. *American Horse Breeder*, November 8, 1908, p. 1039.
10. San Francisco *Call*, August 6, 1909.
11. A Comic Post Card. These were circulated among friends in the early 1900s to encourage opposition to the automobile. In possession of the author.
12. *Ford Fair Lane Papers*, F. Y. P_____, El Paso, Texas, to Henry Ford, June 8, 1909. Accession 94, Box 93.
13. *Otto Gasoline Engines*, Catalogue (Philadelphia, 1899), p. 7.
14. *Wallace's Farmer*, February 13, 1903, p. 247.
15. *Pacific Rural Press*, editorial quoting the *Wall Street Journal*.
16. *Gas Review* (Madison, Wisconsin), September, 1910, p. 8.
17. J. C. Cunningham, "Earthquake," *Motorland* (San Francisco), March–April, 1967, p. 38.
18. *Ford Fair Lane Papers*, letter from Henry Ford to company dealers, May 22, 1933. Accession 2, Box 30.
19. *Gas Review*, September, 1908, p. 20.
20. *The Progressive Farmer*, June 15, 1912, p. 685.
21. *The Southern Cultivator* (Atlanta, Georgia), July 15, 1913, p. 14.
22. *Ford Fair Lane Papers*, James H. B_____, Berea, Ohio, to Edsel Ford, August 26, 1938. Accession 62, Box 3.
23. *Collier's*, April 17, 1909, p. 20.
24. E. A. Knapp, "The Farmer's Cooperative Demonstration Work," United States Department of Agriculture, *Yearbook* (Washington, D.C., 1910), p. 160.
25. Francis R. Allen, *Technology and Social Change* (New York, 1957), p. 107.
26. *Ford Fair Lane Papers*, Charles D. B_____, Altoona, Pennsylvania, to Henry Ford, June 3, 1919. Accession 28; Box 2.
27. Grace Hegger Lewis, *With Love From Gracie: Sinclair Lewis, 1912–1925*, p. 98.
28. *The Fordowner*, January, 1920, p. 120.
29. *Ibid.*, October, 1916, p. 13.
30. *Ford News*, December 15, 1925, p. 3.

31. Letter, Reynold M. Wik, Norbeck, South Dakota, to Elsie Wik, Bethel Academy, Saint Paul, Minnesota, November 12, 1925.

CHAPTER III

1. John Keats, "Reincarnations of the Tin Lizzie," New York *Times* magazine, March 25, 1962, p. 63.
2. Paul H. Bruske, "How the Ford Name Went Round the World," *Pacific Coast Review,* October 1936, p. 15.
3. The Detroit *Journal,* November 12, 1912. Also David L. Lewis, "The Rise of the Model T," *Public Relations Journal* (New York, 1958), p. 8.
4. *The Model T Specialist* (Fordex Editorial Staff, Sales Equipment Company, Detroit, Michigan, 1925), p. 55.
5. San Francisco *Call,* March 26, 1912, p. 4.
6. *Ford Times,* November, 1911, p. 141.
7. Des Moines *Tribune,* October 22, 1912.
8. New York *Herald,* April 13, 1919.
9. *Ford Times,* January, 1915, p. 158.
10. *Ibid.,* vol. 4, 1911, p. 7. Also Detroit *Tribune,* January 13, 1904. The reporter described Ford's record-setting race across the St. Clair River on the ice:
    He's off, was the shout and the 999 came tearing down the straight a way. The four cylinders of the big machine were all working regularly and the roar could be heard before the flying combination struck the third mile. . . . As Ford flashed by it was noticed that he wore no goggles or other protection for his face. Humped over the steering wheel, the tremendous speed throwing the machine in a zig-zag fashion across the 15 foot roadway, Ford was taking chances that no man, not even that specialist in suicide, Barney Oldfield, had dared to attempt. Hanging to the bare side of the machine over the front axle was Spider Huff, the machinist. . . . The judges confer . . . . joyful shouts announced the successful completion of the mile and the hands of the driver and his plucky helper were wrung till they ached. Ford was a bit pale from the awful ordeal. He added, "I knew I could do it."
11. Lewis, *op. cit.,* p. 8.
12. *Ford Fair Lane Papers,* Report to Branch Managers, December 29, 1924. Accession 285, Box 234.
13. *Ibid.,* "Releases to the Press," January 17, 1925. Accession 380, Box 14.
14. *Ibid.,* Dodge Estate. Accession 96, Box 10.
15. *The Farm Journal,* September, 1924, p. 32.
16. Edgar A. Guest, "Henry Ford Talks About His Mother," *The American Magazine,* July, 1923, p. 18.
17. *Ford Fair Lane Papers,* letter from Mrs. Clifford M———, no date or address, Accession 1, Box 111.
18. Telegram, Henry Ford, Dearborn, Michigan, to Branch Manager, Poughkeepsie, New York, February 22, 1922. Accession 1, Box 3.
19. *Ford Fair Lane Papers,* Henry Ford Notebooks. Accession 1, Box 2.

20. Sarah T. Bushnell, *The Truth About Henry Ford* (Chicago, 1922), p. 96.
21. *Ford Fair Lane Papers*, Andrew W. Mellon, Washington, D.C., to Henry Ford, Dearborn, Michigan, March 16, 1922. Accession 1, Box 111.
22. *Ibid.*, E. G. Liebold, Dearborn, Michigan, to Andrew W. Mellon, Washington, D.C., March 22, 1922. Accession 1, Box 111.
23. *Ford Times*, June, 1915, p. 399.
24. *Ford Fair Lane Papers*, "Reminiscences," Fred L. Black, Oral History, p. 16.
25. *Ibid.*, E. G. Liebold, Oral History, vol. 6, p. 441.
26. *Ibid.*, Fred L. Black, Oral History, p. 18.
27. James Francis Cooke, "Start the Day with a Song," *The Etude*, vol. 54, no. 4, April, 1936, pp. 203-4.
28. Rome (Georgia) *News*, May 28, 1926. Dr. Carlton Simon, of New York City, claimed the skull structures of both Ford and John D. Rockefeller were of the genius type.
29. *The Ford Dealer Story, op. cit.*, p. 25.
30. *Ford Fair Lane Papers*, H. B. B____, Big Timber, Montana, to Henry Ford, Detroit, Michigan, November 7, 1927. Accession 62, Box 5.
31. Frederick Lewis Allen, *Only Yesterday* (New York, 1930), p. 1962.
32. Chicago *Tribune*, June 23, 1916.
33. New York *World*, August 1, 1919.
34. The Calhoun (Georgia) *Times*, August 7, 1919.
35. New York *World*, August 6, 1919.
36. Chicago *Herald*, July 16, 1919, p. 10.
37. John W. Spaulding, "The Radio Speaking of William John Cameron," *Speech Monographs*, vol. 36, no. 1, March, 1959, pp. 47-55.
38. *Ford Fair Lane Papers*, W. J. Cameron, Dearborn, Michigan, to Ray Priest, St. Louis, Missouri, September 30, 1938. Accession 44, Box 9.
39. Spaulding, *op. cit.*, p. 55.
40. *Ford Fair Lane Papers*, no name, no address, letter addressed to W. J. Cameron, Dearborn, Michigan, February 8, 1942. Accession 44, Box 2.
41. *Ibid.*, "World's Fair, New York," August 7, 1939. Accession 1, Box 122.
42. *Ibid.*, "Advertising Expenses, 1934-1939." Accession 572, Box 10.
43. *Ibid.*, "Greenfield Village Reports." Accession 1, Box 89.
44. Interview with Ford officials in the Ford Rotunda, July 26, 1960.
45. *Ford Fair Lane Papers*, Harold M. Cordell, "Reminiscences," Oral History Series, p. 8.
46. William L. Stidger, "Henry Ford Talks at Eighty," *Woman's Home Companion*, July, 1943, p. 4.
47. *Ford Fair Lane Papers*, letter, National Steel Corporation to George R. Fink, May 10, 1937. Accession 1, Box 122.

CHAPTER IV

The source for virtually all of the evidence submitted in this chapter is the *Ford Fair Lane Papers*, Experimental Engineering, W. T.

Fishleigh Files, Accession 94, Boxes 1 to 214. These files contain letters from hundreds of thousands of rural Americans who made suggestions for the improvement of the Model T cars, as well as other technological matters. The answers to these letters are also in these files.

1. Henry Ford and Samuel Crowthers, *My Life and Work* (New York, 1925), p. 72.
2. Sacramento (California) *Union*, September 4, 1912.
3. Roger Sherman Hoar, *Patents* (New York, 1926), p. 88.
4. *Ford Fair Lane Papers*, a letter in the Ford-Ferguson File, No. 108,771, stated that the Ford Motor Company would pay for inventions or improvements in the Model T. This statement also appeared in the *Ford Times*, in 1913. This erroneous comment may have accounted for the wide belief of this rumor.
5. *Ibid.*, W. T. Fishleigh, Experimental Division, Ford Motor Company, Dearborn, Michigan, to Mrs. L. E. May, Ennis, Texas, September 5, 1925. Accession 380, Box 18.
6. *Ibid.*, E. G. Liebold, Dearborn, Michigan, to W. B. Moore, Kansas City, Missouri, November 11, 1925. Accession 380, Box 15.
7. Heated stones and hot flatirons were also used to warm passengers, as well as blankets, buffalo robes, overshoes, scarfs, and ear-lap caps.
8. Francis R. Allen, *Technology and Social Change* (New York, 1957), p. 123. Also New York *Times*, February 2, 1956. Total deaths from auto accidents from 1903 to 1956 were 1,149,724.
9. Aberdeen *Daily News*, October 13, 1965.
10. Floyd Clymer, *Henry's Wonderful Model T; 1900–1927* (New York, 1955), pp. 195–218.
11. Quoted in *The New Yorker*, July 18, 1936, p. 6.
12. *Ford Fair Lane Papers*, R. L. Sotegast, Providence, Rhode Island, to Henry Ford, Detroit, Michigan, June 8, 1926. Accession 375, Box 2.
13. *Nebraska Farmer*, December 1, 1915, p. 1176.
14. John A. Kouwenhoven, *Made in America* (New York, 1948), p. 217.

CHAPTER V

1. William Hurst and Lillian Church, *Power and Machinery in Agriculture*, United States Department of Agriculture, Miscellaneous Bulletin no. 157 (Washington, D.C., April, 1933), pp. 7–11.
2. Reynold M. Wik, *Steam Power on the American Farm*, pp. 87–88, 150. The Froehlich tractor mounted a 30-horsepower Van Duzen gasoline engine, manufactured in Cincinnati, on a running gear made by the Robinson Company of Richmond, Indiana. Another early tractor was the William Patterson two-cylinder tractor built in 1892 in the factory of the J. I. Case Company of Racine, Wisconsin. Although the engine did some farm work, its inadequate ignition and cooling system made it impractical. The motor was started by firing a cartridge, which sometimes shattered the cylinder heads. In addition, several portable Otto engines were used for threshing in South Dakota in 1893. The Huber Manufacturing Company of Marion, Ohio, in 1894, built a one-cylinder gasoline tractor.

3. The word "tractor" is in the *Oxford Dictionary* of 1856. It was used by George H. Edwards of Chicago on his patent number 425,600 in 1890. Later, W. H. Williams, sales manager of the Hart-Parr Company of Charles City, Iowa, popularized the word in 1907 because he thought "gasoline traction engine" was an awkward expression when used in advertising.

4. *Transactions of the American Society of Agricultural Engineers* (St. Paul, Minnesota, 1908), vol. 3, p. 21.

5. *Ford Fair Lane Papers*, "Reminiscences," by Joseph Galamb, p. 59. Oral History Series, Accession 65.

6. *Hart-Parr Tractor Catalogue* (Hart-Parr Company, Charles City, Iowa, 1910), pp. 2–3.

7. Barton W. Currie, *The Tractor and Its Influence upon the Agricultural Implement Industry* (Philadelphia, 1916), p. 137.

8. L. W. Ellis and Edward A. Rumely, *Power and the Plow* (New York, 1911), p. 2.

9. *Ford Fair Lane Papers*, letter by an executive of the Minneapolis Steel and Machinery Company, Minneapolis, Minnesota, to Henry Ford, Dearborn, Michigan, September 26, 1914.

10. Grand Rapids (Michigan) *Herald*, June 25, 1915.

11. *The Implement and Machinery Review* (London), May 1, 1915, quoting the London *Times*.

12. *Ford Fair Lane Papers*, telegram, Percival Perry, London, to Edsel Ford, Dearborn, Michigan, April 7, 1917. Accession 62, Box 519.

13. The London *Times*, September 28, 1915, p. 9.

14. *Ford Fair Lane Papers*, letter, David Lloyd George, 10 Downing Street, Whitehall, S. W., First Lord of the Treasury, London, England, to Percival L. Perry, London, June 28, 1917.

15. The London *Times*, October 22, 1917, p. 9.

16. Oakland *Tribune*, October 6, 1918, p. 4.

17. *Ford Fair Lane Papers*, an unsigned letter entitled, "Tractor Farming a Farmette's Way," by a girl in the Berry School in Rome, Georgia, July 6, 1918. Ford-Ferguson File, 45632.

18. *Ford Fair Lane Papers*, C. F. Elmer, "Fordson Production Figures." Accession 268, Box 1. C. F. Elmer was Head of the Accounting Department of the River Rouge Plant.

19. *Ibid.*

20. New York *Times*, January 27, 1926, p. 11.

21. *Ford Fair Lane Papers*, Walter H. W_____, Atlanta, Georgia, to Henry Ford, Detroit, Michigan, April 11, 1921. Ford-Ferguson File, no. 04628.

22. *Ibid.*, H. B. S_____, Aurora, Colorado, to Henry Ford, Detroit, Michigan, March 14, 1921.

23. *Ibid.*, Ford-Ferguson File, no. 06234.

24. Martin R. Cooper, Glen T. Barton, and Albert P. Brodell, *Progress of Farm Mechanization*, Miscellaneous Publication, no. 630, United States Department of Agriculture (Washington, D.C., October, 1946), p. 85.

25. Interview with F. Lee Norton, Racine, Wisconsin, December 28, 1946.

26. *Ford Fair Lane Papers*, George R. S_____, Groton, South Dakota, to Henry Ford, July 4, 1921. Accession 62, Box 27.
27. Douglas R. A. Drummond, *The Musings of a Tramp Engineer* (St. Joseph, Missouri, 1918), p. 32.

CHAPTER VI

1. *Ford Fair Lane Papers*, Charles R_____, Cresbard, South Dakota, to Henry Ford, Detroit, Michigan, September 3, 1922. Accession 380, Box 13.
2. Detroit *News*, January 13, 1924.
3. *Ford Fair Lane Papers*, Idus Sapp, Cedar Springs, Georgia, to Henry C. Wallace, United States Department of Agriculture, Washington, D.C., December 13, 1921. Accession 234, Progress Dr. 595.
4. *Ibid.*, Mrs. H. B. H_____, Davis, South Dakota, to Henry Ford, Detroit, Michigan, March 25, 1922. Ford-Ferguson File, Accession 380, Box 2.
5. *Ibid.*, Lillian M. M_____, Latta, South Carolina, to Henry Ford, Ford-Ferguson File. Accession 380, Box 9.
6. Robert L. Duffus, *The Valley and Its People: A Portrait of T.V.A.* (New York, 1944), p. 53.
7. National Archives of the United States, Washington, D.C., James A. Metcalf, Atlanta, Georgia, to President Warren G. Harding, The White House, Washington, D.C., September 2, 1921. War Department, Office Chief of Engineers, File number, 121502/1277.
8. *Ibid.*, F. E. McCoy, Morgan, Kentucky, to John W. Weeks, Secretary of War, Washington, D.C., October 17, 1921. War Department, Office Chief of Engineers, File number 121502/1262.
9. Robert L. Duffus, "Ford's Muscle Shoals Case Under Fire," New York *Times*, April 20, 1924.
10. New York *Times*, January 15, 1922.
11. *Ford Fair Lane Papers*, William G. Wilcox, Tuskegee Normal and Industrial Institute, Tuskegee, Alabama, to Henry Ford, Dearborn, Michigan, November 20, 1923. Accession 285, Box 249.
12. *Ibid.*, J. W. Worthington, Washington, D.C., to E. G. Liebold, Dearborn, Michigan, August 14, 1921. Accession 285, Box 81.
13. *Ibid.*, "Give Henry Ford an Opportunity," pamphlet, written by Thurman Hendricks McCoy, National Director, Atlanta, Georgia. Accession 380, Box 12.
14. *The Nation*, June 19, 1920, p. 816.
15. *Ford Fair Lane Papers*, John B. Toll, Secretary of the National Fertilizer Association, Philadelphia, January 14, 1922. Accession 380, Box 16.
16. *Pipp's Weekly*, July 15, 1922, 3:6.
17. New York *Times*, March 6, 1924.
18. Richard Lowitt, *George W. Norris: The Making of a Progressive, 1861–1912* (Syracuse, New York, 1963).
19. New York *Times*, June 18, 1922.
20. *Pipp's Weekly*, August 12, 1922, 3:4–11.
21. New York *Times*, April 28, 1924.

22. *Ibid.*, May 3, 1924.
23. *Ford Fair Lane Papers*, Calvin Coolidge, The White House, to Henry Ford, Dearborn, Michigan, October 18, 1924. Accession 1, Box 12.
24. *Ibid.*, H. L. A____, Birmingham, Alabama, to Henry Ford, Detroit, Michigan, October 28, 1924. Accession 572, Box 6.
25. *Ibid.*, Mary Lee H____, Sheffield, Alabama, to Henry Ford, Detroit, Michigan, November 5, 1924. Accession 285, Box 211.
26. *The Farmer* (St. Paul, Minnesota), June 30, 1919, p. 8.
27. *Ford Fair Lane Papers*, E. G. Liebold, Dearborn, Michigan, to O. S. Fisher, Extension Agronomist, United States Department of Agriculture, Washington, D.C., February 2, 1924. Accession 380, Box 1.
28. *Ibid.*, Charles B____, Gadsden, Alabama, to Henry Ford, May 8, 1923. Accession 380, Box 22.

CHAPTER VII

1. Joseph G. Knapp, *The Rise of American Cooperative Enterprise: 1620–1920* (The Interstate Printers and Publishers, Inc., Danville, Illinois, 1969), p. 432.
2. *Ibid.*, pp. 431–32.
3. Topeka *Daily Capital*, March 23, 1925.
4. National Archives of the United States, Washington, D.C., Department of Agriculture Files, Frank Stuby, Radom, Illinois, to W. M. Jardine, Secretary of Agriculture, Washington, D.C., March 9, 1925. Accession 234, Progress Dr. 529.
5. *Ford Fair Lane Papers*, Senator Henrik Shipstead, St. Paul, Minnesota, to Henry Ford, Dearborn, Michigan, June 3, 1924.
6. National Archives of the United States, Washington, D.C., *op cit.*, Evelyn Harris, Betterton, Maryland, to Secretary Jardine, Washington, D.C., November 25, 1925. Accession 234, Progress Dr. 529.
7. "Congress and Cooperative Marketing," *Congressional Digest* (Washington, D.C., October, 1925), pp. 255–56. Over 4,000 livestock shipping associations handled stock valued at 100 million dollars.
8. Merle Crowell, "Nothing Could Keep This Boy Down," *American* magazine, 95:138–39.
9. Grace H. Larsen and Henry E. Erdman, "Aaron Sapiro: Genius of Farm Co-operative Promotion," *The Mississippi Valley Historical Review*, September, 1962, 49:250.
10. Aaron Sapiro, "Co-Operative Grain Marketing," address given Co-Operative Grain Marketing Conference of All Farm Orgnaizations, LaSalle Hotel, Chicago, July 23 and 24, 1920.
11. *American Fruit Grower Magazine*, June, 1926, p. 16.
12. *Ford Fair Lane Papers*, "Cross Examination of Sapiro: Mr. Sapiro's Professional Income by Years," Aaron Sapiro Case, Accession 48, Box 94.
13. *Ibid.*, mms. by Andrew S. Wing, editor of *Farm and Fireside*. Accession 48, Box 39. Apparently this manuscript was not published.
14. *Ibid.*, p. 2.
15. Robert Morgan, "Exploiting Farm Organization," *Dearborn Independent*, April 12, 1924, pp. 4–5.
16. *The Regina* (Saskatchewan) *Leader*, February 18, 1924, p. 1.

17. *Ford Fair Lane Papers*, letter of Joseph Passoneau, Director of Markets, Denver, Colorado, to *The Regina Leader*, February 10, 1924. Accession 48, Box 23.
18. *The Regina Leader*, September 23, 1925.
19. Dallas *Daily Times Herald*, February 3, 1925.
20. Memphis Press *Samitar*, March 24, 1927.
21. New York *Times*, July 24, 1927. Section I.
22. *Ford Fair Lane Papers*, Raymond M. M_____, Manning, South Carolina, to Henry Ford, March 21, 1927. Accession 48, Box 17.
23. *Ibid.*, excepts taken from letters in Accession 48, Boxes 14, 15, 16, and 17.
24. *Ibid.*, excerpts taken from letters in Accession 48, Boxes 17, 18, 19, 20, 21, 22, and 23.
25. *Kansas Farmer*, May 3, 1924, p. 4.
26. Danville (Virginia) *News*, April 22, 1924.
27. Allan Nevins and Frank Hill, *op. cit.*, p. 322.
28. New York *Times*, April 18, 1927.
29. Knapp, *op. cit.*, p. 435.

CHAPTER VIII

1. *Ford Fair Lane Papers*, see *Ford News*, January 1, 1926, p. 2.
2. Walter H. Pay, "Industrial Alcohol," *The Natal Agricultural Journal* (London), vol. II, March, 1909, pp. 577–83.
3. *Ford Fair Lane Papers*, F. B. W_____, San Francisco, California, to Henry Ford, Detroit, Michigan, January 15, 1917. Accession 13, Box 26.
4. *Ibid.*, Ernest G. Liebold, Dearborn, Michigan, to Rudolph Schroeder, Hoboken, New Jersey, May 19, 1917. Ford-Ferguson File, no. 6,5924.
5. New York *Herald-Tribune*, September 14, 1938.
6. *Ford Fair Lane Papers*, W. J. Cameron, Dearborn, Michigan, to Charles S. Johnson, Centerville, South Dakota, July 9, 1938. Accession 380, Box 25.
7. Allan Nevins and Frank Hill, *Ford: Expansion and Challenge, 1915–1933* (New York, 1957), p. 231.
8. *Ibid.*, p. 238.
9. *Farm and Fireside*, September, 1925, p. 4.
10. Grand Rapids *Review*, February 22, 1921.
11. Centralia (Washington) *Hub*, February 2, 1921.
12. Great Falls *Times*, February 10, 1921.
13. Vancouver *Daily World*, March 23, 1921.
14. *Ford Fair Lane Papers*, "Reminiscences," H. G. Ukkleberg, Oral History Series, p. 4. Accession 65, Box 8.
15. James Sweinhart, *The Industrialized Barn* (Ford Motor Company, Dearborn, Michigan, 1934), pp. 4–18.
16. "Henry Ford Talks About Flax," *Textile World*, July 26, 1926, p. 8.
17. R. A. Boyer, "Soybean Protein Fibers," *Modern Plastics*, February, 1942, pp. 2–3.
18. "Business Suits from Soybeans," *Progress Guide*, vol. 5, no. 2 (Chicago), September, 1943, pp. 343–44.

19. *Ibid.*, p. 343–44.
20. *Ford Fair Lane Papers*, "Reminiscences," J. L. McCloud, Oral History Series, p. 197.
21. *Ibid.*, Harold M. Cordell, Oral History Series, p. 3. Accession 65, Box 2.
22. "The Soybean as a Food," The Madison Survey (Nashville Agricultural Normal Institute, Madison, Tennessee), vol. 13, no. 28 (December 9, 1931), pp. 99–100.
23. *Ford Fair Lane Papers*, "Reminiscences," Dr. Edsel A. Ruddiman, Oral History Series, p. 6. Accession 65, Box 1.
24. Paul W. Chapman, "Cowless Milk," Atlanta *Journal*, April 16, 1944, p. 3.
25. Katherine Dos Passos, "Science and the Beanstalk," *Woman's Home Companion*, September, 1942, pp. 14–15.
26. United States Bureau of the Census, *Statistical Abstracts of the United States: 1955* (Washington, D.C., 1955), p. 664.
27. *The Boll Weevil Problem*, United States Department of Agriculture, Farmer's Bulletin, no. 1329 (Washington, D.C., June, 1923), pp. 1–30.
28. *Ford Fair Lane Papers*, R. R. Moton, Tuskegee, Alabama, to Hon. Martin B. Madden, Chairman Appropriations Committee, House of Representatives, Washington, D.C., January 22, 1923. Letter included speech of January 17, 1923. Accession 572, Box 5.
29. Rackham Holt, *George Washington Carver* (New York, 1943), p. 314.
30. *Literary Digest*, June 12, 1937, p. 20. See also *Time*, June 14, 1937, p. 54.
31. *Ford Fair Lane Papers.* Accession 23, Box 47.

CHAPTER IX

1. New York *Times*, November 1, 1923, p. 2.
2. The Hastings (Nebraska) *Tribune*, May 13, 1916, p. 2.
3. Theodore Roosevelt and Charles Evans Hughes were write-in candidates.
4. Ellis O. Jones, "Those Henry Ford Votes," *Independent*, 86, May 15, 1916, pp. 241–42.
5. *The Nebraska State Journal*, April 27, 1916, p. 4.
6. Detroit *Times*, April 19, 1916. The Topeka *Daily Capital*, May 1, 1916, stated that "Ford put the fist in pacifist."
7. Joseph B. Bishop, *Theodore Roosevelt and His Time* (New York, 1920), vol. II, p. 387.
8. Boston *Traveler*, quoted in *Literary Digest*, December 11, 1915, vol. 51, p. 1334.
9. London *Times*, January 8, 1916, p. 7.
10. Christian A. Sorenson, "Personal Papers," State Historical Society and Museum, Lincoln, Nebraska, Box 80.
11. Walter Millis, *The Road to War: America 1914–1917* (New York, 1935), p. 243.
12. *Ford Fair Lane Papers*, mms. "Henry Ford and His Peace Mission; A Discourse at Temple Keneseth Israel," by Rabbi Joseph Krauskopf, Philadelphia, December 19, 1915. Accession 66, Box 6.

13. *Ibid.*, Ike W_____, Charlotte, North Carolina, to Henry Ford, Detroit, Michigan, May 3, 1916. Accession 63, Box 4.
14. *Ibid.*, Rev. V. K. B_____, Cascade, Maryland, to Henry Ford, Detroit, Michigan, July 20, 1916. Accession 63, Box 33.
15. *Ibid.*, Walter T_____, Duluth, Minnesota, to Henry Ford, Detroit, Michigan, July 25, 1916. Accession 63, Box 28.
16. *Ibid.*, Simon P. A_____, Parker, South Dakota, to Henry Ford, Detroit, Michigan, May 17, 1916. Accession 63, Box 19.
17. *Ibid.*, Daniel Poling, "America and the World," keynote speech, National Prohibition Convention, St. Paul, Minnesota, July 19–21, 1916, bulletin. Accession 62, Box 13.
18. Grand Rapids *Press*, June 8, 1916. The votes on the first ballot were: Hughes, 253½; Weeks, 105; Root, 103; Cummins, 85; Burton, 77½; Fairbanks, 74½; Sherman, 66; Knox, 36; Ford, 32; Brumbaugh, 29; La Follett, 25; DuPont, 25; Willis, 4; Borah, 2; McCall, 1; Wood, Harding, and Wanamaker, 0. Ford received 32 votes out of 987.
19. Allan Nevins and Frank Hill, *Ford: Expansion and Challenge, 1915–1933*, (New York, 1957), p. 117.
20. *Ford Fair Lane Papers*, E. G. Liebold, "Reminiscences," Oral History Series, p. 388. Accession 62, Box 20.
21. Nevins and Hill, *op. cit.*, p. 119.
22. New York *World*, August 22, 1918.
23. *Ford Fair Lane Papers*, "Henry Ford for Senator Election Circular," 16 pp. Accession 63, Box 60.
24. Chicago *Tribune*, quoted in (Nashville) *Tennessean*, August 27, 1918, p. 9.
25. *Collier's*, July 14, 1923, p. 5. The votes for the other candidates were: McAdoo, 19,000; Borah, 3,904; Cox, 16,268; Davis, 3,317; Hoover, 9,907; Hughes, 13,761; Johnson, 14,493; La Follette, 6,963; Smith, 14,676; Underwood, 3,720; Wood, 4,116; Roosevelt, 20; Taft, 15; Pershing, 15; Bryan, 138; Debs, 455; Lowden, 2,036.
26. *Ibid.*, p. 5.
27. *Kansas Farmer*, July 24, 1923, p. 2.
28. Boston *Daily Globe*, July 11, 1923, p. 14.
29. Birmingham (Alabama) *Herald*, May 16, 1923.
30. Detroit *Times*, May 27, 1923.
31. New York *Times*, June 10, 1923.
32. *Collier's*, August 26, 1923, p. 6.
33. *Ford Fair Lane Papers*, Lea J. L_____, Milwaukee, Wisconsin, to Henry Ford, Detroit, Michigan, July 25, 1923. Accession 63, Box 16.
34. *Ibid.*, Dr. H. C. S_____, Huntington Beach, California, to Henry Ford, Detroit, Michigan, April 3, 1923. Accession 63, Box 11.
35. New York *Times*, October 18, 1923.
36. Baltimore *Sun*, July 23, 1923.
37. *Life*, March 20, 1919.
38. Nevins and Hill, *op. cit.*, p. 127.
39. Champaign (Illinois) *Gazette*, January 3, 1919.
40. Nevins and Hill, *op. cit.*, p. 311.

41. Dearborn *Independent*, May 22, 1920. These articles were later published in four volumes, entitled *The International Jew*, and sold for 25 cents a volume.
42. *The International Jew* (Dearborn Publishing Company, Dearborn, Michigan), November, 1920, pp. 1–10.
43. *Progress*, vol. II, March, 1923, pp. 12–13. See also John Spargo, *The Jew and American Ideals* (New York, 1921), p. 99.
44. New York *Times*, December 20, 1926, p. 23.
45. *Ford Fair Lane Papers*, J. Emil N_____, Minneapolis, Minnesota, to Henry Ford, December 21, 1923. Accession 63, Box 16.

CHAPTER X

1. Raymond L. Bruckberger, *Image of America* (New York, 1959), p. 195.
2. Alfred B. Rollins, Jr., *Depression, Recovery, and War: 1929–1945* (New York, 1966), p. 9.
3. William Leuchtenburg, *Perils of Prosperity* (Chicago, 1958), p. 90.
4. Frank Kent, "Mr. Coolidge," *American Mercury*, August, 1924, pp. 385–90.
5. *Ford Fair Lane Papers*. Roy A. Batteen, "A Look at the Economy of the United States," unpublished mms., June 6, 1933. Accession 380, Box 24.
6. Kenneth Galbraith, *The Great Crash* (New York, 1955), p. 182.
7. Frederick Lewis Allen, *Since Yesterday* (New York, 1940), p. 86.
8. Caroline Bird, *The Invisible Scar* (New York, 1967), p. 81.
9. *Congressional Record*, Seventy-second Congress, second session, vol. 76, pt. 4, pp. 4316–17.
10. Bird, *op. cit.*, p. xi.
11. T. Harry Williams, Richard Current, Frank Freidel, *A History of the United States Since 1865* (New York, 1964), p. 502.
12. Remley J. Glass, "Gentlemen, the Corn Belt," *Harper's*, July, 1933, pp. 200–206.
13. David A. Shannon, *The Great Depression* (New York, 1960), p. 26.
14. Allan Nevins and Frank Hill, *Ford: Decline and Rebirth: 1933–1962* (New York, 1962), p. 3.
15. Alliance (Ohio) *Review*, May 28, 1930.
16. Allan Nevins and Frank Hill, *Ford: Expansion and Challenge, 1915–1933* (New York, 1957), p. 571.
17. *Ibid.*, p. 588.
18. *Good Housekeeping*, July, 1933, p. 24.
19. *Ford Fair Lane Papers*, John S_____, Novi, Michigan, to Henry Ford, Detroit, Michigan, October 2, 1930. Accession 274, Box 273.
20. *The Nation*, August 12, 1931.
21. Professor S. M. Levin, dean of the Economics Department, Detroit City College, and member of the Detroit Mayor's Unemployment Committee, letter released to Universal Service, Washington, D.C., December 28, 1931. Accession 274, Box 198.

22. *Ford Fair Lane Papers,* James Hedges, Grass Valley, California, to Henry Ford, Detroit, Michigan, December 19, 1930. Accession 380, Box 13.
23. *Ibid.,* Hans S____, Bloomer, Wisconsin, to Henry Ford, Detroit, Michigan, April 30, 1931. Accession 234, Box 6.
24. *Ibid.,* James S____, Wabash, Indiana, to Henry Ford, Detroit, Michigan, June 7, 1932.
25. *Ibid.,* W. L. Spillman, Washington, D.C., to E. G. Liebold, Ford Motor Company, Dearborn, Michigan, June 8, 1924. Accession 380, Box 13.
26. W. J. Cameron, "Decentralization of Industry," *Mechanical Engineering,* July, 1937, pp. 483–92.
27. Drew Pearson, "Henry Ford Says Farmer-Workman Will Build Automobile of the Future," *Automotive Industries,* August 28, 1924, p. 389.
28. Ford Motor Company, *Henry Ford on Farm and Factory* (Dearborn, Michigan), May 30, 1932, p. 4.
29. New York *Times,* October 22, 1933.
30. St. Paul *News,* October 15, 1928, and *Ford Fair Lane Papers,* Robert J. W____, Faith, South Dakota, to Henry Ford, Detroit, Michigan, October 17, 1933. Accession 285, Box 234.
31. *Ford Fair Lane Papers,* Earl B____, Harvey, Illinois, to Henry Ford, Detroit, Michigan, May 12, 1938. Accession 234, Box 22.
32. Donald Day, *Autobiography of Will Rogers* (New York, 1962), p. 206.
33. *Ibid.,* p. 251.

CHAPTER XI

1. Dearborn *Independent,* March 10, 1923, p. 5.
2. *Journal of the National Education Association,* vol. 23, no. 7, November, 1934, p. 210.
3. *Ford Fair Lane Papers,* "Report of the Superintendent of the Henry Ford Trade School," October 10, 1917. Accession 572, Box 5.
4. *Ibid.,* financial statements. Accession 1, Box 44.
5. *Ibid.,* L. J. Thompson, Financial Records. Accession 384, Box 1. See also New York *Times,* April 17, 1925, and March 11, 1930.
6. *Ibid.,* Tom Phillips, "Reminiscences," Oral History Series, interview, November, 1951, p. 1. Accession 62.
7. *Ibid.,* Dr. C. F. Holton, "Reminiscences," Oral History Series, interview, June, 1951.
8. *Ibid.,* "Edison Institute Schools and Greenfield Village," mms. Accession 572, Box 5.
9. Allan Nevins and Frank Hill, *Ford: Expansion and Challenge, 1915–1933* (New York, 1957), p. 497.
10. *Ford Fair Lane Papers,* T. R. Ward, "Henry Ford and the Scotch Settlement School," mms., p. 13. Accession 572, Box 4.
11. *Ibid.,* Harold M. Cordell, "Reminiscences," Oral History Series, p. 62. Accession 572, Box 5.

12. *The Madison Survey*, Nashville Agricultural Normal Institute, Nashville, Tennessee, December 14, 1938, p. 186.
13. Eunice Fuller Barnard, "Henry Ford Invents a School," New York *Times* magazine, April 13, 1930, section V, pp. 1–19.
14. *Ford Fair Lane Papers*, C. J. Sullivan, "Reminiscences," Oral History Series, December, 1951, p. 2. Accession 65.
15. Schools in northern Michigan were located at Pequoming and in L'Anse Township. Schools at the Ford Village Industries were at Macon, Nankin Mills, Cherry Hill, Saline, and Alberta, all in Michigan. Accession 384, Box 9.
16. Frazier Hunt, "Henry Ford's 1940 World," *Hearst's International*, January, 1922, p. 72. See also New Orleans *Times Picayune*, July 22, 1934.
17. Roger Butterfield, "Ford and History," in John B. Rae, *Henry Ford* (Englewood Cliffs, New Jersey, 1969), p. 170.
18. Henry A. Haigh, "Henry Ford's Typical Early American Village at Dearborn," *Michigan History Magazine*, summer, 1929, p. 515.
19. Bruce Bliven, "Mr. Ford Collects," *New Republic*, April 28, 1937, p. 352.
20. Nevins and Hill, *op. cit.*, p. 502.
21. Joe Rynda, interview, New Ulm, Minnesota, August 12, 1947.
22. *The Story of Mary and Her Little Lamb* (Mr. and Mrs. Ford, Dearborn, Michigan, 1928), p. 27.
23. San Francisco *Chronicle*, February 15, 1930.

CHAPTER XII

All letters not cited in a specific footnote in this chapter are located in the *Ford Fair Lane Papers*, Accessions 1, 2, 23, 265, and 380.

1. *Ford Times*, March, 1914, no. 6, vol. VII, p. 253.
2. Detroit *Free Press*, March 14, 1915.
3. Edgar A. Guest, "10,000 People a Week Ask Henry Ford for Gifts," *American* magazine, January, 1924, p. 84.
4. William Greenleaf, *From These Beginnings* (New York, 1964), p. 9.
5. *Ford Fair Lane Papers*, Franklin D. Roosevelt, Fidelity and Deposit Company, 120 Broadway, New York, New York, to Henry Ford, Dearborn, Michigan, January 17, 1924. Accession 23, Box 8.
6. New York *Herald*, August 4, 1918.
7. *Neueste Nachrichten* (Munich, Germany), February 10, 1924.
8. Cameron Wilkie, "If You Could Talk for an Hour with Ford," *Christian Herald*, July 20, 1929, p. 4.
9. *Ford Fair Lane Papers*, "Special Data. List of Ford's Interests and Statistical Tables." Accession 285, Box 58.
10. Detroit *Journal*, January 7, 1914. Ford said it cost as much to feed the baby of a floor sweeper as the child of an engineer.
11. Cincinnati *Times Star*, January 9, 1914.
12. *World's Work*, September, 1924, p. 540.

13. Henry Ford and Samuel Crowthers, *My Life and Work* (New York, 1925), p. 209.
14. Eugene V. Debs, "Poverty Makes Criminals," Terre Haute *Post*, February 4, 1916.
15. *Ford Fair Lane Papers*, Clarence Darrow, Cannes, France, to Henry Ford, Dearborn, Michigan, March 6, 1930. Accession 512, Box 5.
16. St. Louis *Daily Globe Democrat*, February 3, 1927.
17. *Ford Fair Lane Papers*, "Henry Ford on Charity," mms. 1934. Accession 274, Box 2.
18. *Ibid.*, Financial Records. Accession 384, Box 1.

CHAPTER XIII

1. Melvin Kransberg and Carroll W. Purcell, Jr., *Technology in Western Civilization*, vol. II (New York, 1967), p. 358.
2. *Ford Fair Lane Papers*, "Special Data. List of Ford's Interests and Statistical Tables." Accession 285, Box 58.
3. Allan Nevins and Frank Hill, *Ford: Decline and Rebirth, 1933–1962* (New York, 1962), p. 295.
4. John B. Rae, *Henry Ford* (Englewood Cliffs, New Jersey, 1969), p. 91.
5. William Greenleaf, *From These Beginnings* (Detroit, 1964), p. 178.
6. Booton Herndon, *Ford* (New York, 1969), p. 100.
7. Henry Ford and Samuel Crowthers, *My Life and Work* (New York, 1925), p. 73.
8. *Farm Implements* (Chicago), p. 8, quoting *The Mark Lane Express*, London, June 4, 1901, p. 4.
9. Charles E. Duryea, Peoria, Illinois, to the editor of *Horseless Age*, January 31, 1896. Published in *Horseless Age*, February, 1896, p. 19.
10. Detroit *News-Tribune*, February 8, 1903.
11. Mitchell Wilson, *American Science and Invention* (New York, 1954), p. 326.
12. *Collier's*, April 13, 1907, p. 6.
13. Allan Nevins and Frank Hill, *Henry Ford: The Times, The Man, The Company* (New York, 1954), pp. 275 and 646.
14. Bryan Donkin, *A Textbook on Gas, Oil and Air Engines* (London, 1911), p. 21.
15. *Mechanic's Journal*, 2nd series, 1864, 9:248–49.
16. *Ford Fair Lane Papers*. Accession 1, Boxes 23–35, Section V, Shelf 5.
17. *Ibid.* Accession 7, Box 4.
18. Rae, *op. cit.*, p. 71.

Index

Aberdeen *Daily News*, 69, 105
Adams, Henry, 6
Agriculture, U. S. Department of;
  see United States Department of
  Agriculture
Alfonse of Spain, King, 217
Alger, Horatio, 42
Allen, Fred, 56
Allen, W. C., 84
American Agriculturist, 21, 24, 236
American Farm Bureau, 128, 131–32
American Magazine, 44
American Mercury, 181
American Peace Society, 165
American Review of Reviews, 7
American Sunday School Union, 31
American Thresherman, 13
"Amos n' Andy," 46
Anderson, G. S., 168
Anderson, John W., 234
Anti-Saloon League, 144
"Argol," 154–55
Ashurst, F., 174
Atlantic Monthly, 9
Avery, Clarence W., 238

Baekland, Leo, 151
Baker, M. M., 21
Baker, Newton, 108
Baltimore *Evening Sun*, 45

Barnes, Julius H., 142
Barnum, P. T., 34
Barton, Bruce, 8
Baruch, Bernard, 108, 138
Beach, Lansing H., 109
Beardsley, J. A., 75
Bell, Alexander Graham, 237
Benz, Karl, 238
Berliner, Emile, 237
Berry, Martha, 199–201
Berry Schools, 94, 109, 199–201
Best and Hott engines, 83
Bird, Caroline, 184
Black, Fred, 47, 55, 159, 177
Bliven, Bruce, 208
Borah, William, 122
Bornholdt, Oscar, 238
Boston *Globe*, 174
Boston *Traveler*, 166
Breeder's Gazette, 15–16
Bridgeport *Standard*, 92
Brisbane, Arthur, 4, 46, 54, 122
British Ford Motor Co., 89
Bruckberger, R. L., 180
Bryan, William Jennings, 6–7, 12,
  26, 122, 130, 165, 171
Bryant, Clara (Mrs. Henry Ford),
  12
Bryant, Marvin, 87
Bryce, James, 12

Buck, Pearl, 159
Bull Moose Party, 165
Bull Tractor Co., 87, 91
Burbank, Luther, 92, 158, 165, 190, 207
Burlingame, Roger, 5
Burroughs, John, 109, 158, 215–17
Bushnell, Sarah T., 45
Butterfield, Roger, 206
Byrd, Richard E., 46

Cameron, William J., 56, 132, 145, 157, 173, 177
Camping, early automobile, 26–29
Canadian Thresherman, 84
Capper, Arthur, 115, 135
Carnegie, Andrew, 219, 228
Carver, George Washington, 154, 158, 203–4
Casadesus, Robert, 55
Case Co., J. I., 97–98
Centralia Hub, 148
Chambless, Edgar, 190, 194
Chaplin, Charlie, 41
Chapman, Paul V., 153
Chicago American, 86
Chicago Tribune, 12, 121, 170, 203; lawsuit, 51–55
Chicago World's Fair (1933), 149
Christian Advocate, 7
Christian Science Monitor, 192
Cincinnati Post, 192
"City Service Concert," 55
Cleveland Plain Dealer, 110
Cobb, Irvin S., 49
Cody, Buffalo Bill, 240
Coker, Francis W., 53
Collier's, 21, 25, 121, 174
Commager, Henry, 181
Cooke, James F., 47
Coolidge, Calvin, 104, 115–16, 121–23, 126, 135, 179–81, 183
Cooper, Max, 69
Cordell, Harold M., 5, 57, 153, 203, 213

Country Gentleman, 20
Couzens, James, 5, 162, 176, 238
Crooks, Richard, 55
Crowthers, Samuel, 233
Cummins, Albert B., 164
Cunningham, J. C., 22
Cylmer, Floyd, 72

Dahlinger, Ray, 159
Dailey, J. B., 76–78
Daimler, Gottlieb, 238
Dakota Farmer, 20, 84
Danville News, 139
Darrow, Clarence, 221
Daugherty, Harry, 117
Davis, John, 122
Deal, N. B., 105
Dearborn Independent, 113, 121, 124, 132–33, 136, 138–40, 163, 173, 177–79, 190
Debs, Eugene V., 221
Deere Co., John, 97
Degener, Gus, 238
Denver Express, 49
Department of Agriculture, U. S.; see United States Department of Agriculture
DePew, Chauncey, 4
Depression, Great, 147–48, 180, 232
Detroit, Ironton and Toledo Railroad, 11
Detroit Drydock Co., 82
Detroit Free Press, 45, 154, 192, 212
Detroit News, 46, 177
Detroit Times, 45
Dewey, John, 190, 196
Diehl, Fred, 238
Dodge Brothers, lawsuit, 51
Donald, David, 181
Dos Passos, Katherine, 155
Drucker, Peter F., 5, 231
Duffus, Robert L., 119
Dunning, William A., 53
Duryea, brothers, 14
Duryea, Charles E., 20, 235, 238

Duryea, Frank, 238
Duveen, Joseph, 10

Eads, James, 176
Eastern Implement Dealer, 95
Eckhardt, William G., 132
Ecology; *see* Ford, Henry
Edison, Thomas A., 14, 38, 88, 92, 109, 113–14, 143, 145–46, 158, 165, 176, 202, 207–8, 210, 215–17
Edward VII, King, 214
Edwards, Gus, 235
Eggleston, Edward, 32
Emde, Carl, 238
Emerson, Ralph Waldo, 8
Estabrook, Henry D., 164
Etude, 47

Fair Lane, 2, 101, 224
Fair Lane Papers, 81
Farkas, Gene, 87
Farm and Fireside, 43, 132, 147
Farm and Home, 123
Farmer, 123
Farm Journal, 43
Farm Machinery Power, 93
Federal Reserve System, 106
Federal Trade Commission, 110
Ferguson, Harry, 97
Firestone, Harvey, 109, 145–46, 158, 215
Fisher, Bud, 49
Fisher, Carl, 77–78
Fishleigh, W. T., 60
Fishwick, Marshall W., 5
Fleischhacker, Mortimer, 138
Ford, Henry: and the boll weevil, 155–57; and ecology, 157, 161; and education, 196–211; and foods, 152–54; and Muscle Shoals, 103–25; and Peace Ship venture, 165–67; and plastics, 151–52; and politics, 162–79; and science, 142–61; and soybeans, 148–51, 155

Ford, Clara (Mrs. Henry), 10, 12, 43, 173, 197, 199–201, 226–27
Ford, Edsel, 3, 25, 38, 45–46, 53, 55, 89, 171
Ford and Son Tractor Division, 87
Ford Archives, 2–3, 27, 81, 137, 142, 201, 214, 220, 225, 228
Ford Clubs, 36
Ford Days, 37, 111
Ford for President Clubs, 173
Ford for Senator Clubs, 170
Ford Foundation, The, 211
Ford joke books, 49
Ford Museum, 57, 83, 203, 206–7
Fordson tractor, 87–94
"Ford Sunday Evening Hour," 55, 157
Ford Times, 18, 27, 35, 40, 212
Ford Trade Schools; *see* Henry Ford Trade School
Fortune, 58
Foster, C. R., 50
Foster, Stephen, 48
Foy, Eddie, 39
Frank, Glenn, 8
Frankfurter Zeitung, 4
Franklin, Benjamin, 9
Froelich, John, 84

Galamb, Joseph, 84, 238
Galbraith, Kenneth, 5, 182
Gallagher, William H., 135
Garland, Hamlin, 25
Garvin, Francis P., 154
Gas Review, 22, 24
Gay, Byron, 50
General Motors Corp., 58, 97
"Gillette Community Sing," 55
Gladden, Washington, 219
Glass, Remley J., 184
Goldman, Emma, 53
Goodyear, Charles, 145
Graham, William J., 108
Grand Rapids *Herald*, 87, 119
Grant, U. S., 181

Gray, Harold, 46
Great Falls *Times*, 148
Greenbackers, 11
Greenfield Village, 40, 47, 57, 83, 158, 203–4, 206–8
Greenleaf, William, 213
Guest, Edgar A., 44, 213, 225
Guggenheim, Robert, 40
Gurko, Leo, 9
Gustav of Sweden, Crown Prince, 217

Hale, Sarah J., 210
Halifax *Chronicle*, 55
Hall, Harvey M., 146
Hamilton, E. W., 84
Harding, E. L., 75
Harding, Warren G., 104, 111, 116–17, 122, 172, 174–75, 179–80
Harpers, 184
Harrison, Pat, 174
Hart-Parr Co., 84–85, 143
Haynes, Elwood, 14
Hearst, Randolph A., 217
Heflin, Thomas, 120
Helme, James W., 169
Henry Ford Trade School, 197
Herring, Clyde L., 43
Hetch-Hetchy Watershed, 120
Highland Park Ford Plant, 84
Hill, Frank E., 140, 203, 234
Hill, James J., 162
Hockett, James A., 20
Holiday, 233
Holten, C. F., 202
Hoover, Herbert, 8, 117, 122–23, 126, 179, 181, 183–87, 191, 195
Hopkins, Harry, 5
Horseless Age, 19, 23, 235–36
Howard, J. R., 132
Huff, Spider, 34
Hughes, Charles E., 163–64, 169
Hyatt, John, 151

Implement and Machinery Review, 91
Ingersall, E. P., 19
International Harvester Company, 53, 84, 96–97, 121, 236

Jardine, William M., 104, 126–28
Jefferson, Thomas, 3, 6
Johnson, Hiram, 122
Jordan, David Star, 166

Kahn, Julius H., 108
Kahn, Otto H., 138
Kaltenborn, H. V., 4
Kansas City *Packer*, 135
Kansas City *Post*, 89
Kansas Farmer, 110, 139, 174
Kent, Frank, 181
Keynes, John Maynard, 181
King, Mackenzie, 134
Kingsley, Philip, 12
Kinnard-Harnes Co., 84
Kirkland, Wemouth, 52
Klann, William C., 238
Knapp, E. A., 26
Knapp, Joseph G., 140
Knoxville *Sentinel*, 24
Knudsen, William, 238
Kouwenhoven, J. A., 78
Krass, Nathan, 178
Krauskopf, Joseph, 167
Kreisler, Fritz, 217
Kropotkin, Peter, 53
Kuen-Loeb Co., 115
Ku Klux Klan, 178, 140
Kulick, Frank, 39

La Follette, Robert, 103, 122
Landon, Alf, 179
Lane, Rose Wilder, 38
Langen, Eugen, 238
Lardner, Ring, 39, 49
Larsen, Grace H., 129
Laurel and Hardy, 41

Lavassor, Emil, 238
Lazar, J. Aaron, 178
Legge, Alexander, 188
Leibold, E. G., 45, 47, 60, 121–22, 163, 169, 172–73, 177, 203, 213, 218, 220
Lenoir, Jean Etienne, 20, 237
Leopold, Wilhelm, 157
Levy, David, 138
Lewis, David L., 41
Lewis, Gracie (Mrs. Sinclair), 1, 28
Lewis, Sinclair, 28
Lindbergh, Charles A., 241
Lindsay, Ben, 166
"Little Orphan Annie," 46
Livingston, Seyburn, 87
Lloyd George, David, 90
Lockner, Louis, 58
Lodge, Henry Cabot, 172
London *Times*, 89–90, 166
Longworth, Nicholas, 119
Love, Harry, 238
Lovett, Benjamin, 223
Lowden, Frank O., 134–35
Lucking, Alfred, 52
"Lucky Strike Hit Parade," 55

Madison, James, 183
Malcomson, Alexander T., 234
Manufacturer's Record, 117
Markham, Edwin, 3, 218
Mark Lane Express, 89
Marquis, Samuel S., 43, 53, 219, 225, 240
Martin, P. E., 238
Mayback, William, 238
Mayo, William B., 114
McAdoo, William, 122, 181
McCloud, J. L., 147
McCormick, Colonel, 52–53, 55
McCormick, Cyrus, 237
McCormick Deering tractors, 97
McCullum, E. V., 148
McDonald, H. Y., 135

McGuffey School, 204–5
McGuffey, William Holmes, 204, 210
McKenzie, J. C., 112
Mellon, Andrew, 8, 45, 117, 162, 182, 188
Menlo Park, 207
Mergenthaler, Otto, 237
Merz, Charles, 4
Michigan Car Co., 82
Michigan Farmer, 111
Miller, James Martin, 121–22
Millis, Walter, 167
Milner, Lord, 90
Minneapolis *Journal*, 15, 17
Moody, Dwight L., 31
Moody, Paul, 31
Morgan, J. P., 7, 10, 61, 115
Morgan, Robert, 132–33, 139
Moton, R. R., 156
Motor Age, 21
Muir, John, 158
Munich *Neueste Nachrichren*, 157, 218
Muscle Shoals, 106, 120–24, 156–57, 163, 175, 179, 199, 231; *see also* Ford, Henry
Myrick, Herbert, 123

Nashville *Banner*, 111
Nation, 116
National Defense Act of 1916, 108
National Waterways Commission, 107
Nebraska Farmer, 20, 164
Nelson, Marie, 241
Nestos, R. A., 101
Nevins, Allan, 5, 140, 177, 181, 203, 234, 236
Newark *Star-Eagle*, 92
Newberry, Truman, 169–72, 175
New Deal, 55, 123, 179, 183–84, 195, 232
Newman, Ray, 159

New York *Call*, 88
New Yorker, 10
New York *Herald*, 218
New York *Mirror*, 46
New York *Times*, 4, 34, 92, 112–13, 119, 122, 157, 192, 231
New York *World*, 4
New York World's Fair (1939), 57, 150
Nicholas II, Czar, 40
Non-Partisan Leaguers, 11
Norris, George W., 104, 119–23
North American Review, 15
Northcliffe, Lord, 49, 89, 91–92
Norton, F. Lee, 98

Octopus, 12
Ogburn, William F., 26
Olds, Ransom E., 14, 235
Olson, Sidney, 3
Omaha *Daily Bee*, 88
Omaha *World-Herald*, 58
Ormandy, Eugene, 55
Osborn, Chase, 169
Oscar II, 51, 166–67
Otto, Nikolaus A., 20, 237–38
Otto, William, 238
Outlook, 7

Pacific Rural Press, 25
Pacifism, Ford's, 164–67, 170, 175
Panhard, René, 238
Passoneau, Joseph, 134
Peace Ship mission, 51, 90, 165–67, 175, 231
Pearson, Drew, 191
Pearson, James, 164
Perry, Lord, 89
Philadelphia *Bulletin*, 110
Philadelphia *Public Ledger*, 15
Phillips, Tom, 202
Pinchot, Gifford, 119
Pioch, William, 238
Pipp, E. G., 5, 177–78

Pipp's Weekly, 95, 118
Plank, Eddie, 41
Plastics, Ford and, 151–52
Poling, Daniel B., 168
Populists, 10–11
Pound, Arthur, 9
Prairie Farmer, 4, 111
Progress Guide, 151
Progressive Farmer, 24, 80

Quadricycle, Ford's first, 12

Racing, Ford and, 39–40
Rae, John B., 6
Raymond, F. S., 135, 140
Redstone School, 205, 210
Reed, James A., 135, 138–39
Regina *Leader*, 134
Richards, Carl, 174
Richmond Hill School, 202–3
Rider and Driver, 16
River Rouge Plant, 1, 6, 57, 92, 157, 159
Robinson, James Harvey, 7
Rockefeller, John D., 6–7, 121, 162, 174, 217, 228
Rogers, Will, 4–5, 8–9, 179, 181, 195, 211
Rolvaag, Ole, 25
Roosevelt, Franklin D., 56, 123, 179, 183, 193, 195, 214
Roosevelt, Theodore, 6, 39, 58, 163, 165, 168, 170, 200, 216
Rose, Philip S., 86
Ross, Lanny, 55
Roulstone, John, Jr., 210
Ruddiman, Edsel A., 152–53
Rumely, Edward A., 86
Rural New Yorker, 4, 111, 175
Ruth, Babe, 241

Sacco and Vanzetti Case, 222–23
St. Joseph *News Press*, 110
San Francisco *Call Bulletin*, 38

San Francisco earthquake, 22
Sapiro, Aaron, 128–40; Sapiro Plan, 129; Sapiro lawsuit, 5, 135–40, 179
Saskatoon *Star*, 134
Sawyer, Mary Elizabeth, 210
Scott, B. W., 40
Schwimmer, Rosika, 165
Seattle *Times*, 119
See, Elmer, 159
Seldon Patent Case, 51
Shakespeare, William, 3
Simpson, William G., 163
Singer, Charles A., 20
Smith, D. J., 40, 84, 238
Smith, Fred, 5, 209
Smith, J. Janney, 220
Smith, William Alden, 163
Smith, William H., 146, 156
Smut, Jan, 40
Sorensen, Charles E., 87, 90, 96, 239
Sorensen, Christian A., 166
Southern Cultivator, 12, 24
Southern Dairy Products Journal, 153
Southern Pacific Railroad, 12
Southwest School, 205
Sowerby, A. C., 143
Soybean, Ford and the, 148–51, 155
Spanish-American War, 6, 170
Spaulding, John W., 56
Spillman, W. L., 190
Stalin, Joseph, 4
Standard Oil Co., 7, 45, 53, 145
Steber, Eleanor, 55
Stern, Philip Van Doren, 14
Stevenson, Elliott G., 52–53
Stidger, William, 57–58, 151
Stoll, Elmer R., 77
Street, Robert, 237
Strout, Lee, 72
Successful Farming, 43
Sullivan, Mark, 6
Sunday, Billy, 40
Swinehart, James, 46

Taft, William Howard, 39–40, 165
Tarbell, Ida M., 6
Taylor, Walter, 16
Teapot Dome, 8, 119
Tennessee Valley Authority, 123
Thayer, Webster, 223
Thompson, J. D., 46
Thompson, L. J., 159
Thompson, William Hale, 13
Thoreau, Henry, 158
"Tobacco Road," 41
Toledo *Blade*, 87
Tolstoy, Leo, 214
Topeka *Daily Capital*, 76, 88
Tractors, early, 84–102
Traubel, Helen, 55
Tucker, James G., 52
Tulsa *Tribune*, 116
Turner, Frederick Jackson, 9

Ukkleberg, H. G., 146
Underwood, Oscar, 108
United States Department of Agriculture, 26, 83, 110, 115, 124, 135, 142–43, 146, 149, 155, 190, 229

Vancouver *Daily World*, 148
Vandenberg, Arthur, 5, 119
Veblen, Thorstein, 15
Villa, Pancho, 51, 241
Von Krupp, Baron, 217

Wadell, William, 213
Wadsworth, James W., 108
Wadsworth-Kahn Bill, 108–9
Wagner, Robert F., 183
Wagoner, Mike, 186
Wallace, Henry A., 101, 104
Wallace's Farmer, 20
Wall Street, 7, 10–11, 105–6, 112, 115–16, 123, 145, 163, 178, 187, 231
Wall Street Journal, 22, 121, 187, 189, 231

Walsh, Tom, 128
Waring, Fred, 55
Washington, George, 32, 53, 105,
    183, 209
Washington *Evening Star*, 192
Wayside Inn, 205
Wayside Inn School, 205
Way's Station, 202
Weeks, John W., 109, 111, 117,
    121
Weinstock, Harris, 129
Welch, Mrs. Marion, 48
Welliver, Judson C., 7
Welt Archiv, 4
Western Brewer, 143
White, E. B., 72
Whitehall Library, 91
Whiteman, Paul, 55
Whitney, Eli, 237
Wichita *Eagle*, 110

Wickham, Henry A., 145–46
Wilhelm, Kaiser, 214
Wills, C. Harold, 238
Wilson, Meredith, 55
Wilson, Mitchell, 235
Wilson, Woodrow, 6, 39, 51, 58,
    88, 108, 163, 165–66, 168–70, 190
Wing, Andrew S., 43, 132
Winnepeg Plowing Trials, 85
Winton, Alexander, 14
Wisconsin *Agriculturist*, 144
Wisconsin *News*, 5
Woman's Home Companion, 155
Worthington, J. W., 109, 115–16
Wright, brothers, 237

Young, Brigham, 5
Young, William P., 49

Zahnov, Charles, 212

Selected Ann Arbor Paperbacks
Works of enduring merit

AA 4   THE SOUTHERN FRONTIER, 1670-1732   Verner W. Crane
AA 9   STONEWALL JACKSON   Allen Tate
AA 13 THOMAS JEFFERSON: The Apostle of Americanism   Gilbert Chinard
AA 18 THOMAS MORE   R. W. Chambers
AA 21 THE PURITAN MIND   Herbert W. Schneider
AA 28 ANTISLAVERY ORIGINS OF THE CIVIL WAR IN THE UNITED STATES   Dwight Lowell Dumond
AA 31 POPULATION: THE FIRST ESSAY   Thomas R. Malthus
AA 34 THE ORIGIN OF RUSSIAN COMMUNISM   Nicolas Berdyaev
AA 35 THE LIFE OF CHARLEMAGNE   Einhard
AA 49 THE GATEWAY TO THE MIDDLE AGES: ITALY   Eleanor Shipley Duckett
AA 50 THE GATEWAY TO THE MIDDLE AGES: FRANCE AND BRITAIN   Eleanor Shipley Duckett
AA 51 THE GATEWAY TO THE MIDDLE AGES: MONASTICISM   Eleanor Shipley Duckett
AA 53 VOICES OF THE INDUSTRIAL REVOLUTION   John Bowditch and Clement Ramsland, ed.
AA 54 HOBBES   Sir Leslie Stephen
AA 55 THE RUSSIAN REVOLUTION   Nicolas Berdyaev
AA 56 TERRORISM AND COMMUNISM   Leon Trotsky
AA 57 THE RUSSIAN REVOLUTION and LENINISM OR MARXISM?   Rosa Luxemburg
AA 59 THE FATE OF MAN IN THE MODERN WORLD   Nicolas Berdyaev
AA 61 THE REFORMATION OF THE 16TH CENTURY   Rev. Charles Beard
AA 62 A HISTORY OF BUSINESS: From Babylon to the Monopolists   Vol. I   Miriam Beard
AA 65 A PREFACE TO POLITICS   Walter Lippmann
AA 66 FROM HEGEL TO MARX: Studies in the Intellectual Development of Karl Marx   Sidney Hook
AA 67 WORLD COMMUNISM: A History of the Communist International   F. Borkenau
AA 69 THE MYTH OF THE RULING CLASS: Gaetano Mosca and the Elite   James H. Meisel
AA 72 THE MERCHANT CLASS OF MEDIEVAL LONDON   Sylvia L. Thrupp
AA 74 CAPITALISM IN AMSTERDAM IN THE 17TH CENTURY   Violet Barbour
AA 76 A HISTORY OF BUSINESS: From the Monopolists to the Organization Man   Vol. II   M. Beard
AA 77 THE SPANISH COCKPIT   Franz Borkenau
AA 78 THE HERO IN AMERICA   Dixon Wecter
AA 79 THUCYDIDES   John H. Finley, Jr.
AA 80 SECRET HISTORY   Procopius
AA 86 LAISSEZ FAIRE AND THE GENERAL-WELFARE STATE   Sidney Fine
AA 88 ROMAN POLITICAL IDEAS AND PRACTICE   F. E. Adcock
AA 94 POETRY AND POLITICS UNDER THE STUARTS   C. V. Wedgwood
AA 95 ANABASIS: The March Up Country   Xenophon   Translated by W. H. D. Rouse
AA 100 THE CALCULUS OF CONSENT   James M. Buchanan and Gordon Tullock
AA 103 IMPERIALISM   J. A. Hobson
AA 104 REFLECTIONS OF A RUSSIAN STATESMAN   Konstantin P. Pobedonostsev
AA 110 BAROQUE TIMES IN OLD MEXICO   Irving A. Leonard
AA 111 THE AGE OF ATTILA   C. D. Gordon
AA 114 IMPERIAL GERMANY AND THE INDUSTRIAL REVOLUTION   Thorstein Veblen
AA 115 CIVIL LIBERTIES AND THE CONSTITUTION   Paul G. Kauper
AA 118 NEGRO THOUGHT IN AMERICA   August Meier
AA 119 THE POLITICAL IDEAS OF THE ENGLISH ROMANTICISTS   Crane Brinton
AA 120 WILLIAM PENN   Catherine Owens Peare
AA 122 JOAN OF ARC   Jules Michelet   Translated by Albert Guerard
AA 124 SEEDTIME OF REFORM   Clarke A. Chambers
AA 126 LECTURES ON THE PRINCIPLES OF POLITICAL OBLIGATION   T. H. Green
AA 133 IMPRESSIONS OF LENIN   Angelica Balabanoff
AA 137 POLITICAL HERETICS   Max Nomad
AA 139 REBEL VOICES: An I.W.W. Anthology   Joyce L. Kornbluh, ed.
AA 160 PATTERNS OF SOVIET THOUGHT   Richard T. De George
AA 172 DEATH AND LIFE IN THE TENTH CENTURY   Eleanor Shipley Duckett
AA 173 GALILEO, SCIENCE AND THE CHURCH   Jerome J. Langford
AA 179 SEARCH FOR A PLACE   M. R. Delany and Robert Campbell
AA 181 THE DEVELOPMENT OF PHYSICAL THEORY IN THE MIDDLE AGES   James A. Weisheipl
AA 186 CAROLINGIAN CHRONICLES   Translated by Bernhard Walter Scholz with Barbara Rogers
AA 187 TOWARD A MATHEMATICS OF POLITICS   Gordon Tullock
AA 192 CRISIS IN WATERTOWN: The Polarization of an American Community   Lynn Eden
AA 193 HENRY FORD AND GRASS-ROOTS AMERICA   Reynold M. Wik

For a complete list of Ann Arbor Paperback titles write:
THE UNIVERSITY OF MICHIGAN PRESS ANN ARBOR